The Mystical and Prophetic Thought
of Simone Weil
and Gustavo Gutiérrez

The Mystical and Prophetic Thought
of Simone Weil
and Gustavo Gutiérrez

REFLECTIONS ON THE MYSTERY
AND HIDDENNESS OF GOD

Alexander Nava

State University of New York Press

Published by
State University of New York Press

For information, address the State University of New York Press,
90 State Street, Suite 700, Albany, NY 12207

Marketing by Fran Keneston • Production by Bernadine Dawes

Library of Congress Cataloging-in-Publication Data

Nava, Alexander, 1967–
    The mystical and prophetic thought of Simone Weil and Gustavo Gutiérrez : reflections
on the mystery and hiddenness of God / Alexander Nava.
        p. cm.
    Includes bibliographical references and index.
    ISBN 0-7914-5177-1 (alk. paper) — ISBN 0-7914-5178-X (pbk. : alk. paper)
        1. Weil, Simone, 1909–1943. 2. Gutiérrez, Gustavo, 1928– 3. Mysticism—History—20th
century. 4. Sociology, Christian (Catholic)—History of doctrines—20th century. I. Title.

BV5095.A1 N38 2001
230'.092'2—dc21

                                                                              2001031454

1   2   3   4   5   6   7   8   9   10

A mi familia,
Los Nava

Contents

Acknowledgments

The task of acknowledging the individuals who have contributed to the completion of this work is a difficult undertaking. With one's first book, the temptation to include everyone who played an important role in your life is difficult to resist. From family and relatives to professors and friends, the list is long of those to whom I feel indebted. First and foremost, I am indebted to my family (my parents Eduardo and Alicia and my siblings Andrew and Melinda) for instilling in me a love of learning. My cousin Robert Robinson also has been a constant source of friendship and laughter since the days of our childhood. While in graduate school I received invaluable encouragement and support from Siovhan Sheridan and Michael Ferguson. I am deeply grateful for the spiritual and intellectual companionship that they provided me.

On an academic note, Professors Robert Burns, OP, and Heiko A. Oberman were pivotal influences in my life as an undergraduate student at the University of Arizona. Their gifts as both teachers and scholars played a crucial role in provoking in me a love of theological reflection and causing me to redirect the course of my studies and career from premed to the humanities. At the University of Chicago, I am grateful to Bernard McGinn and Anne Carr, who read early versions of this book and contributed many valuable suggestions. Finally, it would be hard to overstate David Tracy's influence on my own intellectual development. His ideas fill the pages of this book even when unacknowledged in the text. I am equally grateful for the friendship that David and his mother, Ms. Eileen Couch, shared with me during my time in Chicago.

Abbreviations

WORKS BY SIMONE WEIL

FLNB	First and Last Notebooks
FW	Formative Writings
GG	Gravity and Grace
ICAG	Intimations of Christianity among the Greeks
LP	Lectures on Philosophy
LTP	Letter to a Priest
NFR	The Need for Roots
NB	The Notebooks of Simone Weil
SNLG	On Science, Necessity, and the Love of God
OL	Oppression and Liberty
SE	Selected Essays
SL	Seventy Letters
MA	Simone Weil: An Anthology, edited by Sian Miles
WFG	Waiting for God

WORKS BY GUSTAVO GUTIÉRREZ

ELC	Entre las calandrias
GL	The God of Life
LC	Las Casas: In Search of the Poor of Jesus Christ
MIC	Mysticism and Institutional Crisis
OJ	On Job
PPH	The Power of the Poor in History
STH	Sobre el trabajo humano
TL	A Theology of Liberation
TSMYF	The Truth Shall Make You Free
WDOW	We Drink from Our Own Wells

Introduction:
A New Saintliness for Our Time

> Today it is not nearly enough merely to be a saint, but we must have the saintliness demanded by the present moment. . . . The world needs saints who have genius, just as a plague-stricken town needs doctors.
>
> —Simone Weil

In one account of the life of Socrates by Xenophon, one of the interlocutors of the dialogue—a dialogue concerning the meaning of justice—perhaps exhausted from the endless round of questions by this wise man who claims to know nothing, finally remarks that Socrates would do better to simply say, once and for all, what justice is. Socrates replies: "If I don't reveal my views on justice in words, I do so by my conduct."[1] An aspect of the irony of Socrates concerns the tension between Socrates' love of dialogue and ideas, on the one hand, and the equal insistence on ignorance, on the limitations of reason and language. Justice cannot be defined in an absolute manner; it must be lived. Those intellectuals who offer not just theories of justice or truth, but provide us with hints and suggestions on how we are to live our lives, have a peculiar appeal. If their ideas offer us glimpses of the meaning of justice, their examples can be gifts that unveil and more fully disclose the meaning of justice. It is the integrity and union of their ideas with their lives, of their daring and uncompromising passion for truth or justice, that has the potential to ignite a spark in the heart of others. The passion that these sages display in their lives is more contagious and alluring than theories or speculations divorced from practice and separate from the narrative of a life. If we are attentive to these individuals, the unity of their ideas and lives has the potential to effect a change in our own mode of being-in-the-world.[2]

1

As a college undergraduate, I recall being captivated by the life and philosophy of Simone Weil. I also remember my burgeoning interest in the theology of Gustavo Gutiérrez and especially my admiration for this dedicated Peruvian priest's life. The Platonic tradition and hermeneutical philosophy speak of a "shock of recognition," and that would not over-state the impact of their ideas and lives on my own direction. Surely, the power that they began to exert on my life had its source in the manner in which they represented not only intellectuals but also individuals engaged in historical and social struggles. The thought of Gustavo Gutiérrez illu-minated for me the conditions of life in the "third world" of Latin America: the pervasive and destructive poverty, the history of violence and oppres-sion, the vulnerability of the people to disease and natural disasters, the unjust distribution of resources. He awakened as well my awareness of the growing presence of refugees and immigrants in my own "backyard" of Tucson, Arizona. Tucson's proximity to the U.S.-Mexican border made my hometown an ideal place for many refugees to seek asylum and work. It became obvious to me that the United States was, after all, part of the Americas and that the destiny of the North was inextricably linked with that of the South. The thought of Gutiérrez shed light not only on the distant world of Latin America but also on the world that I inhabited in the United States.

Simone Weil's life and philosophy resonated with me for reasons that will only become obvious in the course of this book, but one dimen-sion of her life was especially captivating: her brilliant intellectual achieve-ments were inseparable from her commitment to manual labor, especially factory work. Her reflections on working conditions in factories in Eu-rope in the 1920s and 1930s were born of her own painful experiences. Far removed from other more abstract, speculative thoughts on the na-ture of industrial capitalism, her reflections communicate a lived involve-ment and solidarity with the common laborer. I believe her thoughts re-main relevant in the contemporary postmodern world of capitalism, given the growing presence of oppressive and exploitative working conditions in the proliferating factories of third world countries. The number of U.S. companies moving their enterprises across the border in order to avoid paying living wages, to avoid decent and safe work conditions, and to escape environmental restrictions is alarming. Given this reality at the start of the new millennium, the insights of Weil are only more perspica-cious and prophetic.

Make no mistake about it: both Weil and Gutiérrez are great intellectuals, not simply activists. They are intellectuals, however, who discern with great lucidity and passion the shortcomings of intellectual, academic life. When Simone Weil writes, "Intellectual: a bad name, but we deserve it. . . . ," she states nicely the ambivalence she feels toward her undeniable intellectual gifts and proclivities. Gutiérrez too is an intellectual and academic who finds much that is abstract and unreal about the self-contained ideas of the academic community. For both Weil and Gutiérrez, the world of ideas and beliefs is only legitimate when it thoughtfully articulates the experiences and struggles of the poor and afflicted and, moreover, inspires solidarity with such communities and histories. When Simone Weil wrote that a new saintliness was required for our times, she certainly had in mind the need for sages who would be capable of addressing in thought and action the problems and injustices that confront our contemporary situation. Weil and Gutiérrez offer us outlines and hints at how to forge a saintliness for our time.

The central argument of this book is that Weil and Gutiérrez provide philosophical and theological visions that creatively integrate themes and perspectives often separated in modern thought or treated as mutually exclusive, such as mystical and prophetic thought, spirituality and politics, theory and practice, justice and love, and, more generally, the human experiences of goodness and beauty, on the one hand, and terror and evil, on the other. If the thought of Weil and Gutiérrez teaches us anything, one crucial lesson is how incomplete, how deficient Christian thought is when one of the above pairs is held in opposition to the other, when separation gives rise to either neglect or to a suspicion of the importance and value of the other.

Consider the case of spirituality today. In both academic circles and popular culture there has been an explosion in the interest of spirituality and mysticism (witness not only individual book titles, but entire sections devoted to spirituality in many major bookstores). Many such books (especially of the New Age or occult kind) promise to provide therapy for individual brokenness, healing and self-affirmation for a troubled soul. The self-help variety of spiritual texts hope to nurture the individual to psychological health and, perhaps, to instill some sense of mystery of both the cosmos around us and the depths of the human spirit. In many instances, however, such attention to the spiritual life often fails to even consider the threats and interruptions of the human spirit in the form of injustice, inequality, prejudice, poverty, and oppression. Absent in many considerations of spirituality (not only in popular culture but in academic circles as well) is a social consciousness and an awareness of the social and political fabric of our lives. The mystical dimension is considered without attention to the prophetic.

Precisely the opposite temptation is often prevalent in considerations of the prophetic tradition: namely, the eclipse of a spiritual and mystical element in the interest of promoting social and economic justice. The single-minded attention to conditions of inequality or the exposure of the realities of injustice comprises the heart of a prophetic sensibility. It is not surprising that these prophetic concerns, concerns that are ineluctably public issues, look with distrust and suspicion in the direction of mysticism. In their reading, mysticism is all-too-private, purely individualistic, and inevitably only concerned with the interior realm of the spirit—and hence the material necessities of life are neglected. In many cases, however, such a passion for social change, and the requisite emotion of anger and fury, is easily debased into a stance of bitterness, spite, and vengeance when a mystical and spiritual dimension is absent. Human energy and purpose easily become spent when the prophetic tone is that of denunciation and rebuke. A prophet who adopts such a tone is soon tempted by a complete and total repudiation, even hatred, of the enemy. As many great prophetic figures testify, the maintenance and cultivation of a mystical, spiritual element is indispensable and makes possible a more complete, more humane, and more soulful pursuit of justice and peace.

For Weil and Gutiérrez, this uniting of mystical and prophetic thought is a key aspect of the union between justice and love. For both of them, justice without love is in danger of lapsing into a spirit of vengeance, resentment, and anger. Without love and forgiveness, justice may degenerate into the cycle of violence so characteristic of revolutions and war (as in the history of revolutions of Latin America so well explored in the literature of Gabriel García Márquez, Isabelle Allende, Carlos Fuentes, and others). Love without a spirit of justice, on the other hand, suffers from an incompleteness that distorts true love into a sentimental emotion, a purely individualistic ethic, or an attitude of condescending pity toward the afflicted. The appeal to justice, in this case, ensures that love is manifested in the public domain of society and culture and not only in the private sphere.

The uniting of the mystical and prophetic dimensions of Christianity, Weil and Gutiérrez contend, may create an understanding and appreciation for both contemplative and prayerful withdrawal and committed action in the world; for spirituality and politics; for an appreciation of beauty and a demand for ethics; for love and justice.

While this book is not a biography of Weil and Gutiérrez, and indeed primarily is a study of their ideas and beliefs, it would be a mistake to ignore the uniqueness of their lives in a study of this kind. Toward this end, I would like to discuss some characteristics of each of them prior to considering their original intellectual contributions in light of the mystical and prophetic dimensions of the Christian tradition.

SIMONE WEIL

One common description of many ancient philosophers was *atopos*, meaning strange, out of place, or unclassifiable. The lives of many of the ancient philosophers struck the average citizen as bizarre. Their dissatisfaction with wealth and comfort, their contempt for power or status, and their disrespect for conventional ways of life had the effect of rendering these figures "strangers to the world." That pretty well begins to describe the life of Simone Weil. She was "set apart" from a very early age. Many stories illustrate her sensitivity to the suffering of others and, concomitantly, her willingness to makes sacrifices for the good of a cause or the well-being of others. We are told that at five years old she refused to eat sugar because the French soldiers fighting against the Germans lacked it. Even upon her deathbed, after being diagnosed with tuberculosis at the age of thirty-four, she refused to eat any more than the ordinary French people under Nazi occupation. Whether or not such a decision contributed to her death—or as some critics argue, was suicidal—no one can doubt her total devotion to her convictions.

At the age of seventeen she wrote an essay about Alexander the Great, who, while crossing the desert with his army poured out his allotment of water so as to share his army's suffering. Her comments on this story foreshadow her entire life. "His well-being, if he had drunk, would have separated him from his soldiers," she writes. "Sacrifice is the acceptance of pain, the refusal to obey the animal in oneself, and the will to redeem suffering men through voluntary suffering. Every saint has poured out the water; every saint has rejected all well-being that would separate him from the suffering of other men."[3]

A few years later, when preparing to take the entrance exam for the prestigious Ecole Normale, she was approached by the young Simone de Beauvoir. Reports of Weil's intelligence, her ascetic way of life, and her sensitivity to the suffering of others, including a story that some students had found Weil weeping in response to the news that a famine had just broken out in China, had created a reputation that fascinated this other young female intellectual. Beauvoir managed to strike up a conversation, and in it Weil proclaimed that the only thing that mattered in the world today was the revolution that would feed all the starving people on the earth. Beauvoir responded by saying that the problem was to find the reason for human existence. Weil then proceeded to look her up and down and retorted, "It's easy to see that you've never gone hungry."[4] Weil herself had been born the daughter of a doctor and had the privilege of an excellent education, but it is clear she was determined from her youth to know what it was like to hunger and to suffer in body and spirit.

Her education was indeed exceptional. At the age of sixteen, she was a student of the distinguished philosopher Alain. By the age of nineteen she passed the entrance exam to the prestigious Ecole Normale Supérieure, scoring the highest on that exam, with the second highest score going to Simone de Beauvoir. It was at the Ecole Normale that she began reading Marx and dedicating herself to issues pertaining to the working classes, the poor, and the cause of France's unions. By twenty-one she finished her thesis, "Science and Perception in Descartes," and soon began teaching philosophy to young girls in the town of Le Puy. At Le Puy she allied herself with the unemployed of the city and led a demonstration before the city council. Her concern with the issue of colonialism was also ignited at this time. In response to an article on the condition of France's colonies and the suffering of the Indo-Chinese, she remarked that she could hardly bear the description of "the condition of the Indo-Chinese, their wretchedness and enslavement, the perennially unpunished insolence of the whites."[5] Her activism in the community of Le Puy displeased the school's administrators, and she was soon transferred to Auxerre. Her term did not last long there either, because she refused to teach her students the kind of rote learning the school expected.

By 1933, now twenty-four years old, she was teaching again at Roanne. During this time she participated in the March of the Miners, a major demonstration on behalf of miners and the unemployed. This only confirmed her growing reputation as a dangerous leftist. During these years, Weil was struggling to clarify the nature of her vocation and the direction of her life. Was she to be an intellectual or an activist on behalf of political and economic justice? Her decision was to choose neither a purely intellectual vocation nor one of political activism: she decided to work in a factory to get firsthand experience of the daily circumstances of the working poor. Simone Petremont insisted that this choice of hers was in part due to the fact that she had reached an impasse in her theoretical thought, that she was trapped in an epistemological crisis. In the words of Petremont: "She was forced to think that where theoretical thought could not find a solution, actual contact with the object might suggest a way out. The object was the misery for which remedies had to be found. If she herself plunged into this misery, she would be able to see more clearly what remedies were appropriate to it."[6] Another biographer, Robert Coles, also emphasizes the shift from mind to body, from mental to physical labor: "She was convinced that hard physical work was essential for an intellectual, lest the mind become all too taken with itself, all too removed from the concrete realities of everyday life, the burdens that rest upon the overwhelming majority of the earth's population."[7] If Simone Weil was an intellectual, she was one who clearly recognized the limits of pure theory and the necessity of committed action in history and society.

In 1935 she took up work in a Renault factory. The physical pain and exhaustion that she endured in the factory was compounded by severe migraine headaches. Seeing her in this worn-out condition, her parents convinced her to come with them on vacation to Portugal. In a small Portuguese village, on the day of the festival of its patron saint, the conviction was born in Weil that Christianity is a religion of slaves and that she could not help being one of them (WFG, 67). Such a conviction supported her belief that the simple faith of the lowly—in this case the peasants of this Portuguese village—imparted a wisdom that is born from their experiential contact with suffering, a wisdom inaccessible to many privileged individuals. The outcasts and the poor are bearers of truths about God, the human condition, and even nature—truths that, in the words of St. Paul, shame the powerful and wise of the world (1 Cor. 26ff.).

Prior to this time in Weil's life interest in Christianity or religion was noticeably absent. Weil had been raised in a secular Jewish home and was not exposed to any regular form of worship or religious belief. Her education, shaped by the classics of Western thought from Greek tragedy and philosophy to Descartes and Marx, did not have a religious focus. It is true that she took up the question of God in her thesis on Descartes; however, in this case the God being considered was an abstract object of theory and was primarily defined by his omnipotence. The God that she would later witness to as the Good is quite different from this all-powerful and conceptual God.[8] This experience in Portugal, then, represents a turning of her soul that was to profoundly mark the direction of her life.

In 1937 and 1938 she claimed to have even more intense experiences of God. In 1937 she wrote later that something compelled her for the first time in her life to go down on her knees at Assisi (WFG, 67–68). In

1938, she was at Solesmes following the liturgical celebrations from Palm Sunday to Easter. She describes the beauty of these celebrations (the music, ritual, the architecture of the churches) as filling her with pure joy. She met a young English Catholic at Solesmes who introduced her to the metaphysical poets of the seventeenth century. Weil was particularly taken with one particular poem, *Love* by George Herbert. She made herself meditate on this poem during one of her violent headaches. "I used to think I was reciting it as a beautiful poem," she writes, "but without my knowing it the recitation had the virtue of a prayer. It was during one of these recitations that, as I told you, Christ himself came down and took possession of me" (WFG 68-69). It was because of her critical, skeptical mind, Weil later explains, that God had prevented her from reading the mystics; He wanted it to be evident to her that she had not invented this completely unexpected contact.

Following these events, the ideas and experiences of various mystics increasingly occupied her thoughts and concerns. In addition to her unflagging love of Plato (whom she regarded as a mystic) Weil began reading some of the classic Christian mystics, especially Eckhart and John of the Cross. She also was fascinated by the stories of St. Francis of Assisi, especially his marriage to Lady Poverty and the participation of Francis in the cross of Christ through the stigmata. While Weil clearly read some of the classic mystics, we are never sure how thoroughly and exhaustively she studied them. The echoes of many mystical voices are noticeably present in several of her mystical metaphors and symbols, but she does not reference them as a historian or scholar of mysticism might. This is not surprising, however. Weil is not, after all, a historian. As a philosopher and mystic herself, she is interested in the constructive and contemporary significance of mysticism, especially for modern life.

Her early death at the age of thirty-four meant that Weil never had the opportunity to fully explicate and clarify her thoughts on the mystical traditions, and many of her reflections on mysticism come from her very unsystematic notebooks. For this reason, in what follows in this book, I pinpoint some of the affinities between Christian mystical traditions and Weil's own thought. Weil's own mystical vision shares many characteristics with the classic mystics, and even when she is unaware of the points of contact with previous mystics, the echoes and similarities between them are unmistakable.

We might suggest the intriguing possibility that different individuals, in different historical and cultural settings—though still sharing a similar religious, cultural, and linguistic tradition, e.g., the Jewish and Christian paradigm of the West—have similar experiences and express similar ideas, attitudes, and worldviews. That there exist analogies (such as the Otherness of the divine, the role of silence, the centrality of love, the epiphany of beauty, and so on) between various mystics, between Weil and other Christian mystics in this case, is one hypothesis of the present work.

While the encounters in 1937 and 1938 were profound and decisive in their impact on Weil's life, one potential implication certainly did *not* follow: namely, an abandonment of her commitment to justice in history and society. Hers was not a dualistic spirituality; her concern for addressing the material needs of the human spirit was just as passionate as before her religious transformation, but now it was more consciously related to an awareness of the presence of the crucified Christ in the faces of the afflicted. Her involvement in the Young Christian Worker's Movement illustrates her interest in imbuing social and political reform with a Christian spirit. Weil's nascent mystical consciousness only intensified and deepened her attention to the invisible and powerless in history and society.

Given this powerful interest in Christianity—and in particular Catholicism—why is it that she refused to be baptized? Her answer to that question is a further instance of the strength and depth of her convictions. She tells us that her love of non-Christian traditions and spiritualities (including those of ancient Greece, Egypt, India, and China) kept her from entering the Church (WFG, 94-95). Weil felt that a decision to enter the Church would signify a betrayal of the wisdom and truth that lies outside the Church. This fidelity reveals her desire to be in solidarity with "all the countries inhabited by colored races," in her words (WFG, 75). Thus, while Weil confesses that she loves "God, Christ, and the Catholic faith" (WFG, 49), she understood her vocation to be one in exile from the Church; she sought to be a witness to the truth of Christ wherever she discerned truth to exist.

The list of figures influenced and inspired by Simone Weil is quite extensive. Albert Camus said that her essays dealing with Marx and social and political themes, collected under the title *Oppression and Liberty*, were "more penetrating and more prophetic than anything since Marx."[9] The poet T. S. Eliot remarked in the introduction to her work *The Need for Roots* that "we must expose ourselves to the personality of a woman of genius, of a kind of genius akin to that of the saints" (NFR, vi). The inaugurator of Vatican II, Pope John XXIII, mentions Simone Weil as a significant influence on the development of his thought. Such testimonies by these very different individuals communicate well how widely influential Simone Weil has been. Of course, not all the responses to her life and

thought are affirmative. Without mincing words, Charles de Gaulle remarked: "She's out of her mind" (OL, xii). Georges Bataille called her
with disgust "the Christian" and created a character based on her in his
work *The Blue of the Sky*: "She wore black, ill-fitting, and dirty clothes . . .
I felt that such an existence would only have sense for men and a world
doomed to misfortune."[10] Perhaps Weil would have conceded that her
existence would be unintelligible in a world devoid of affliction and misfortune; tragically, the presence of these experiences are all too real in the
time and space that we inhabit. In Weil's own perspective, the suffering
of the world—the mark of slavery and the mark of the cross—had entered
into her person and contributed to the construction of her inimitable
and transgressive identity.

Indeed, this is another reason why Weil became dear to me, precisely
for being an anguished soul, for being able to communicate in her writing
and in her life the weight of suffering. In her hands mysticism is not
tempted by facile, overly optimistic solutions. Her lucid awareness of the
gravity that grounds the human condition to the earth prevents her from
succumbing to a version of mysticism that heedlessly flees the agonies of
history.

Even the form of her writing—direct, honest, unsentimental, precise,
bare—is indicative of her way of life. In this light her close friend Gustave
Thibon expresses well the unity of theory and practice, form and content,
in her life: "She did not write one line which was not the exactest possible
expression of an irresistible inspiration and, at the same time, an invitation and an engagement to remain faithful to this inspiration, to embody
in her whole life and to the very depths of her being what her spirit had
glimpsed."[11] While Weil's life came to an untimely end at the young age
of thirty-four, it is clear that she lived a life of such integrity, veracity, and
passion to make her life and philosophy a rich source of learning.

GUSTAVO GUTIÉRREZ

Gustavo Gutiérrez was born in a poor region of Lima, Peru, in 1928. He
is a mestizo, part Hispanic and part Quechuan Indian. Between the ages
of twelve and eighteen he lived as an invalid, bedridden with osteomyelitis.
In addition to this experience of physical suffering, he notes that another
important memory of his early years was the economic difficulties his
family faced.[12] While such memories are painful to him, he also mentions
the affection and love that he received from his parents and family during

that time. He speaks of his mother's influence as instilling in him a simple and gratuitous love for everyone, especially the poor and needy. "I think her simple faith made me understand something that I later worked out theologically."[13] Indeed, as we will see in the course of this book, the critical and theoretical moment of theological reflection in Gutiérrez is grounded in an attentiveness to the insights, struggles, and suffering of the simple and uneducated masses of Latin America and beyond.

It is no wonder, then, that he insists his work is primarily pastoral and only secondarily theological. His decision to become a priest, for instance, was grounded in his commitment to others and his passion for justice as a key component of his love of intellectual work. Even though entering the seminary allowed him great educational opportunities, he did not become a priest only for intellectual reasons. He has stated:

> I have always believed that my work as a priest is essentially pastoral, fundamentally that of accompanying the lives and the journey of the people and of trying to preach the Gospel out of this experience. Circumstance has led me to express in writing some reflections on this experience. But I want to insist that I have never frankly and honestly considered my writing to be the most important part of my work. . . . I feel very much absorbed in my pastoral work, engulfed by it and by the cruel situation lived by the poor. I have always wanted to make my life a life of daily close contact and shared experience, a shared journey and shared hope, with the poor.[14]

Gutiérrez certainly does not intend to devalue intellectual work and his own theological writings. As we will see, his ideas are insightful and important in raising the consciousness of others and in drawing attention to experiences and perspectives that remain mute and overlooked when not communicated in written form. He nevertheless maintains that intellectual work should operate with a profound modesty and recognition of the limits of pure ideas. Words can offer us only hints of the realities they intend to capture. Gutiérrez writes, "I feel that words can express this world [the world of the poor] only very partially. And so, perhaps, there is a certain reticence about trying to write on a reality that with each passing day appalls me more."[15]

Attention to the appalling situation of the majority of the world today is a cornerstone in Gutiérrez's understanding of theology's fidelity to the "signs of the times." Theology has the unwelcome task of disturbing the complacency and apathy of many of us toward global realities. Far from soothing our conscience, theology serves to make us uneasy and troubled. Indeed, this is one purpose of Gutiérrez's theology as well as Simone Weil's. Gutiérrez insists on the primacy of experience in a country riddled with violence:

> It means not becoming accustomed to seeing the newspapers filled day after day with pictures of mutilated corpses, of mass graves, of innocent people being mowed down. It means not getting used to the fact that fellow human beings must search the garbage to find something to eat, that they must trick their stomachs by eating dirt. . . . It means maintaining a permanent attitude of shock and rejection in the face of all these indignities. Not to do so would be to compromise one's own human dignity.[16]

At its very best liberation theology seeks to give voice to the presence of affliction and injustice in history and to evoke in others this permanent attitude of shock and rejection in the face of these dehumanizing conditions. These realities are what is at stake; the justification of a school of theology named "liberation theology" is not the primary issue. Gutiérrez states clearly, "Personally, the meaning of my life is not liberation theology; it is to be close to my people, to participate in their struggles for liberation and for a just world, and to share their faith and hope."[17]

While these personal experiences and pastoral commitments are crucial in understanding the theology of Gutiérrez, it would be inappropriate to overlook the intellectual trends that shaped his thought. In addition to stimulating in him a love of reading, one of the effects of his childhood illness was the cultivation of an interest in medicine. He pursued this interest at San Marcos University in Peru before deciding to become a priest. After feeling the call to the priesthood, he began his study of philosophy and theology at the seminary of Santiago, Chile. Because he demonstrated much potential for academic work, he was sent for theological training to Europe, studying in Belgium, France, and Rome. During this time he was exposed to much of progressive European theology, from Yves Congar and Karl Rahner to Maurice Blondel and Gerhard von Rad. In Louvain, he also continued his interest in the human sciences, writing his master's thesis on Freud.

He also developed a friendship with Camilo Torres, a radical Latin American priest who later would leave the priesthood to join a guerilla force. Upon leaving the priesthood, Torres once remarked that he would not celebrate the Eucharist until there is justice in the world. Gutiérrez responded, "If we can't celebrate the eucharist until we have attained a perfect society, then we will have to wait until we get to heaven, in which case the eucharist will superfluous."[18] Gutiérrez's comment suggests both a defense of liturgy (and hence a refusal to reduce religion simply to a matter of ethics) and an awareness of the incompleteness of human action and the concomitant need for divine grace. While Gutiérrez is not the "utopian pessimist" that Simone Weil was, he is far from naïve about the construction of a perfect kingdom of God on earth.[19]

The fruit of his education also led him to an understanding of theology that would welcome dialogue with culture and contemporary thought, whether religious or secular in nature. He speaks of such an understanding of theology as "incarnational," that is, as a form of religious thought that discerns and interprets the concrete and visible manifestation of God vis-à-vis the configurations of culture and the contemporary world. Upon reflecting on this aspect of his education and his early experience in teaching, he writes: "It seemed important to me to take up themes in my classes that would allow an examination of the meaning of human existence and the presence of God in the world in which my students lived. This led me to confront Christian faith with thinkers like Albert Camus, Karl Marx, and others as well as film directors like Luis Bunuel and Ingmar Bergman and writers like José María Arguedas. . . ."[20] While this theological method of incarnation led him to recognize the contributions of the various human sciences, it does not follow that his theology is entirely determined by these methodologies.

It is quite clear, for instance, that the charges of Gutiérrez being a Marxist are deeply misleading and wrong. Many of these accusations come from individuals who have not taken the care to read his work, or from individuals who see in liberation theology a stubborn refusal to recognize the triumph of capitalism (Michael Novak, Richard John Neuhaus). The criticism that has come from the Vatican is more nuanced and balanced. Cardinal Ratzinger, for instance, warns of the alliance of theology and church with Marxist and Communist armed struggle. Contrary to the opinion of many, however, Ratzinger does not deny the validity of the concerns and issues at the heart of liberation theology—such as resistance to hunger and poverty, exploitation and oppression. Meanwhile, Pope John XXIII has made quite clear not only the dangers and abuses of communism but also the inequalities and injustices that capitalism has produced.

The fact that Gutiérrez appreciates aspects of the Marxist tradition does not warrant the imputation of the title "Marxist" to his thought. As he once mentioned, it never occurs to anyone to label him a Freudian because he wrote his master's thesis in Louvain on the subject of Freud. The inappropriateness of calling him a Marxist is especially evident when one notes how central spirituality is to the thought and life of Gutiérrez. His early, classic work A *Theology of Liberation* is clearly preoccupied with how to faithfully and courageously follow in the footsteps of Christ in our contemporary period, especially where poverty and misery abound. The passion that pervades the work of Gutiérrez is nothing less than the demand to remember the agony and death of Christ not as a past event, but as a present reality in the world of injustice and violence. His thought offers us signals and hints on a new saintliness for our time.

For Gutiérrez, the life and martyrdom of Archbishop Oscar Romero, killed in 1980 for his prophetic denunciation of the Salvadoran government's repressive and bloody rule, is an instance of a saintliness for our time. Gutiérrez was at Romero's funeral and witnessed the gunfire and panic that interrupted the event. Many were trampled and Gutiérrez attended one of them in his capacity as a priest as she lie dying.

With this brief biographical description in mind, perhaps we can understand the well-verified story of why Gutiérrez failed to receive an honorary doctorate from Yale University. Yale requires that the recipient receive the degree in person. Gutiérrez could not make it because he had already agreed to lead a retreat for laypeople. While to many academics such a story is a case of missed opportunity, for Gutiérrez academic achievement is only meaningful and real when it is incarnated in solidarity and communion with others.

THE MYSTICAL-PROPHETIC THOUGHT OF SIMONE WEIL AND GUSTAVO GUTIÉRREZ

Central to this book is the suggestion that dialogue between the mystical and prophetic trajectories of the Christian tradition should prevail over any binary opposition. The reflections of Simone Weil and Gustavo Gutiérrez are provocative and extraordinary for their creative ability to engage both the mystical and prophetic traditions. As this book hopes to show, both Weil and Gutiérrez are suspicious of forms of mysticism that ignore or minimize the harsh reality of suffering and violence in history and society; conversely, they reveal a serious mistrust of prophetic traditions that deny the contributions of mystical interpretations, practices, and ways of speaking about the divine mystery. They ratify both expressions of God's transcendence and mystery in the mystical tradition, on the one hand, and God's hiddenness in the prophetic and tragic traditions, on the other. In the former case, the emphasis placed on the "mystery of God" suggests the limits of any conceptual, intellectual comprehension of God. The divine is wholly Other to the human mind. In the case of divine hiddenness, however, the accent is less on the intellectual incomprehensibility of God; rather, interpretation of the "hiddenness of God" expresses a concern about God's absence in the face of suffering, especially innocent suffering. In this light, the problem of evil is raised—an issue that is key to both Simone Weil and Gustavo Gutiérrez.

Insofar as Weil and Gutiérrez embody distinct perspectives and interpretations, attention to important differences in their thought cannot be ignored. In regards to mysticism, I will argue that Simone Weil contributes a more intense and developed understanding of mysticism than that of Gutiérrez. While this does *not* suggest that mysticism is absent in Gutiérrez, I believe that Weil incorporates aspects of mysticism in a manner that is exceptional and original. This presence of mysticism in her life and thought is due, in large part, to her profound and penetrating knowledge of Plato and the Platonic tradition, on the one hand, and to her own mystical encounters with God and Christ, on the other. The intensity and excess of mysticism in her life endows this young woman with an aura of fascination and mystery. Gutiérrez's interpretation and appropriation of the prophetic Israelite tradition, however, provides an important corrective and critique of Weil's tendentious dismissal of much of the Old Testament. Gutiérrez's reading of Exodus, the prophets, the Psalms, and especially Job is important in retrieving the Jewish roots of the west. Weil adds her own contribution to the prophetic tradition, however, by her creative interpretation of Greek tragedy vis-à-vis the Christian passion narratives. I believe that bringing these thinkers into dialogue might not only spark an interest and appreciation for these two important thinkers as individuals but also in the ways they enrich each other. It is the hope of this work that a focus on the mystical and prophetic traditions will awaken an attentiveness to the possible glimpses of the face of God in acts of justice and love, in epiphanies of beauty and joy, and in moments of suffering and anguish. The suggestion of this book is that in reading Weil and Gutiérrez together we might possibly be led down a path of challenging ideas and insights, guiding us to new, unexplored possibilities in the course of our own lives and in the circumstances of our world.

I ✍

Mysticism, Marx, and Work in Simone Weil

In a move quite original in the history of Christian mysticism, Simone Weil breaks with those aspects of mystical traditions that have overlooked or minimized the suffering of history as manifested in war, class oppression, and exploitative work conditions. Since Platonism and Christian mysticism have both been accused of neglecting history and being excessively optimistic, it is no small accomplishment to combine a mystical consciousness with an awareness of the dark and destructive presence of power and violence in human history and nature. This is the formidable project that Simone Weil tackles so creatively.[1] With Plato, Weil contends that a central goal of the philosophical life is the remembering of forgotten truth (ICAG, 76). In the thought of Weil, however, the major cause of the loss of memory is the destructive presence of force in human life. Force in the form of conquest, slavery, rape, and oppressive conditions of work uproots the human spirit from community and tradition and destroys human thought and attention. Whole traditions and spiritualities are forgotten and lost at the hands of force.

In addition to the damaging effects of force and violence, Weil contends, the modern world and the notion of historical evolution have influenced this loss of memory, especially in regards to the exclusion of the defeated of history, the victims of force (NFR, 219). "No attention is paid to the defeated. . . . They become naught" (NFR, 212). In this view, the central task of philosophy is to love that part of the past which is "inarticulate, anonymous, and which has vanished" (NFR, 222). To do so requires a creative attention that sees what is invisible, what has been destroyed by force. This vision of the invisible past is contemplation for Weil and, following Plato, it is love (WFG, 149; ICAG, 134).

In the perspective of Weil, this love of the invisible and anonymous

17

past militates against the modern illusion and bias regarding the present. We moderns believe that we have evolved beyond the primitive thought of the past. Among other things, Simone Weil's notion of decreation is an interruption and critique of this modern bias. The idea of decreation in Weil is a decentering and emptying of the self in regard to both space and time. As she observes in her notebooks: "To annul perspective in time as we do in space. Eternity. Hence the power of memory..." (*FLNB*, 85). The decentering of the self in time makes possible a reception of other voices beyond the monotone voice of modernity. The decentering of the self in space makes possible a reception of other voices beyond, firstly, the political and economic elite of society, and secondly, beyond European and "first world" countries.

Most persuasive in Weil's retrieval of the past (forgotten truth) is her refusal to lend this task a reactionary and romantic form. "Love of the past has nothing to do with any reactionary political attitude" (*NFR*, 49). Indeed, the retrieval of spiritual treasures of the past is to inspire a resistance against the subjugation of marginalized voices. An honest recognition of the destructive impact of force with regard to such powerless voices is the condition for the possibility of spirituality.

> There is nothing more cruel towards the past than the commonplace according to which force is powerless to destroy spiritual values; by virtue of this opinion we deny that civilizations obliterated by the violence of arms ever existed. . . . So we slay a second time what has perished. . . . Piety enjoins reverent attention to the traces, however scarce, of destroyed civilizations, and an attempt to conceive what their spirit was. (SE 43)[2]

Central to the thought of Weil is the preservation of past spiritual treasures for the enrichment and inspiration of workers and the poor. In attending to the voices of workers and mystics, Weil seeks to expose the narrow and oppressive features of the modern age, the age of the scientific revolutions and industrial capitalism. The Enlightenment is in part culpable for the marginalization of the voices and lives of mystics and workers, contends Weil. "We are living at time when most people feel, confusedly but keenly, that what was called enlightenment in the 18th century, including the sciences, provides an insufficient spiritual diet. . . . There is an urgent need to refer back to those great epochs which favored the kind of spiritual life of which all that is most precious in science and art is no more than a somewhat imperfect reflection" (*SL*, 131). Weil's reflections on the mysticism of work are central to her retrieval of both the voices of workers and the voices of the mystical traditions as resources for filling the void created by the "insufficient spiritual diet" of the Enlightenment. As Weil insists, however, we cannot be negligent in recognizing the major obstacles to the cultivation of mystical and spiritual values constituted by oppressive and dehumanizing conditions of work. In Weil, then, the experience of work can aid in the formation of a mystical consciousness, but it also can destroy the human spirit. The central task of this chapter is to interpret and clarify the relationship between Weil's ideas of mysticism and her reflections on force and necessity in relation to human labor.

SPIRITUALITY AND MYSTICISM IN
THE THOUGHT OF SIMONE WEIL

While Simone Weil never clearly defined the terms "spirituality" or "mysticism," she does use the term "spirituality" in a more general and inclusive manner than that of "mysticism." While "spirituality" may include non-Christian forms of thought and practice (i.e. Greek, Eastern, or even Marxist forms), "mysticism" in the thought of Weil is employed with a more specific Christian meaning and is usually related to an explicit and intense consciousness of God, on the one hand, and to apophatic discourse, on the other.

"The word spirituality doesn't imply any particular affiliation. . . . It would not be difficult to find in Marx quotations that can all be brought back to the reproach of a lack of spirituality leveled at capitalist society . . ." (NFR, 93). Indeed, Weil's understanding of spirituality is quite broad. In her book *The Need for Roots* Weil cogently articulates a notion of spirituality that she hopes will imbue society with a greater humility and piety. Her promotion of the term "spirituality" is not undertaken, however, without a certain misgiving. With good justification she is afraid that the conception will be corrupted. "But one can only lay hold of such a conception in fear and trembling. How can we touch it without soiling it, turning it into a lie?" (NFR, 93). In addition to her fear of spirituality being reduced to a sentimental feeling of consolation or special state of experience ("feel-good religion," as we say these days), Weil worries that it might also become the unholy rationale for a movement, regime, or nation in promoting its cause, especially in the case of colonialism or warfare (NFR, 93). If this corruption of spirituality is avoided, however, the nurturing of the human spirit may enrich society and lead to an expression of thought guided by humility, beauty, and justice.

In keeping with some contemporary postmodern thinkers, moreover, Weil suggests that this kind of spirituality may remedy "the lack of balance due to a purely material development of technical science" (NFR, 94). In this sense, the retrieval of spiritual resources from the Western tradition, and indeed from non-Western traditions as well, will instill the modern world with a rootedness sorely lacking. Such spiritual roots may function to create and strengthen a continuity with both the past (the memory of the dead) and with future generations.[3] "But no one thinks nowadays about his ancestors who died fifty or even only twenty or ten years before his birth; nor about his descendents who will be born fifty or even only twenty or ten years after his death" (NFR, 95).

Simone Weil's conception of philosophy is also linked with spirituality. As in ancient Greek and Roman philosophy, Simone Weil understood the *love of wisdom* that defined the philosophical enterprise to be a comprehensive training of the human spirit, to be a "way of life" before it was an affair of theory and abstract speculation. "Philosophy (including problems of cognition, etc.) is *exclusively* an affair of action and practice. That is why it is so difficult to write about it. Difficult in the same way as a treatise on tennis or running, but much more so" (FLNB, 362). The subject matter of philosophy (wisdom, justice, good, beauty, and ultimately God for Weil) is incapable of being captured by rational thought and speculation alone. One must play tennis to learn it, experience music to know it, experience art to understand it, and finally engage in spiritual exercises in order to come to know truth, justice, beauty, love, and God.

The insufficiency of objective and rational knowledge is especially obvious if, as Weil contends, an awareness of suffering and affliction is the key to wisdom. A village idiot may possess a greater wisdom by virtue of her suffering than the most intelligent man of talent (MA, 67–70). Weil insists that certain people have a privileged contact with the most important knowledge of all: the reality of misfortune (NFR, 169). Thus, in the thought of Weil the experience of suffering can give rise to a mystical wisdom, but spiritual exercises of work, detachment, and attention must first prepare the spirit for the reception of the divine. While the experience of suffering per se is not constitutive of mysticism, it can become a source of mystical insight when attention and awareness are cultivated by spiritual exercises. The need for spiritual exercises and the insight that suffering may engender both imply the limitations of purely objective, rational theory in the search for truth.

Related to this claim, Weil insists that there are two kinds of philoso-phers: those who construct systems of thought to represent objective real-ity and those who orient the form of philosophy to provoke a transforma-tion in the students or readers.[4] It is the latter, Weil claims, who are the true masters of thought. They recognize that "philosophic reflection de-pends on an effort of detachment that goes beyond the intelligence and involves the whole man. . . . 'One must turn toward the truth with one's whole soul'" (FW, 288). For Weil, this Platonic philosophy results in trans-formation and conversion. It is spirituality.

Certainly it should be noted that not all forms of philosophy have spirituality at their heart. Indeed, central to the contention of Weil is that the modern world has impoverished the classic understanding of philoso-phy by separating theory from practice and philosophical questioning from spiritual training.[5] Weil argues that the seeds of such a separation are already present in Aristotle and come to full bloom in modernity. Thus, philosophy can be considered a form of spirituality only if and when the central task of philosophy is to instigate a transformation in the life of the student. An engagement in the philosophical life will demand a commit-ment by the entire human person, body and soul.

If we understand the task of philosophy in this sense (as a way of life and a spiritual discipline at odds with objective and detached scientific models of thought), we can begin to appreciate the thought of Weil in relation to a wide variety of contemporary thinkers. The French philoso-pher Pierre Hadot, for instance, is worthy of greater attention for his in-sistence that among the ancients, philosophy operated with the purpose of training the philosophical disciple to incarnate a different mode of being in the world than the average person. Each philosophical school had spiritual exercises that were "designed to insure spiritual progress toward the ideal state of wisdom, exercises of reason that will be, for the soul, analogous to the athlete's training or to the application of a medical cure."[6] Philosophical works or dialogues were employed with the primary intention of training and *forming* rather than simply *informing* the philo-sophical disciple.

Another theme that is a part of the Greek philosophical tradition, especially Plato, and important for understanding Weil's mystical thought is the theme of ineffability or incomprehensibility concerning the One or the Good. In book 6 of Plato's *Republic*, the Form of the Good is said to be "not being but more than being," and in the *Parmenides* (142a) Plato concludes that the One is beyond time and being: "Then the One has no name, nor is there any description or knowledge or perception or opinion of it. . . ." While much of Western apophatic language (*apophasis* understood as a language of unsaying, of speech about God that is a failure of speech)[7] is fully developed only in later Platonism and in Christian mysticism, certainly the roots of this tradition are already present in Plato himself. In the mysticism of Weil, the spiritual exercises and apophaticism inherent to her mystical vision are grounded in these traditions, but they are radically transformed in light of her Christian consciousness, especially of the suffering God of the cross.[8]

We might say that for Simone Weil mysticism is an entire way of life connected to an explicit consciousness of God's immediate presence and, no less, of God's absence from all human conceptions and experiences. While such a vision has affinities with the spirituality of ancient Greek thinkers, especially Plato, Weil's growing Christian faith led her to an understanding of mysticism informed by a theology of the cross. This transformation of the Greek tradition by a central metaphor of Christianity—Christ crucified—is the foundation for her development of a mysticism of work. Work is a daily death, a bearing of the cross. The absence of the idea of work among the Greeks, according to Weil, amounts to a failure to ground spirituality in a concrete, historical praxis.

It is with Weil's developing Christian belief that God is manifested within history—on the underside of history, to be exact—that her mysticism departs from the Greek tradition of philosophy and spirituality. The departure from the Greeks is even more radical if one considers that for Simone Weil the cross is manifested not merely in a personal manner but in the faces of whole groups of afflicted and oppressed persons, such as factory workers or colonized peoples. It this moment which adds a Christian character to the general understanding of mysticism.

The scholarship of Bernard McGinn has contributed much to our understanding of mysticism in the Christian tradition. McGinn makes a very important suggestion that mysticism should be interpreted in the following ways: "mysticism as a part or element of religion; mysticism as a process or way of life; and mysticism as an attempt to express a direct consciousness of the presence of God."[9] Spirituality in the thought of Weil should be interpreted in relation to the first two more general headings, but in regard to the third heading ("mysticism as an attempt to express a direct consciousness of the presence of God") we would be more precise in calling this, in particular, the mystical element in Weil's thought. Of course, mysticism certainly includes the first two elements as well, but more specifically can be defined, in McGinn's work, as the "preparation for, consciousness of, and reaction to . . . the immediate or direct presence of God."[10]

Thus, while the first two elements of McGinn's interpretation of mysticism are characteristic of all spirituality, the third element is distinctive of a spirituality that becomes mystical. For Simone Weil, then, philosophical schools can be understood to be forms of spirituality when and insofar as they are concerned with ultimate value, transcendence, and a new way of life. Mysticism, on the other hand, only emerges with an expression of a more immediate and direct consciousness of God, on the one hand, and with an apophatic consciousness, on the other. Such an understanding of mysticism becomes increasingly clear in Weil's own accounts of God's revelation in her life.

In her own maturing consciousness of God's presence, Weil noted a change in her life. After her mystical contacts, Weil explains that the "name of God and Christ have been more and more irresistibly mingled with my thoughts" (*SL*, 140). Prior to that time she was closer to the thought of the Greeks. "Until then my only faith had been the Stoic *amor fati* as Marcus Aurelius had understood it. . . ." (*SL*, 140). Her deepening Christian faith takes her more and more in the direction of mysticism that, to be sure, incorporates the Greek philosophical and spiritual tradition, but also transforms it in relation to a Christian theology of the cross as well as in the direction of apophatic discourse.

As mentioned in the introduction, at this time she began to read many of the classic Christian mystics. She mentions that, if anything, she formerly had been turned off by the reputation of mystical authors. Apparently the association of mysticism with special states or miraculous events left a distaste with the idea of mysticism—a distaste, it seems to me, that would have only been intensified if she had lived to witness the range and idiosyncrasy of phenomena that are considered "mystical" in today's world. Following her own unexpected and surprising encounters, however, she began to rethink her position and allowed herself to read and appreciate the contributions of many of the major Christian mystics.

Certainly, the significance Weil attached to the phenomenon of mysticism went much deeper than her reading and knowledge of the classic Christian mystics. It is with mystical epiphanies in her own life that we witness her emergence as a Christian mystical figure. It is only then that she begins to speak so poignantly and with such great conviction of the mystical dimension of Christianity. In no uncertain terms she says that Christ came down and took possession of her (*WFG*, 69). She likens this encounter to the presence of a love, "like that which one can read in the smile on a beloved face" (WFG, 69).

It is important to note that this event occurred during an episode of one of her frequent migraine headaches. If Weil was privileged to receive certain epiphanies and revelations, it was hardly an experience of pure consolation or sweetness; the experience of affliction, rather, was the vehicle for her experiences of God. The manifestation of Christ in her life had the effect of heightening her consciousness of God in a more immediate and explicit manner and, no doubt, of giving her a more profound sense of the crucified Christ. In her view, God is most inclined to manifest himself to the outcasts and rejects, to those who lack power, glory, and majesty (WFG, 72).

Concerning the question of mysticism in the thought of Weil, however, we need to consider more than her autobiographical accounts. To challenge distortions of mysticism, especially those that reduce mysticism to a special or bizarre feeling or experience, Weil insists that a method is necessary for the study of mysticism. "The supreme and perfect state of mystical contemplation is something that is infinitely more mysterious still, and yet St. John of the Cross wrote treatises on the method of attaining to such a state . . ." (NFR, 180). Her contention is that mysticism is not an arbitrary or magical state of experience. If this is what constitutes mysticism, as we will see later, she was hostile toward "mysticism." As I mentioned, she had been put off by accounts of miracles and special states that ostensibly described the experience of God (WFG, 69). To reduce mysticism to a feeling or experience is to run the risk of creating the kind of sentimental and consoling opiate that she spent so much of her life criticizing. As such, mysticism will be indistinguishable, Weil argues, from the experience of the effects of a drug. "The mistake lies precisely in the search for a particular state" (WFG, 173). Weil names this kind of mysticism "ersatz mysticism."

This suspicion toward the association of mysticism with special states or extraordinary experiences is related to the suspicion Weil expresses toward belief in miracles. For example, she insists that miracles in Jesus' life were ambiguous and neutral in themselves. False prophets are also portrayed as possessing powers to perform signs and wonders, so miracles are an inadequate sign of the presence of God. It was not the miracles of Jesus that revealed his authenticity, but instead the extraordinary quality of his entire life: the poverty and purity of his life, his compassion, the beauty of his words (NFR, 256).

Along similar lines, Weil states that there are two kinds of figures in the history of mysticism: "There are people who simply experience states of ecstasy; there are other people who devote themselves almost exclusively to the study of these states, who describe and classify them and, so far as it is possible, induce them" (*SL*, 123). Weil then suggests that it is the latter who have been generally considered mystics! The title of "mystic" is improperly imputed only on the basis of an extraordinary state of experience.

This claim, I believe, agrees with much of contemporary scholarship on mysticism. As scholars have pointed out, many mystical thinkers of the Christian tradition have abstained from providing the readers with autobiographical accounts. Such a focus on autobiographical descriptions of experience has led to a neglect of a hermeneutics of mystical texts.[11] Of course, the presence of autobiographical accounts does not disqualify one as a mystic. What I am insisting upon, in fidelity to Weil's thought, is that special experiences as such do not constitute mysticism. Not only Simone Weil but also classic figures such as John of the Cross and Meister Eckhart are examples of mystics who would agree that experience itself can be deceptive and is an insufficient, even dangerous, feature by which to define mysticism.

The problem with this reduction of mysticism to a feeling or experience is that it obscures the significance of spiritual exercises and practices as preparation for the consciousness of God as well as overlooking the life lived as a reaction to the consciousness of God. The entire process of the mystical life is thereby given slight attention.[12] For Weil spiritual exercises are crucial for preparing for the reception of divine grace or inspiration, but equally important is the way of life following upon a vision of God, the return to the cave of the transformed person (*LP*, 221).

In her essay "Forms of the Implicit Love of God," for example, she claims that love of neighbor, love of the beauty of the world, love of religious ceremonies, and friendship are all ways to prepare for the presence of God. "The combination of these loves constitutes the love of God in the form best suited to the preparatory period, that is to say a veiled form. They do not disappear when the love of God in the full sense of the word wells up in the soul; they become infinitely stronger and all loves taken together make only a single love" (*WFG*, 138). The cultivation of these implicit, preparatory loves involves a kind of apprenticeship or spiritual training closely linked with her understanding of mysticism. Note that in this case, it is *love*, not any kind of *feeling*, that constitutes mysticism per se.

In the Christian Platonism of Weil, the key moment of mystical consciousness concerns the transformation or turning of the soul. Through

Platonic images Weil suggests that consciousness of our blind and ignorant situation in the cave (our exile) is the beginning of our movement
toward the light of the sun. "We are unconscious of our misery" and
unaware of our blindness and misery inside the cave (*SNLG*, 109). This
insight into our exiled state takes on a more explicit Christian meaning in
her association of human exile with the fall in Genesis and the concomitant curse of Adam and Eve with regard to the pain of labor (*NFR*, 285–
86). Weil interprets this sense of exile in Plato (and Greek tragedy) vis-à-
vis a theology of the cross and the pain of work. In a concrete manner,
work heightens our consciousness of our exile, namely, our subjection to
time, suffering, monotony, cross.

The consciousness of God thus begins with the consciousness of our
misery and blindness (not unlike Luther). Yet in the vision of Weil this is
the beginning of the mystical life, not the culmination. Again following
Plato, but relating it to her own notion of attention, Weil claims that the
consciousness of God needs further training and illumination. The ascent of the soul outside the cave is cultivated by (1) mathematical and
scientific exercises, (2) philosophical dialectics, (3) apprenticeship in beauty,
(4) ethical exercises, and (5) contemplation or vision of God. Weil argues
that the culminating point of contemplation (*theoria*) is a transcendence
or transgression of pure intellectual theory: it is love. "Sight is then the
faculty which is in relationship with the good. Plato, in the *Symposium*,
says as definitely as possible that this faculty is love. By the eyes, by sight,
Plato means love" (*ICAG*, 134). Love thus makes possible a consciousness
of God that is both a vision of and assimilation to God (*ICAG*, 77). This
renewed consciousness brings a new knowledge of the self, neighbor, cosmos, and God. As many classic mystics claimed, love is a form of knowing (*amor ipse notitia est*).

Weil also uses the formula of "descent, ascent, and redescent" to describe the journey of the soul in the mystical life. First and foremost, the
descent is an imitation of the kenotic, self-emptying God incarnated and
crucified in Jesus Christ.[13] The descent corresponds to the embrace of the
finite, limited, fragile, and historical character of human existence. It is
an awareness of and consent to pain and suffering; that is, the descent is
our bearing of the cross. A mystical theology that seeks to ascend beyond
the world by fleeing time, death, and suffering is another form of false
mysticism, according to Weil. "To escape from time—that is a sin" (*NB*,
28). This form of specious mysticism flees from historical existence in
order to evade the pain of time, especially the consent to necessity via
human labor (*NB*, 269). Labor makes obvious our subjection to time and

is a "daily death" (NFR, 286-87). For Weil, the Christian virtue of humility is central to the meaning of mystical descent; humility is, first and foremost, recognition of human finitude in time and space (NB, 235). Thus, for Weil, a "descending movement is a condition precedent to an ascending movement" (NFR, 221).

Finally, the development of a mysticism of work by Simone Weil challenges the separation of sacred and profane spheres of culture and society. Spirituality in the modern age has the task, Weil creatively suggests, of cultivating a form of "life in which the supernatural truths would be read in every kind of work, in every act of labor, in all festivals, in all hierarchical social relations, in all art, in all science, in all philosophy" (FLNB, 173). A spirituality that speaks to our age should not seek to exacerbate the separation of religion from secular and public life, but rather imbue it and transform it with its spirit. The relationship between mysticism and work is at the heart of such a transformation (not annulment) of secular life. Thus a peasant working in the fields or a worker in the factory may be as prayerful as a monk in his cell, Weil contends.[14]

Weil's interpretation of mysticism echoes that of previous mystics, even when she does not explicitly note them. Meister Eckhart, for example, states: "Because truly, when people think that they are acquiring God more in inwardness, in devotion, in sweetness and in various approaches than they do by the fireside or in the stable, you are acting just as if you took God and muffled his head up in a cloak and pushed him under a bench."[15] This quote sums up well both a critique of mysticism as a private, inward experience and as a form of religion separate and isolated from the public and "profane" world. Eckhart was part of a general trend in the late Middle Ages of lay movements of mysticism and spirituality that made use of vernacular languages, giving them an access to spiritual involvement otherwise denied them by the monasteries and the language of the educated elite, Latin. Such a trend made mysticism accessible to whole groups traditionally excluded, especially women and the common folk. Simone Weil continues in this tradition and takes it in a new direction, especially in regard to work.

THE ACCESSIBILITY OF MYSTICISM

In the late Middle Ages various lay groups and movements, such as the Beguines or the Devotio Moderna, erupted into prominence as a reaction against the monopoly of mysticism by monastic and mendicant communities. Eckhart's vernacular sermons proved to be especially appealing in their insistence that no one, even if illiterate or poor, is incapable of mystical consciousness.[16] Simone Weil takes this attitude one step further and maintains that mysticism is not only accessible to the poor and afflicted, but that they even have a privileged insight. Contemplatives or mystics, philosophers or scholars, run the risk of losing contact with real, concrete history, Weil argues. Work makes it impossible to do so. "He who is aching in every limb, worn out by the effort of a day of work, that is to say a day when he has been subject to matter, bears the reality of the universe in his flesh like a thorn. The difficulty for him is to look and to love. If he succeeds, he loves the Real. That is the immense privilege God has reserved for his poor" (WFG 170). Workers and the afflicted can have, if their attention is vigilant, a more truthful and unsentimental vision of the painful reality of suffering and cross in history and nature.

For Weil, it is not that the working poor are necessarily more ethical than other, more privileged groups. What is at issue is their cognitive insight into reality brought to light by their suffering. Since Weil believed that the cross is the supreme source of wisdom, it is not surprising that she considered the destitute and disenfranchised as bearers of wisdom. "The Cross of Christ is the only gateway to knowledge" (NB, 444). While the passion narratives conveyed this insight, Weil also believed that Greek tragedy articulated a kind of experiential knowledge that is born of suffering (ICAG, 56–59). For this reason, she felt that the poor would be capable of understanding and appreciating tragic poetry or the Christian passion narratives in a unique and creative manner. What does one learn by suffering? The wisdom that grace brings violently (Aeschylus) teaches us of our human vulnerability, our fragility, and our limits (ICAG).

The insights inspired by her reading of tragedy take on a more forceful reality in her own experience of factory work. The purpose of her factory work was, in addition to her desire to be in solidarity with the working classes, to deepen her knowledge and to continue her studies. Simone Petremont mentions that Weil had reached an impasse in her theoretical thought. The time of factory work was to bring clarification and illumination on the social, political, and economic issues of the time.[17] This was to lead to a solution that would inspire change and alleviation of social oppression. Thus the time of factory work was not simply a question of "experience" for Weil but rather, in keeping with our understanding of mysticism, an opportunity to cultivate a consciousness of society and humanity. Evident in Weil's attitude toward the working classes and the afflicted, therefore, is an eagerness to learn from their struggle and plight.

   This appreciation for the potential wisdom inherent in the marginalized groups of society has a philosophical foundation in the thought of Weil. In the early writing of Simone Weil it is already clear that she claims that truth is accessible to all, not merely to an elite class. "Thus any man, however mediocre his intelligence and talents may be, can, if he applies himself, know everything that is within man's reach . . ." (*FW*, 48; *WFG*, 64). This quote from her thesis on Descartes has as its target the scientific knowledge of the modern world. She complains that science shows a confident scorn for the intuition of the common person (*FW*, 32–34). The authority of science reigns unchallenged in its monopoly of what will count as knowledge. The norms of valid knowledge promulgated by science exclude the potential insights among the poor and uneducated masses.

   Weil's understanding and experience of factory work led her to an appreciation of the wisdom and courage implicit in the lives of workers. She believed that in actual work what is involved is not merely an "insight" in an intellectual sense but also a vision as *theoria* in the Platonic sense (*theoria* suggesting contemplation or vision of the Good). In other words, the "sight" or vision that is implicit in the act of work gives rise, in the thought of Weil, to a mysticism of work. The workers bear within them the wisdom that may blossom, with proper attention and spiritual training, into mystical glimpses of God. This is especially true because, for Weil, the beginning of mystical consciousness is an acceptance of our state of exile, of human misery, finitude, and fragility. For Simone Weil it is the common person, especially the workers and the poor, who is in the best position to recognize this truth of the human condition.

WORK AS AN OBSTACLE AND BRIDGE
TO MYSTICAL CONSCIOUSNESS

"The suffering which degrades and that which ennobles are not the same" (*NB*, 79). While Simone Weil believes suffering and pain in human labor to be an inescapable consequence of our natural state of exile, there are certain forms of oppression and exploitation that are abnormally destructive. In the former case, confronting suffering is interpreted by Weil as a heroic overcoming of adversity that engenders wisdom, whereas in the latter case, suffering has the power to actually crush the human spirit of any impulse of resistance and decimate any knowledge. Weil locates the idea of "affliction" in the context of the degrading, not ennobling, effect of suffering. Extreme affliction brings death to the self before the self is capable of attentively consenting to its own decreation. The different forms of suffering lead, then, to either a nihilistic annihilation of the self or to an annihilation in God. "Just as there are two voids, two silences, etc., the one above and the one below—so perhaps also, if death is annihilation, there are two annihilations, annihilation in nothingness and annihilation in God" (NB, 463).

Weil's thoughts on affliction are shaped by her interpretation of Greek tragedy and the Christian passion narratives. In her interpretation of the passion narratives, for example, she insists that unlike the heroic deaths of the Christian martyrs (often in emulation of a Greek hero, e.g., Socrates), Jesus trembled in the garden prior to his death and during the crucifixion cried out in agony and loneliness. "The accounts of the Passion show that a divine spirit, incarnate, is changed by misfortune, trembles before suffering and death, feels itself, in the depths of its agony, to be cut off from man and God" (MA 192). In Weil's interpretation of the passion narratives, the humanity of Christ makes evident the fragile and vulnerable character of human nature. No account of suffering that obscures the weakness of the human spirit in the face of force and oppression will be able to shed light on the human condition. Even a Stoic who had to endure the oppressive conditions of the modern factory would be degraded, Weil remarks (SL, 38).

The differences between these two forms of suffering lead, then, to either decreation or destruction. In the case of decreation, suffering is the path to the loss of the self and the discovery of another agent deep within the self—God. In the case of destruction, the self is lost without any such breakthrough. "Suffering is to move either towards the Nothingness above or the Nothingness below" (FLNB, 117; also 142, 220, 310, 339). In terms of work, Weil suggests a similar contrast in her image of a squirrel revolving in its cage. Akin to an animal, we work to eat and eat to work. This cycle can be either supreme wretchedness or supreme splendor (NB, 496). Elsewhere, Weil contrasts a base, servile humility or waiting (humiliation) with a Christlike humility (NFR, 135). In the factory, the worker is made to wait for orders in the former sense. It breeds a humiliating passivity and absence of thought and initiative (FLNB, 20).

Work, or suffering in general, can be either an obstacle or bridge to mysticism. What is the key for fostering the latter? For Weil, the answer to that question begins with the actual struggle against oppressive conditions themselves. This struggle for just conditions is a condition for the possibility of mysticism. Of course, the struggle for justice in itself does not constitute mysticism anymore than human deeds constitute salvation in Christianity. There is a tension between the demand for just conditions of work and the fact that mystical insight occurs as a result of the free and unmerited manifestation of God. Ultimately, for Weil, the development of the mind, spirit, and attention among the workers is more central to mysticism per se than reforming the conditions of the factories. Such a development is intent on heightening the consciousness of workers and of fostering their *consent*, key for the passage to mystical insight. Such consent makes possible mystical decreation as opposed to the destruction of the self. Decreation of the 'I' happens from within, while destruction occurs from without (*NB*, 337, 342). Because of Weil's lucid and tragic recognition of the brutal and dehumanizing impact of force in society, however, she insists that any mystical thought should begin with a study of oppression and the struggle for justice. She realized that too often the conditions in the factories prohibited the free consent of workers and destroyed the seeds of any authentic spirituality. Her own insights regarding social oppression were deeply shaped by her study of the problems in the industrial factory.

Work as an Obstacle to Mystical Consciousness

The destructive capability of affliction became quite clear to her during her time in the factory, the place where Weil sought to shed light on the conditions of workers not by a theoretical analysis, but through a participation in the lives of those who struggle for their daily bread. Against heroic conceptions of suffering as ennobling, Weil could not fail to notice in the factories the loss of dignity and humanity in the encounter with brute force. Her conception of affliction illustrates this and accentuates the vulnerable and fragile character of the human spirit. Her understanding of *human misery* should be seen in light of this human fragility and *not* simply in terms of human sinfulness. What exactly is affliction for Weil?

First of all, affliction takes possession of the soul and brands the soul with the mark of slavery. It is a humiliating degradation of human dignity. Second, affliction includes physical suffering, the pain of the body. Third, affliction is the loss of all social consideration. One's life is seen as an ignominious shame, as with criminals. Lastly, affliction strikes the soul and produces self-hatred and self-contempt, even a feeling of guilt (*SNLG*, 170–75). "There is not real affliction unless the event which has gripped and uprooted a life attacks it, directly or indirectly, in all it parts, social, psychological, and physical" (*SNLG*, 171). The general condition of the afflicted is a terrifying experience of God's absence, and it is affliction that causes our absence from God. "Men struck down by affliction are at the foot of the Cross, almost at the greatest possible distance from God. It must not be thought that sin is a greater distance" (SNLG, 175). Oppressive conditions of work have the power to thrust a human spirit into a state that is the equivalent of death.

One of Weil's major criticisms of Marx is that he never fully understood the debasing reality of affliction. Marx claims that there exists a revolutionary spirit among the proletariat. During Weil's time in the factory, the complete absence of a radical spirit was most striking. "Marx's assertion that the regime would produce its own gravediggers is cruelly contradicted every day; and one wonders, incidentally, how Marx could ever have believed that slavery could produce free men. . . . The truth is that, to quote a famous saying, slavery degrades man to the point of making him love it . . ." (OL, 117). The conditions of the factory engendered submission and docility, not revolt (SL, 16, 35, 47, 57). Marx underestimated the power of force. He failed fully to recognize the effectiveness and pervasiveness of force and ideological legitimation—that is, the way in which the sentiments and interests of the masters are internalized and appropriated by the slaves. In other words, the scorn and disregard that the masters show for those who obey is internalized by the slaves and directed against themselves. "The man who obeys, whose movements, pains, pleasures are determined by the word of another, feels himself to be inferior, not by accident, but by nature" (OL, 144).

Even if Marx underestimated the debilitating effect of affliction, there was much in Marx that Weil affirmed. Marx's analysis of capitalism was unsurpassed in demonstrating the effects of specialization as well as the separation of theory and work in the factory. The result of specialization placed the task of thought and initiative in the arms of the ruling classes, while the workers were stripped of any self-determination. "The rationalized factory, where a man finds himself shorn, in the interests of a passive mechanism, of everything which makes for initiative, intelligence, knowledge, method, is as it were an image of our present day society" (OL, 13). Theoretical culture came to be monopolized by the ruling classes and as such only legitimized social oppression. "The false conception so formed tends to prolong the duration of the oppression, in so far as it causes this separation between thought and work to seem legitimate" (OL, 30, 156).

Thus, Weil argues that the factory destroys the thought, creativity, and initiative of the workers. The factory puts the interests of production and material products before the human person. This brings about a subordination of the subject to the object (*OL*, 33). The products come out refined and polished, while the workers come out debased. "In crafts-manship the worker's limbs formed a living machine; in the factory, there is dead machinery which is independent of the worker, of which they are a part like living cogs in a machine" (*LP*, 147). Oppressive conditions of the factory make one into a reified thing. The ability of force to transform one into a thing is at the heart of her later essay "The Iliad." There she defines force as "that x that turns anybody who is subjected to it into a thing" (*MA*, 163). In the factory, it produces a blind and servile passivity in fearful deference to orders from above.

Weil also makes clear that time became an unbearable burden in the factory (*FW*, 225). The pain and suffering of work seemed to slow the passing of time. The burdensome character of time in the factory was only exacerbated by the demand for increased speed in production.[18] In this light, "time is the most profound and the most tragic subject which human beings can think about. . . . So, there is nothing in us which does not protest against the passage of time, and yet everything, in us, is subject to time" (*LP*, 197–98). In the factory, Weil came into contact with the tragic and onerous face of time. The destructive effect of this experience of time gave her the sense of bad infinity, the infinity of a squirrel revolv-ing in his cage time and time again. The wretched haste demanded of the workers in the factory is without rhythm, grace, and dignity (*SWR*, 61). It is a barren monotony ruled by the time clock, the opposite extreme of the beautiful monotony of a Gregorian chant or the uniform succession of the days and seasons (*SWR*, 69). The bad infinity of the modern factory is a vicious obstacle to a breakthrough to divine infinity.

The factory uproots and thrusts the human spirit into exile without fostering a sense of belonging in the world. "Time drags for him and he lives in a perpetual exile. He spends his day in a place where he cannot feel at home" (*SWR*, 62). In Weil's later work, she insists that the sense of belonging in the world is nothing else than a feeling for the beauty of the world. The conditions of the workers, however, produces a "horror of ugliness. The soul that is prevented by circumstances from feeling any-thing of the beauty of the world, even confusedly . . . is invaded to its center by a kind of horror" (*WFG*, 168). This horror is the tearing up of our roots from their connection with the infinity of the cosmos (*WFG*, 180).

In short, the factory for Weil is a "festering-ground of evil" (*SWR*, 72). Clearly, in her view the conditions of the modern industrial society are an obstacle to the cultivation of any form of thought, much less that of mys-tical consciousness. A transformation of such conditions, therefore, is key to create a nourishing soil of spirituality. "Marx's truly great idea," Weil writes, "is that in human society . . . nothing takes place otherwise than through material transformations" (OL, 45). This transformation demands a thoughtful and reflective social theory. "Only on this condition could political action become something analogous to a form of work . . ." (OL, 60). Social theory joined with practice plays a part in the Weilian understanding of work.

One might suggest that such a materialistic study of society was part of Weil's early work and came to be nullified by her deepening Platonic and Christian vision. I believe that it is clearly inappropriate to think so. To be sure, the materialistic understanding of her early work undergoes a transformation. Nevertheless, as late as the year of her death (1943), she was writing on Marx's "indestructible" contribution, namely, the methodological study of relations of force in society (OL, 164). "Here we have an idea of genius. . . . It is not a doctrine; it is an instrument of study, research, exploration . . ." (OL, 171). This methodological contribution of Marx's makes him, she says, more attractive to the Christian than to atheists (OL, 177). Her demand for intellectual honesty required, she says, of herself, an openness to all ideas, including materialism and atheism (WFG, 85).

It is true, however, that there is a change in her later thought. The change corresponds to her development of a Platonic and Christian mysticism. In her later thought, the study of the relations of force demands spiritual training in order to transform it. "Working out a social theory means, instead of worshiping the beast [Plato's metaphor], to study its anatomy, physiology, reflexes, and, above all, to try to understand the mechanism of its conditioned reflexes, that is to say find a method for training it" (OL, 165). In Simone Weil, this method of training the beast combines a social theory with a mystical *theoria*. In other words, mysticism has the task of imbuing social analysis with a vision that transforms the public sphere in a new light. This new light is provided by a form of contemplation that unites intellectual and manual work at a higher level (MA, 254). Such a mystical theory will be brought to bear on the entire social realm, including the political sphere. The effect of this vision will transform the nature of politics from being a "power game" to being an enterprise that is attentive to the powerless and weak in history and society.

In *The Need for Roots* Weil argues that frequently politics is debased to being a "technique for acquiring and holding on to power" (NFR, 209). A political vision inspired by a Christian and Platonic *theoria*, on the contrary, has detachment from, and annihilation of, the will-to-power as its central end. Through spiritual training, social change becomes nothing less than a hunger and thirst for justice. Politics should be inspired by a view of justice formed by supernatural compassion—that is, a compassion that resists the natural inclination for the strong to dominate the weak. Such compassion inspires the renunciation or annihilation of the will of the strong out of sympathy for the weak. "The sympathy of the strong for the weak, being in the opposite direction, is against nature" (*WFG*, 147–49). Attention to the weak and afflicted demands a creative spirituality that sees what is invisible and embraces what is repulsive. This political vision, she claims, "could be defined as being that of a director of conscience on a national plane" (*NFR*, 206).

At its best, the fruit of such an analysis, via social theory and mystical *theoria*, is the creation of conditions for the possibility of mysticism for all people and groups, not merely among privileged classes. One metaphor that Weil uses to signify the importance of social and political conditions for the mystical life is the growth of a plant. "One must remember that a plant lives by light and water, not by light alone. So it would be a mistake to count upon grace alone. Energy from this world is also needed" (*FLNB*, 348; also *MA*, 255–56). The task of the farmer is to prepare the soil so that the plant might be able to receive light. "It is not the farmer's job to go in search of solar energy or even to make use of it, but to arrange everything in such a way that the plants capable of using it and transmitting it to us will receive it in the best possible conditions" (*SNLG*, 151). "This shows that good descends from heaven upon earth only to the extent to which certain conditions are in fact fulfilled on earth" (*NFR*, 252).

Clearly then, oppressive conditions of force, as in the factory, are obstacles to the mystical life, and analysis and transformation of these conditions should occupy the attention of spirituality. It should be obvious that Weil's formulation of mysticism is grounded in historical and social realities. The rule of force in history, the burden of time in the factory, the loss of dignity and the potential for reflection in affliction—these are all addressed by Weil as key moments in her mystical theory. Her major insight in this regard is her refusal to reduce mysticism to an ahistorical and otherworldly pursuit, as in gnosticism. One variety of a spurious mysticism "consists in only being prepared to recognize obligations towards what is not of this world. . . . It is only through things and individual beings on this earth that human love can penetrate to what lies beyond" (*NFR*, 150–51).

This concern of Simone Weil does not, however, lead us to conclude that once certain conditions of justice are established mystical decreation immediately follows. Insofar as decreation involves the graced discovery of God at the core of our being, Weil will insist that decreation is not exactly dependent on any material condition any more than God's grace is dependent on human works. Furthermore, even if the reform of social conditions is effective, it does not follow that individuals in this context are protected from the capricious rule of force. Force may still strike a person, group, or nation. There is no way of shielding ourselves from affliction. Suffering in human life is indeed inevitable. What is suggested in this position of Weil is that the establishment of a nurturing soil may allow for the cultivation and advancement of the mystical life and the diminution of, insofar as possible, destruction. A nurturing soil will allow for the cultivation of attention and, concomitantly, the capacity for recognizing and responding to the gift of grace.

Work as a Bridge to Mystical Consciousness

The tragic vision of Weil asserts, against Marx, that no ultimate escape from human pain, toil, and suffering is possible in human history. The Good or the kingdom of God is otherworldly. The ineluctable reality of pain and misery in human life is due to the fact that necessity, not the good, is supreme in our state of exile. Marx's optimism that the curse of work will be lifted and necessity evaded was part of the illusory faith in social evolution of the time, charges Weil (OL, 43). That revolution itself would bring about a utopian society was no more than an imaginative and dangerous dream, Weil thought. Revolution, not religion, is the opiate of the people. "The hope of a revolution to come satisfies a craving for adventure, of escaping from necessity, which again is a reaction against misery" (MA, 247). Even with the transformation of conditions of work to a less servile form, suffering and pain remain. In less servile conditions of work, however, the exercise of the mind is more possible. Transformation of conditions of force into necessity is a key ingredient in making possible human consent. When contemplation and consent are present, necessity and suffering can bring a wisdom and insight into the human condition.

Weil had hoped to create conditions of society that would enable the human spirit to come into contact, thoughtfully and attentively, with necessity, pain, and suffering in a way that is enriching and not destructive. "The problem is, therefore, quite clear; it is a question of knowing whether it is possible to conceive of an organization of production which, though powerless to remove the necessities imposed by nature and the social constraint arising therefrom, would enable these at any rate to be exercised without grinding down souls and bodies under oppression" (*OL*, 56). In social oppression, force rules in brutal, cold, and destructive manner. In this case, force is a blind and indifferent mechanism "that freezes all those it touches right to the depths of their souls" (*WFG*, 124–25). These conditions make conscious reflection and attention a rare reality. The workers live in unconsciousness.

Simone Weil offers many practical suggestions concerning the amelioration of the material work conditions. First and foremost, she had hoped that the workers could begin to participate in their work as free and creative subjects. Weil believed that this must involve extending educational opportunities to the common laborers. She suggested the creation of universities in the service of workers, for example (*NFR*, 52). The task of such schools would be to translate the truths and insights of the culture of intellectuals into a form that would be accessible to the masses. Far from being a degradation of such culture, this act of translation would prove not only enriching to the working classes but also would enrich our understanding of cultural classics themselves. "It would constitute an extremely precious stimulant for the former [culture], which would in this way emerge from the appalling stuffy atmosphere in which it is confined, and cease being merely something of interest to specialists" (*NFR*, 65).

At the heart of the cultural training of peasant workers in particular, Weil suggests, should be an awareness of the beauty and regularity of nature. Peasant literature, such as Hesiod, *Piers Plowman*, the complaints of the Middle Ages, should play an important role in heightening the consciousness of the workers (*NFR*, 85).[19] An appreciation and love of the cycle of nature would give the peasants a feeling of participation and belonging to the cosmos. In addition to peasant literature, the parables of Jesus should be an inspiration along these lines, Weil claims. "It is shocking to observe to what extent . . . religion can be divorced from daily life and reserved for a few hours only on Sunday, when one remembers what a preference Christ showed for taking the theme of his parables from country scenes" (*NFR*, 83). Workers might find in Greek tragedy, moreover, a vision that illuminates the misfortune, pain, and struggle at the heart of much of the working condition (*NFR*, 67). Clearly, these educational elements play an important role in the spiritual training of the workers for Simone Weil.

While providing educational training clearly plays an important role in ameliorating the conditions of the working classes, this is an insufficient factor if actual material conditions do not change. Weil believed

that a change of material conditions should include the following: factories operating on a much smaller scale; more decentralization; workers
having a share in ownership and better pay; less dangerous working conditions; doing away with highly specialized jobs; and a less demanding
and stressful production speed (*FW*, 194; *NFR*, 70-71). She also believed
that obedience among the workers must involve thoughtful consent and
not a blind, servile self-immolation.

She sums up many of her ideas in the following sentence: "We must
change the system concerning . . . the type of stimulants which make for
the overcoming of laziness or exhaustion—and which at present are merely
fear and extra pay—the type of obedience necessary, the far too small
amount of initiative, skill and thought demanded of workmen, their
present exclusion from any imaginative share in the work of the enterprise as a whole, their sometimes total ignorance of the value, social util-
ity and destination of the things they manufacture, and the complete divorce between working life and family life" (*NFR*, 52). At the heart of her
proposals, which parallel the major ideas of the Roman Catholic papal
social encyclicals, is the general insistence that the human person should
take precedence over the interests of production.

If these material conditions and faculties of the human person are
transformed and cultivated, necessity and suffering can become an apprenticeship. "The body plays a part in all apprenticeships. On the plane
of physical sensibility, suffering alone gives us contact with that necessity
which constitutes the order of the world . . ." (*WFG*, 131-32). In this
case, one can love necessity (*amor fati*) in a way that is ennobling. "Let us
love the country here below. It is real; it offers resistance to love" (*WFG*,
178). The love of illusions and dreams, by contrast, leads the human person to believe that he or she is unlimited, almighty, even infinite. Power
has this intoxicating effect. Such persons "never think of their own strength
as a limited quantity . . . they conclude from this that destiny has given all
license to them and none to their inferiors" (*ICAG*, 34-35). Weil challenges the illusion that liberty is pure license or simply the capricious
satisfaction of whims. On the contrary, true liberty is the "conscious submission to necessity" (*OL*, 107). When labor is accompanied by attention, liberty is most fully realized.

Necessity teaches us our fragility, limits, and dependency. Necessity is
most obvious to us in the pangs of hunger or thirst, or when we are poor
and needy. "Man is a limited being to whom it is not given to be, as in the
case of the God of the theologians, the direct author of his own existence
. . ." (*OL*, 87). Recognition of the role of necessity in human affairs should

make it clear that we are not, in contrast to God, absolute masters of our destiny. This insight, however, is at the same time an act of freedom. Human nature is the only living species capable of being attentive to this fact. "I am always a dual being, on the one hand a passive being who is subject to the world, and on the other an active being who has a grasp on it . . ." (FW, 78).

The proper relationship with necessity is one of equilibrium, therefore. Simone Weil suggests that there are three possible ways in which humanity is related to necessity. "In fantasy, or by the exercise of social power, it seems to be his slave. In adversities, privations, grief, but above all in affliction, it seems an absolute and brutal master. In methodical action [work] there is a point of equilibrium . . ." (ICAG, 180; also FLNB, 88-90; LP, 88). In work, the ideal equilibrium is established as a "thought in action" that consents to necessity. The ability to consent to necessity, not to force, is true liberty. "Man is free to consent to necessity or not. This liberty is not actual in him except when he conceives of force as necessity, that is to say, when he contemplates it. He is not free to consent to force as such. The slave who sees the lash lifted above him does not consent, nor refuse his consent, he trembles" (ICAG, 182). When a thoughtful and attentive consent is absent, as in the case of oppressive and servile work, force rules in a destructive manner. When the attentive contemplation of force is possible, then force becomes necessity. This requires both the change of material circumstances and educational, spiritual training.

By stating that one ought not give one's consent to force, Weil is seeking to avoid the implication that our attitude toward preventable evil should be one of complacent acceptance. "To imitate this indifference [of the impersonal love of God] is simply to consent to it, that is, to accept the existence of all that exists, including the evil, excepting only that portion of evil which we have the possibility, and the obligation, of preventing" (ICAG, 184). The amor fati that Weil appropriates is the acceptance and affirmation of the here and now of human life even in the face of the dark realities of history and nature (as with Nietzsche). It is not, however, an apathy toward preventable evil!

The recognition of necessity via human labor is nothing else than the awareness of our exile, of the reality of pain, suffering, and cross in human life; as such, it is the beginning of the mystical life. It is the beginning of decreation through participation in the cross (NB, 372). The following quote expresses this well: "This world into which we are cast does exist; we are truly flesh and blood; we have been thrown out of eternity; and we are indeed obliged to journey painfully through time, minute in and minute out. This travail is our lot, and the monotony of work is but one of the forms that it assumes" (SWR, 69).

For Simone Weil, then, the disgust experienced in work makes evident our state of exile. "To admit it to oneself and not yield to it is to rise. This disgust is the burden of Time. It is the cross" (NB, 301; also NFR, 287). The ascent of the mystical life must be preceded by a descent, and labor is a descending movement (NB, 269). As a descending movement it is a humble imitation of the kenotic incarnation and crucifixion of God. "Renouncing dreams out of love for the truth means truly abandoning all of one's goods in the folly of love and following Him who is the Truth . . . and carrying one's own cross. The cross is time."[20] The goal of human life is eternity, but eternity can only be reached through the endurance of the painful pressure exerted upon us by time. "Time leads out of Time" (NB, 278).

The result of the Fall in Genesis, in Weil's reading, is the punishment of humanity through labor and death (NFR, 286). The cross of Christ makes possible our return to the Good, but only if we are willing to consent to suffer death without illusions and consolations. In human labor the bearing of the cross is no longer an abstract ideal, but now a daily duty. "But consent to suffer death can only be fully real when death is actually at hand. . . . Physical labor is a daily death" (NFR, 286). The acceptance of necessity through labor is, thus, the acceptance of our mortality (NB, 60-61).

The concept of affliction, in relation to oppressive work, is an example of the destructive effect of force. With a change in material circumstances and spiritual training to cultivate the mind and spirit, however, suffering becomes a form of training. It is not that the experience of suffering is, in itself, constitutive of the mystical life and of the realization of decreation; rather, it is the heightened awareness and consciousness of suffering and pain in human life that is the beginning of the mystical life—as awareness of our state of exile. The task of such consciousness is at the heart of Weil's notion of attention. Before turning to her mystical vision in greater depth in the next chapter, allow me to conclude this chapter with a brief analysis of work as related to her understanding of mysticism.

THE MYSTICISM OF WORK

Weil's notion of decreation is a key element of her mystical thought and is associated with the annihilation of the self, with the idea that the self is nothing. "We have to know that we are nothing, that the impression of being somebody is an illusion . . ." (*FLNB*, 263). At first glance such an idea might sound unpalatable and troubling, especially to a generation that places so much value in self-affirmation and self-esteem. And how might this idea, this illusion that we are somebody, resonate with workers? Given Simone Weil's analysis of social oppression and the destructive impact of force, is this mystical notion of decreation simply another way of describing the destruction of the self? In other words, if there is a loss of the self under the impact of force and a loss of the self that is consented to in decreation, is there a fundamental difference between the two conceptions? I believe there is.

For Simone Weil, when the soul is destroyed under the oppressive conditions of work, society, or force in general, one is made into a reified thing. The apophatic meaning of decreation, however, is that the mysterious depths of the human person is no-thing at all. The reification of the self in oppressive work conditions leads to a final death, whereas decreation leads to an annihilation that discovers an-Other agent deep within the soul: God.

"God created me as a non-being which has the appearance of existing, in order that through love I should renounce this apparent existence and be annihilated by the plenitude of being" (*FLNB*, 96). Apophatic language of the self—in this case "annihilation" or "nothingness"—is not a literal description of the self. These terms in Simone Weil should not be seen as a final negation of the human person. Indeed, such apophatic terms are a negation of negation. The ego that is abolished through decreation has no true existence. The fruit of annihilation is a plenitude. As with many mystical thinkers, reference to the "nothingness" of God (e.g., by John Scotus Erigena) is debased when read as a form of nihilism. So too with regard to the mystery of the self: the nothingness of the self via decreation is a world apart from the reified nothingness via destructive force. Miklos Veto explains decreation in Simone Weil well when he writes: "Decreation, which is at heart self-knowledge, reduces the human being to nothingness, but curiously this reduction implies an 'intensification' of our reality."[21]

The contrasts between these two states abound in Weil's thought. I mentioned some of them at the beginning of this chapter. The idea of "waiting," for example, takes on completely different meaning in different contexts. In the oppressive conditions of the factory, waiting is a humiliating condition of slavery. "Whoever is subdued to the arbitrary is suspended on the thread of time; he is obliged to *wait* (the most humiliating state! . . .) for what the next moment will bring . . ." (*FLNB*, 20). But waiting in regard to Weil's important mystical notion of attention is the condition for receiving truth, beauty, good, love. "In our acts of obedience to God we are passive; whatever the difficulties we have to surmount, however great our activity may appear to be, there is nothing analogous to muscular effort; there is only waiting, attention, silence, immobility . . ." (*WFG*, 194). Weil continues that the model of such passivity is the humble (not humiliating) example of Christ at the cross.

The humility that Weil here advocates is a renunciation of one's own ego and will. For her, such a renunciation repudiates the will-to-power through charity. This renunciation of the will and all its motives, intentions, and desire for rewards and honor is the acceptance of the void. In order to allow for grace to descend into the void, neither false consolations nor illusions must be entertained. The void thus acts in the form of idolatry-critique. It is a critique of and detachment from all our possessions and worldly goods. Necessity and void, not the Good, are supreme here and now. The void is inextricably related to work when, in the form of contemplative action, work renounces all desires of the ego and will. "Work is like a death if it is without an incentive. To act while renouncing at the same time the fruits of action" (*NB*, 79). The seeking of fruits of action is, for Weil, tantamount to the sin of Adam and Eve (*NB*, 517). They sought the fruit of the tree and were punished. The cross, on the contrary, has no fruit; it is the model of the renunciation of the seeking of honor, power, possessions, wealth.[22] Is action possible in this detached form?

> Detachment, indifference (in the elevated sense). One says to oneself: I no longer have any incentives; how am I to act? Why am I to act? But therein lies the miracle of the supernatural. Silence all the motives, all the incentives in yourself, and you will nevertheless act, impelled by a source of energy which is other than the motives and the incentives. (*NB*, 247)

The result of the decreated or the detached life is clearly not inaction. It is action performed solely for "the salvation of others."[23] It is action that wills and knows nothing. In the words of the medieval mystic Marguerite Porete: "Thus the soul wills nothing, says Love, since she is free; for one is not free who wills something by the will within him, whatever he might will. For when one is a servant of oneself, one wills that God accomplish

His will to one's own honor. . . . To such a one, says Love, God refuses His kingdom."[24]

In the thought of Simone Weil decreation means that one is no longer a servant of oneself. Love gives without a why, without motives and intentions. One must not even act "for God," says Weil. "Generally speaking, 'for God' is an unsuitable expression. God must not be put in the dative" (*NB*, 358). Virtue must not, again as in Porete, be seen in terms of "good works" seeking reward. In this sense, Porete speaks of taking leave of the virtues. "It is true that this soul takes leave of virtues, as to their usage and as to the desire for that which they demand, but the virtues never take leave of her, for they are always with her."[25] Virtue is not a means to the earning of rewards or salvation. For Simone Weil, work, too, can be seen in relation to such an apophasis of desire (detachment). By the renunciation of the fruits of action in work, Weil means that work is, in itself, crucial to the fulfillment of human nature. Work should not be debased to a concern for increased rewards or wages. Human labor is the realm in which the human spirit is fully incarnated in the world. In this light, the transformation of the actual conditions of labor is a more important duty than any increase in wages or other rewards (*NFR*, 6-7, 51-54, 58, 70).[26]

Eckhart is famous for developing some of the above ideas on the detachment of the will while, at the same time, defending a life of intense worldly activity. His well-known reading of the Mary and Martha story is exemplary in illuminating the meaning of "contemplative action" or "inactive action" in Simone Weil. Eckhart reverses the traditional privileging of the contemplative role of Mary over the activity of Martha. In a similar manner, Weil challenges the privileging of the contemplative life over the life of work (or *theoria* over praxis) in the Greek tradition. For Eckhart, Martha is the model of the detached (virgin) soul who lives without a why. Such virginity does not result in sterility, but on the contrary, in a fruitful life of activity and the giving of birth to others. Bernard McGinn sums up Eckhart's creative reading of Martha: "Martha is the type of soul who in the summit of the mind or depth of ground remains unchangeably united to God, but who continues to occupy herself with good works in the world that help her neighbor and also form her total being closer and closer to the divine image."[27] Such a vision of praxis is animated by contemplative *theoria*. The ideal Christian life is, as the Jesuit tradition has it, "contemplatives rooted in action."

Weil is creative and innovative in relating this mystical tradition to human labor. In connecting us to the painful and harsh aspects of reality, work is a participation in the cross in a daily manner. In the form of monotony and disgust, work is a clue to the human state of exile and the burdensome face of time. In a bodily and spiritual manner work realizes the decreation of the self. It helps foster detachment and is even an apophatic practice and form of idolatry-critique (against idols that conceal our exiled plight and the reality of affliction). If the worker is able to resist filling the void by consolations, motives, fruits of action, and illusions, work opens the worker to the reception of grace, including openness to the order, regularity, and beauty of the cosmos (*FLNB*, 38, 44, 46). Work thereby is the possibility for the mystical life.

The key in the thought of Simone Weil is that some degree of thought and attention, even autonomy, is a prerequisite for work and suffering to be a bridge to, rather than an obstacle to, the mystical life. It is only when one has an attentive self that one can consent to the annihilation of the self. Here the example of Christ enduring and protesting, yet also consenting with attentive love to his destiny (necessity), is the model for the decreated spirit. As St. Paul has it, the decreated spirit has given up her self to make room for God. "I no longer live but now Christ lives within me" (Gal. 2:20).

To further understand the meaning and significance of decreation and union with God in the thought of Weil, it is necessary to comprehensively examine her mystical vision. In addition to this task, the following chapter will enable us to locate the mysticism of Weil in the context of the history of Christian mysticism.

II ⁓

The Mystical-Aesthetical Vision of Simone Weil

What is death for the carnal part of the soul is to see God face to face. That is why we fly from the inner void, because God might steal into it. . . .We know that we cannot see him face to face without dying, and we do not want to die" (*NB*, 623). If the mystics express a yearning to see God face to face, Simone Weil is unambiguous about the sacrifice involved in such a vision. The surrender of one's comforts and attachments, the break with our ambitions of power and wealth, the letting go of the ego's illusions—in the thought of Weil, all such sacrifices reveal themselves in the willingness to face and prepare for death. Central to her mystical thought is an understanding of human mortality and suffering. Such an understanding of mysticism manifests an honesty that refuses to discount the nocturnal face of existence, what Weil calls the void. False consolations, illusions of ego or nation, imaginary thoughts: such fictions aim at veiling the void, ignoring death and suffering (*SNLG*, 155). As such they are idols. The beginning of a mystical vision, in this light, is the deconstruction of idols. "To believe in God is not a decision we can make. All we can do is to decide not to give our love to false gods" (*SNLG*, 148). "This refusal," Weil continues, "does not presuppose any belief. It is enough to recognize, what is obvious to any mind, that all the goods of this world, past, present, or future, real or imaginary, are finite and limited and radically incapable of satisfying the desire which burns within perpetually within us for an infinite and perfect good" (*SNLG*, 158).[1] This recognition of the absence of an infinite Good in the world is the other side of an awareness of force and violence, suffering and mortality, in history and society in Weil's thought. The void is the recognition that God is present in the world only under the form of absence, as the *deus absconditus* (*GG*, 99).[2]

In the thought of Weil, then, confrontation with the void is a necessary moment in the mystical life; it leads to the death of the ego, "but it inflicts a death which leads to a resurrection" (SNLG, 158). The deconstruction of idols is a condition for the reception of God's iconic self-manifestation. As this chapter explains, Weil's interpretation of the void, dark night, detachment, and decreation function in the form of idolatry-critique (or "idoloclasm"). Such a position in Weil begins with an intellectual, apophatic critique of conceptual and experiential idols and proceeds to a critique of idols that divert our attention to affliction and concomitantly to the hiddenness of God. In combining these two aspects of idoloclasm, I am suggesting that idolatry in Weil is that which conceals both the transcendence and hiddenness of God. When such idols are deconstructed, the reception of God's self-manifestation through attention is imaginable.

Bernard McGinn has claimed that such a vision of the hidden God is part of much of the mystical tradition: "If the modern consciousness of God is often of an absent God (absent though not forgotten for the religious person), many mystics seem almost to have been prophets of this in their intense realization that the 'real God' becomes a possibility only when the many false gods (even the God of religion) have vanished and the frightening abyss of total nothingness is confronted. . . . This is why many mystics from Dionysius on have insisted that it is the consciousness of God as negation, which is a form of the absence of God, that is the core of the mystic's journey."[3] As McGinn himself notes, such a vision of mystical thought finds a congenial ally in Simone Weil.

When the false gods have been destroyed and the void confronted, then a reception of the icon's manifestation becomes a possibility. Implicit in Weil's thought on these issues is a distinction between an idol and an icon. While an idol reduces and freezes the Divine in a particular object, image or symbol, an icon manifests the immanence of God, while still preserving the transcendence and Otherness of God. Simone Weil spent much of her life exposing and destroying the idols that distort and soil our ideas of God, but she was equally emphatic about the potential that an icon, as an aesthetic medium, has for fostering a reverent and sacred form of attention.

The iconic gaze is central to Weil's notion of attention. "One of the principal truths of Christianity, a truth that goes almost unrecognized today, is that looking is what saves us. The bronze serpent was lifted up so that those who lay maimed in the depths of degradation should be saved by looking upon it" (WFG, 192–93). Weil warns that such looking is debased when the self determines the gaze by domination and control. "It may be that vice, depravity, and crime are nearly always, or even perhaps always, in their essence, attempts to eat beauty, to eat what we should only look at" (*WFG*, 166). The reception of the icon is possible only when the self is passive and open to beauty.

What is striking about Weil's reading of mysticism is the inclusion of a moment of lament in the mystical life, coupled with a refusal to deny the tangible presence of beauty around us. If the former sensibility teaches us to recognize the mortality and suffering of the human condition, the reality of exile, the latter communicates our belonging and participation in the world. We are led to recognize that, in her words, "this place of the soul's exile is precisely its fatherland" (*SL*, 125–26). These two poles of existence are held together in a fashion that refuses to deny the wisdom of either tragedy or the allure of hope. They are instances of both a prophetic-tragic outlook and mystical-aesthetical vision.

In the previous chapter on work, we have seen that work is related to the void and detachment, to participation in the cross of history. In addition to continuing these reflections on the void, the task of this chapter is to see how Weil understood attention, contemplation, and love in relation to spiritual exercises. Weil articulates a vision in which the mystery of God acts to deconstruct the false gods in order to make room for the graced manifestation of God. Before examining Weil's understanding of the void and the dark night of the soul, it is necessary to mention how these metaphors have been interpreted in the Christian tradition.

THE METAPHORS "DARKNESS" AND "VOID" IN THE CHRISTIAN TRADITION

The metaphors of void or darkness in the Christian tradition have been susceptible to many different interpretations. First, the metaphor of the darkness of God has been associated with an apophatic critique of all human desires, attachments, ideas, images, concepts, and so forth. In this tradition, God is the Divine Darkness (Gregory of Nyssa) who limits and relativizes our attempts to sensibly or conceptually imagine God.[4] Andrew Louth shows how this apophatic tradition stems from the patristic thinkers in particular.[5] This interpretation of the metaphor "darkness" stems from a reading of Moses' encounter with God at Mt. Sinai in Exodus as well as from Plato's allegory of the cave. In the book of Exodus God is portrayed as hidden beneath the cloud of darkness that hovers over the Israelites in the desert. The cloud veils God's being. In Plato's *Republic*, the darkness of the cave is a metaphor for the human condition. Most of us, save for the philosopher, live among the shadows of illusion and appearance, far from the enlightening truth and goodness of the sun (the Good).

Louth argues that among the church fathers, the understanding of "darkness" in these texts is usually employed in an intellectual and theoretical manner. The darkness elucidates the incompleteness of human knowledge, the inevitable failure of our attempts to conceptually circumscribe the divine darkness. Even Moses is denied access to the face of God and, instead, is only shown God's countenance from behind (Exod. 33:18–23). If we catch a glimpse of God it is only, as St. Paul has it, through a mirror dimly (1 Cor. 13:12). Almost completely absent from patristic interpretations of "darkness" is any autobiographical account of personal experiences. Thus, idols in this tradition could include false worldly desires and attachments, on the one hand, and concepts and images that claim absolute knowledge of God, on the other.

In the second model, Louth argues, the metaphor of the darkness of God takes on a more affective, experiential connotation (as an experience of overwhelming love or one of interior pain and suffering). The author of the *Cloud of Unknowing*, for example, claims that only through love can the dark cloud of unknowing be pierced. The best example of this experiential and afflictive interpretation of darkness and void is John of the Cross. In reference to the first apophatic, intellectual tradition, John mentions Pseudo-Dionysius. "This is why St. Dionysius and other mystical theologians call this infused contemplation a ray of darkness. . . . For this great supernatural light overwhelms the intellect and deprives it of its natural vigor."[6] But John goes on to mention another way of interpreting darkness. "Why, if it is a divine light . . . does one call it a dark night? In answer to this, there are two reasons why this divine wisdom is not only night and darkness for the soul, but also affliction and torment."[7] John explains that such a sense of affliction and torment is the experience of God's absence, or even worse, "it seems God is against them and they are against God."[8] The book of Job plays an important role in this sense of darkness or void, as we will see.

A third interpretation of the metaphors of darkness or void is represented by contemporary liberation thinkers. Here the darkness of suffering or affliction is seen in relation to whole groups and histories of oppression. The destructive impact of force produces a void in the lives of its victims. As I hope to show in what follows, Weil incorporates all three of these traditions in her interpretation of the metaphors void, darkness, nakedness, detachment, and decreation.[9]

Void, Dark Night and Detachment in Simone Weil

Concerning the first of the above models, we can distinguish between two aspects of this category: first, the active voiding of our sensual and worldly attachments; second, the voiding of our experiential and conceptual/imaginative idols. While many of these practices of detachment are central to most Christian mystics (or to the Greek philosophical tradition), the experience of suffering is less prominent. The actual experience of affliction and suffering comes to the forefront when negative or apophatic theology becomes a theology of the cross. Here a confrontation with the hiddenness of God is central to the meaning of void or darkness. Simone Weil redirects this meaning of theology of the cross to include the destruction of memory and crucifixion of whole groups of oppressed peoples. The domination of force in history and society is confronted in a way not fully developed in John of the Cross or Luther.

Simone Weil interprets the ideas and practices of void or dark night as instigating three possible effects or responses. The void or dark night may lead either to destruction, decreation, or the filling in of the void by consolations, illusions, fantasies, certain ideas and concepts—in short, idols. Weil says, "Idolatry is a vital necessity in the cave. . . . The imagination is continually working to stop up all the fissures through which grace might pass" (NB, 150). In order to make decreation possible, a voiding, emptying and detachment from all attachments, including experiential and conceptual/imaginative idols, is a prerequisite. The dawn of decreation emerges with the twilight of the idols.

There is, however, a danger in confronting the void. The possibility of destruction is all too real. "Whoever for an instant bears up against the void, either he receives the supernatural bread, or else he falls. Terrible risk; but we have got to run it, and even for an instant without hope. But we must not plunge into it (Second temptation)" (NB, 156). This danger most clearly pertains to affliction and suffering. If one is capable of facing affliction without filling in the void with idols, one passes over to decreation.

The Voiding of Sensual and Material Idols

In John of the Cross, the voiding of sensual idols is named the "active night of the senses." "When the appetites are extinguished—or mortified—

one no longer feeds on the pleasure of these things, but lives in a void and in darkness with respect to the appetites. . . . We are dealing with the denudation of the soul's appetites and gratifications. This is what leaves it free and empty of all things, even though it possesses them."[10] John insists that the soul must become naked, empty, and purified. The process of doing so is the casting out of "strange Gods, all alien affections and attachments."[11] Interestingly, for both John of the Cross and Weil, it is not necessarily the things of the world in themselves that cause damage, but "the will and appetite dwelling within."[12]

Simone Weil finds the metaphors of nakedness, death, void, and detachment to be of the "purest mysticism" (ICAG, 81). She cites the examples of Plato, St. Paul, and John of the Cross. The willingness to confront death and cross is a condition for the possibility of truth. "The truth is not revealed except in nakedness and that nakedness is death, which means the rupture of all those attachments which for each human being constitute the reason for living; those whom he loves, public esteem and possessions, material and moral, all that" (ICAG, 82). For Weil, the person who succeeds in casting off her attachments and facing the void is the just person. In her creative reading of justice in Plato's Republic, she insists that the person who is truly just (not just in appearance) willingly suffers persecution, death, and even public ignominy for the sake of justice. "Plato does not say but he implies that in order to becomes just, which requires self-knowledge, one must become, already in this life, naked and dead" (SNLG, 96). I will return to this point later.

At this level of sensual and worldly detachment, the mystical life begins with carnal privations or asceticism. This is an acceptance of the void at a material level (NB, 137). Philosophizing or praying, Weil adds, is learning how to die to our worldly attachments, namely, our material possessions, public esteem, passions of avarice, anger, hatred, revenge, envy, jealousy, and so forth (NB, 136). The training of the body, Weil says, seeks to transform the egoistic "animals" within us. "These animals are the thing within me which incessantly, in diverse accents of sorrow, exultation, triumph, anxiety, fear, pain, and every other emotional nuance, keeps on crying 'me, me, me, me, me'" (FLNB, 231).[13]

Finally, however, these forms of detachment from our sensual and worldly attachments (as ascetical exercises) are insufficient to lead to a mystical consciousness of God. At best, they are forms of preparation for such consciousness. This is especially true in that the active will and intelligence are involved at this level. In the terminology of John of the Cross, the active night of the senses must give way to the passive nights. The active, ascetical self easily degenerates into, in John's words, spiritual "avarice" or "gluttony." "What I condemn in this is possessiveness of heart. . . ."[14] Thus, in the case of Weil, the will eventually must be exhausted in order to pass over to a consciousness of God (*FLNB*, 326). "They [ascetical exercises] are not useful if they proceed from a resolution" (*FLNB*, 127). Of course, it is important to insist that the insufficiency of active detachment is not only true at this level of sensual asceticism, but also at the level of experiential and conceptual/imaginative detachment. Indeed, for Weil the rule of the active, controlling will is the chief obstacle to attention.

The Voiding of Experiential and Conceptual/Imaginative Idols

Simone Weil is quite innovative in her comprehensive understanding of the potential idols humanity reveres. The idols in need of deconstruction include false consolations, illusions, fantasies; visions and locutions (as putative "mysticism"); the human ego and its will, motives, desires; nationalism, classicism, Eurocentrism, racism; and even many of our conceptions of God. Spiritual nakedness, detachment, or the process of voiding is a cleansing of all such idols.

In his detachment from experiential and conceptual idols, Eckhart may shed light on the mystical elements of Weil. For Eckhart, the mystical way of life is a state of "virginity," free from all experiences, images, concepts, and so on. The mystical life is a renunciation of the will, including all desires, motives, intentions, and even the will to please God. "So long as you perform your works for the sake of the kingdom of heaven, or for God's sake, or for the sake of your eternal blessedness, and you work them from without, you are going completely astray."[15] True poverty or nakedness is longing and wanting nothing. This brings about a freedom that is detached from anxious and pious works that aim to establish or earn one's salvation. This breakthrough makes possible an encounter with God in the depths of the human soul without the need for an awareness of such an encounter. God enters without the need for our knowledge or acknowledgment. "He should be so free of all knowing that he does not know or experience or grasp that God lives in him."[16] The instinctive understanding of God as pure naked simplicity follows upon such nakedness or detachment. God is the nameless One.[17]

John of the Cross is similar to Eckhart in this moment of detachment. Faith is a darkness or nudity that relativizes and annuls all experiential, imaginative, and conceptual idols. "Insofar as they are capable, people must void themselves of all, so that however many supernatural communications they receive they will continually live as though denuded of them and in darkness. Like the blind, they must lean on dark faith, accept it for their guide and light, and rest on nothing of what they understand, taste, feel, or imagine."[18] This understanding of faith as a darkness, as a cloud of unknowing, functions as idoloclasm. It deconstructs all idols of the intelligence, will, and experience. For John the seeking of consolations is an indication of a "spiritual sweet tooth" that reveals one to be an enemy of the cross of Christ.[19] John is particularly critical of any association of "supernatural visions" or "locutions" with faith. "But when there is a question of imaginative visions or other supernatural communications apprehensible by the senses and independent of one's free will, I affirm that at whatever time or season they occur . . . individuals must not desire to admit them, even though they come from God."[20] In a manner reminiscent of Luther, John asserts that Christ was the final and ultimate vision or locution.[21]

John also relates this understanding of faith to a loving attentiveness. This loving attentiveness is devoid of the intellect and will. It may need to use concepts, images, and forms, but "the soul will have to empty itself of the images and leave this sense in darkness if it is to reach divine union."[22] John also compares this "loving attentiveness" to contemplation in which discursive meditation is discontinued.[23]

Thus, in the case of John and Eckhart, a spiritual nakedness or void and a state of virginity function to detach us from all idols of an experiential and conceptual/imaginative nature.[24] In Simone Weil, the critique of idols includes these elements of idoloclasm, but is more explicitly extended in new directions.

In her critique of conceptual/imaginative idols, Weil asserts that the intelligence must become silent in order to discover truths that it would otherwise overlook. "When the intelligence, having become silent in order to let love invade the whole soul, begins once more to exercise itself, it finds it contains more light than before, a greater aptitude for grasping objects, truths that are proper to it. Better still, I believe that these silences constitute an education for it which cannot possibly have any other equivalent and enable it to grasp truths which otherwise would for ever remain hidden from it. . . . Is not this what St. John of the Cross means when he calls faith a night?" (LTP, 58–59). Weil claims that divine mysteries are darkness to the intellect, but a darkness that is more luminous than what is luminous to the intelligence (NB, 226). The significance of contradiction (as with the Zen koan) is to bring the intellect to its knees, to make evident the limits of intellectual knowledge. "The search for the meaning of the *koan* results in a 'dark night' followed by illumination" (NB, 396). The conceptual idols that claim absolute knowledge must be silenced.

In relation to the will, moreover, the dark night or void manifests the impotency of active effort. The will must be annihilated. In a manner not unlike Marguerite Porete's *Mirror of Simple Souls*, Weil states: "[E]xhaust the human faculties (will, intelligence, etc.) so as to pass over to the transcendent" (FLNB, 361). Weil's annihilation of the will insists on the exhaustion of the faculties through actual exercise. "The will and the discursive intelligence which makes plans are adult faculties. We must use them up. We must destroy them by wearing them out" (FLNB, 326). By wearing them out they become humbled by their frailty. "There is no entry into the transcendent until the human faculties—intelligence, will, human love—have come up against a limit, and the human being waits at this threshold, which he can make no move to cross, without turning away and without knowing what he wants, in fixed, unwavering attention. . . . Genius is the supernatural virtue of humility . . ." (FLNB, 335). Genius readily accedes to the finite and limited character of the human intelligence and will.

In exhausting the will, the renunciation of all motives and fruits of action should follow. Love proceeds not for the sake of a "good work" or even "for God," but without a why. "Love without any prospect in view" (NB, 276). "The sufferer and the other love each other, starting from God, through God, but not for the love of God; they love each other for the love of the one for the other" (WFG, 151). "One must labor and sow, not in order to reap, but from pure obedience. Act, while renouncing the fruits of action" (FLNB, 267). She insists that true renunciation is not from action itself, but from seeking fruits of action (NB, 145). Yet again, echoes of other Christian mystics resound in Weil's thought. Eckhart maintains that those who seek God for a purpose, a why, are misguided. "Whoever is seeking God by ways is finding ways and losing God, who in ways is hidden. But whoever seeks for God without ways will find him as he is in himself, and that man will live with the Son, and he is life itself. If anyone went on for a thousand years asking of life: 'Why are you living?' life, if it could answer, would only say: 'I live so that I may live.'"[25] Simone Weil consistently expresses herself in a similar manner. Life is to be lived, love is to be performed, not for self-motivated purposes and intentions, but rather in a spontaneous and instinctive manner.

As we have seen, idols can be objects of the intellect or motives of the will. Equally pernicious, Weil claims, are consoling and imaginative experiences. Like John of the Cross, she sees those seeking such experiences as enemies of the cross of Christ. She declares that Christ had no such experiences on the cross. "He had no visions or voices on the Mount of Olives, nor on the cross" (NB, 272). The danger of such consoling experiences lies in their obstruction of grace. The voiding of these products of the imagination makes possible the reception of grace. "Men exercise their imaginations in order to stop up the holes through which grace might pass, and for this purpose, and at the cost of a lie, they make for themselves idols . . ." (NB, 145). One of these idols can be religion. "Religion in so far as it is a source of consolation is a hindrance to true faith: in this sense atheism is a purification" (GG, 104). No less than Marx or Freud, Weil was very aware of the way in which religion can function as an opiate or as an imaginary fantasy and illusion. When it does, religion soothes and consoles the troubled human spirit, but at the same time it prevents us from confronting reality.

Not only religion, but even the concept "God," can become an idol, asserts Weil.[26] Facing the void and death is a condition for passing over to the true God. "But when God has become as full of significance for one as the miser's treasure has for him, one should keep on firmly repeating to oneself that He doesn't exist, experience the fact of loving him even though He doesn't exist" (NB, 421). When God becomes to us as a treasure to a miser, we need atheism to purify our notion of God. This purification cleanses us from a god created to fulfill our desires, wants, demands. "We must know that nothing that we touch, hear or see, etc., nothing that we visualize to ourselves, nothing that we think of is the good. If we think of God, that is not the good either" (NB, 491). "I am quite sure that there is not a God in the sense that I am quite sure nothing real can be anything like what I am able to conceive when I pronounce this word" (GG, 103). In this case, Weil certainly would have affirmed the sanctity of Eckhart's prayer for God to free us from God.[27]

This stage of the mystical life is one of nonbelief, says Weil. It is a negation of all attempts to understand God by particular experiences or ideas. "In trying to do so it either labels something else with the name of God, and that is idolatry, or else its belief in God remains abstract and verbal. . . . At a time like the present, incredulity may be equivalent to the dark night of Saint John of the Cross . . ." (WFG, 211). The destruction of idols is a crucial stage of the preparation for the consciousness of God. It is a stage that detaches one from allegiance to the idol, but is prior to the reception of the icon's manifestation.

This deconstruction of idols in Weil, as we have said, is also extended in new directions not explicitly developed in the mystical tradition. The meaning of void in Weil is also related to the claim that there is no center in the world. "Just as God, being outside the universe, is at the same time the center, so each man imagines he is situated in the center of the world. The illusion of perspective places him at the center of space . . . and yet another kindred illusion arranges a whole hierarchy of values around him" (WFG, 158). The illusion that Europe is the center of all values is a major target of criticism in Weil. It is no more than a small corner of the globe. Not unlike the liberation theologians, Weil asserts that a recovery of traditions beyond Europe is central to a true catholic vocation. In order for Christianity to be catholic, an embrace of excluded traditions, including "all the countries inhabited by colored races . . . all the traditions banned as heretical" must permeate Christianity (WFG, 75).

The illusion of being the center of space equally applies to the pretensions of modern nations. The idolatry of nations has led to the upsurge of totalitarianism in the modern world. "Nowhere does it appear that any city, or people, should have thought itself chosen for a supernatural destiny" (NFR, 125). In such a case, Weil argues, God is debased into a figure serving a national interest. The idea of the void (as the absence of God) interrupts the confidence that God rules a particular nation through providence. "Christianity became a totalitarian, conquering and destroying agent because it failed to develop the notion of the absence and non-action of God here below" (NB 505). Weil's understanding of the impersonal God is here linked to the critique of a personal, providential idol-god (NFR 259).

In the exceptional essay "The Power of Words," Weil extends the interpretation of modern idols to include the nation, security, capitalism, communism, fascism, order, authority, property, and democracy. "Each of these words seems to represent for us an absolute reality, unaffected by conditions, or an absolute objective, independent of methods of action, or an absolute evil . . ." (MA, 222). She explains that while we live in finite and contingent realities, we "act and strive and sacrifice ourselves and others by reference to fixed and isolated abstractions . . ." (MA, 223). For the sake of empty words with capital letters we are willing to shed blood. The critique of these idols is a central task in the mystical thought of Weil. All concepts, ideas, symbols, myths, narratives, and so forth that pretend to absolute knowledge are in need of demolition.

This deconstructive task is to serve more than the cultivation of a private religious life; it is to further the well-being of the public realm. "To sweep away these entities from every department of political and social life is an urgently necessary measure of public hygiene" (MA, 237). To use qualifying terms, Weil argues, is to perform a critical function. "By reviving the intelligent use of expressions like *to the extent that, in so far as, on condition that, in relation*, and by discrediting all those vicious arguments which amount to proclaiming the dormitive virtue of opium, we might be rendering a highly important practical service to our contemporaries" (MA, 237–38). Such qualifying terms highlight the finitude and limits of human knowledge. Mysticism, in this light, is not to be confined within the realm of "inwardness or devotion," to borrow the words of Eckhart. One can bring mysticism to bear on the public realm.

Void and the Hiddenness of God

In an illuminating essay on Luther and mysticism, Heiko A. Oberman makes an important point regarding the understanding of "darkness" in Luther. Oberman asserts that in Luther "darkness" means more than the apophatic negation of all intellectual attempts to comprehend God, as in the case of Pseudo-Dionysius. "In 1514 it is already clear that 'darkness,'— *tenebrae, umbra*, or *caligo*—shares in the double meaning of *abscondere* and *absconditas*. . . ."[28] It is not simply that God *transcends* our speculations, but that, as the rest of Oberman's essay implies, God is *hidden* from us as long as we have the status of a *viator* (pilgrim).[29] The status of *viator* is an inescapable fact of our finite and exiled human existence. Suffering and cross comprise a part of reality here and now. A mysticism that seeks sweet experiences and ignores suffering is, as John of the Cross says, an enemy of the cross of Christ.

The crucial point, Oberman suggests, is that "true negative theology is 'theology of the cross.'"[30] The "valley of tears" of our exiled existence is identified with the cross of Christ in Luther. A mystical embrace of Christ will not, thus, be sweet and splendorous, but "death and hell." In Luther's words: "God wants us to be trained [by the cross], not absorbed."[31] The mystical ecstasy of Luther is, as Oberman explains, an *excessus* that does not "imply the transcendence of this valley of tears and a rest in the peace of God, but the 'demasquer' of the enemies of truth (i.e. the flesh and the world) and marks the beginning rather than the end of battle."[32] The *viator* is the exiled soldier who brings a sword not peace, but a sword against the complacency and apathy of the world.

For Luther, then, the mark of an authentic Christian mystic is the brand of one who is in agony, who engages in battle (in Greek, *agonia*) against the weight of evil. The sign that Christ is with the mystical theologian will not be found in consoling experiences, visions, or locutions. "Therefore if you look for a sign of the grace of God or wonder whether Christ himself is in you," Luther says, "no other sign is given to you but the sign of Jonah. Therefore if you were to be in hell for three days, *that* is the sign that Christ is with you and you in Christ."[33] True mystical insight is revealed in hiddenness: at the location of the suffering and dying Christ and by human participation in the cross. For Luther, there is no other path to mystical theology. "By living, indeed by dying and being damned, one becomes a theologian, not by thinking and reading and speculating."[34]

John of the Cross's mysticism bears many similarities to this understanding of the *deus absconditas*. In John of the Cross the interpretation of "dark night" is explicitly related to the abandonment of Christ at the cross.

> Second, at the moment of His death he was certainly annihilated in His soul, without any consolation or relief. . . . He was thereby compelled to cry out: *My God, My God, why have You forsaken me?* This was the most extreme abandonment, sensitively, that He had suffered in His life. . . . The Lord achieved this, as I say, at the moment in which He was most annihilated in all things: in His reputation before people, since in beholding Him they mocked Him instead of esteeming Him; in His human nature, by dying; and in spiritual help and consolation from His Father, for He was forsaken by His Father. . . .[35]

John of the Cross concludes that this path of the cross is at the heart of mystical union with God. "This union is the most noble and sublime state attainable in this life. The journey, then, does not consist in recreations, experiences, and spiritual feelings, but in the living, sensory and spiritual, exterior and interior, death of the cross."[36]

With this brief background in mind, we are in a better position to appreciate Simone Weil's understanding of the void and its relation to the hiddenness of God. It is my contention that Simone Weil's conception of the void is a reading of the *deus absconditus* and is a perception of God's presence in the form of absence (theology of the cross) (*NB*, 148–49). Not unlike John of the Cross, Weil interprets the agony of Jesus on the cross as an experience of not only physical suffering but of anguish of spirit. "He was ridiculed like those madmen who take themselves for kings," she writes, "then he perished like a common criminal. There is a prestige belonging to the martyr of which he was entirely deprived. He did not go to his martyrdom in joy, but in a disarray of all the powers of the soul, after having vainly implored his Father to spare him and having vainly asked men to console him" (ICAG, 138).

In imitation of Christ, the journey of the soul in the mystical life must involve detachment from worldly comforts and honors: "In that case, to attain complete detachment, the soul must really suffer the equivalent of what Job experienced, or Christ on the cross: affliction without consolation" (NB, 211). Such an experience of affliction has the potential to communicate to the human soul what is not apparent during a time of well-being: knowledge of human misery. In this sense, the radical distance between humanity and God is what is most striking to Weil; God is God and man is man. "We can only know one thing about God: that he is what we are not. Our misery alone is the image of this. The more we contemplate it, the more we contemplate Him" (NB, 236). The experience of Job allowed him to break through the false ideas and values (of God or humanity) that prevent one from recognizing the pain and suffering of the human condition. Job was able "to view things in their nakedness, and without this fog of false values" (NB 553).

Since the apophatic tradition emphasizes the critique of intellectual and conceptual idols, this move in Luther, John, and Simone Weil toward a more explicit confrontation with suffering and cross is an important corrective of some aspects of mysticism. Despite some important similarities, however, Weil takes her interpretation of affliction in a different direction from Luther and John of the Cross. The hiddenness of God in Weil is not merely a struggle with the Anfechtung (Luther) or the depression (John of the Cross) of the individual self.[37] When John of the Cross, for example, speaks of the emptiness of memory in the dark night, Weil expresses her consent. Nevertheless, for Weil the destruction of memory is most brutally apparent in the oppressive rule of force in history and society. The hiddenness of God (void) is most striking in the faces of whole groups of poor and oppressed peoples. The victims of conquest, imperialism, and totalitarianism; exploited workers; raped women; victims of war; marginalized traditions of spirituality—all are painful examples of the void. This attentiveness to suffering brings Weil close to the liberation theology of Gustavo Gutiérrez.

Decreation

Mystical consciousness in Simone Weil functions to deconstruct the idols of sensual and imaginative/conceptual attachments and the idols that avert our gaze from affliction and that conceal from view the hiddenness of God. Simone Weil interprets this moment of the void as both a preparation for and an actual consciousness of God. The detachment from the idols is a stage in the direction of God's iconic manifestation, but still awaits God's presence. "There is a period when the soul is already detached from the world without being yet able to attach itself to God: void, terrible anguish. (Dark Night.)" (*NB*, 215). This is the stage of nonbelief in which the soul still awaits God's self-disclosure. "It does not rest with the soul to believe in the reality of God if God does not reveal this reality" (*WFG*, 211). Decreation, however, is the culminating point of void, detachment, spiritual nakedness, and dark night in Simone Weil. It is the breakthrough to God *via* knowledge of the misery and nothingness of the self as well as awareness of the presence of affliction and force in history and nature. In other words, at the level of decreation we can say that the void is no longer a mere preparation for the consciousness of God, but instead is an actual breakthrough to God-consciousness.

"Knowledge of the self is knowledge of God" (*NB*, 282). Such an idea has a rich history in Christian mysticism arising from the interpretation of the Socratic maxim (originally from the oracle at Delphi), "Know thyself." For Christian thinkers, knowledge of self should lead us to an acknowledgment of our need for God. Trapped in original sin, the self has a will that is curved in upon itself and that arrogates to itself what is a gift from God. In an Augustinian manner, Bernard of Clairvaux, for instance, maintains that knowledge of both the misery and grandeur of the human condition is crucial for the restoration of our fallen nature and, consequently, for knowledge of God. Humility is that graced virtue which enables us to recognize the nothingness and misery of the human person.[38] For John of the Cross, also, the "dark night" leads to a self-knowledge in which the self "considers itself to be nothing and finds no satisfaction in self. . . ."[39]

In an analogous fashion, the knowledge of the self for Simone Weil is insight into the nothingness and illusory character of the autonomous self. This insight is a divine knowledge and, indeed, a form of contact with God. "To become something divine, I have no need to get away from my misery, I have only to adhere to it" (*FLNB*, 83). In creation, God renounced His autonomous control and possession of history and nature. In order to imitate the nothingness of God, we must be willing to die to all that constitutes the ego. Sin, in this light, is the unwillingness to let go of our clinging, possessive self (*FLNB*, 218). Sin is the failure to recognize human wretchedness. The more we contemplate our wretchedness, the more we contemplate God (GG, 110). "To consent to being a creature and nothing else. It is like consenting to lose one's whole existence" (*FLNB*, 217).

Since the discussion of this negation of autonomy in Simone Weil is well known and has been explored by many scholars, I would like to focus on a neglected feature of decreation in Simone Weil, namely, the union with God through justice.[40]

In Meister Eckhart the just person is the detached, annihilated self who is "equal to nothing" (the nothingness of the Godhead and justice).[41] For Simone Weil, the decreated person is, likewise, a just individual. The decreated person is the (materially and spiritually) naked, detached spirit. In her reading of Plato's *Republic*, the just person is devoid of prestige, "naked without honor, divested of all the brilliance which the reputation of justice gives" (*ICAG*, 142). The decreated/just person has renounced his will and no longer sees himself as the center of all desires and values. "To give up our imaginary position as the center, to renounce it, not only intellectually but in the imaginative part of our soul, that means to awaken to what is real and eternal . . ." (*WFG*, 159). The just person accepts the void, therefore, and awakens to the reality of justice. The decreated one gives up his imaginary position at the center in order to be attentive to others.

Weil claims that the true just person will thus be assimilated to justice. "Just (or righteous) men are simply very close to justice itself, they have a very large share in it. But in order that a man 'in no way differs from justice itself,' should be the same in all respects as justice, 'divine Justice, from beyond the skies, must descend upon earth'" (*ICAG*, 140). Assimilation to God occurs through the just person (*ICAG*, 139). For Weil, the just person who descends upon earth is none other than Christ: he who suffered, died, and was buried as a consequence of his justice. "During the days when Christ was, as Plato would have him, completely stripped of all appearance of justice, even his friends themselves were no longer wholly conscious of his being perfectly righteous" (*ICAG*, 142). The model for the decreated-just person is explicitly Christ on the cross in Weil (unlike in Eckhart's mystical thought).

The incarnation of justice in Christ is the model for human assimilation to God through justice. "Plato says in the *Theaetetus* that justice is assimilation in God. . . . Whoever is just becomes to the Son of God as the Son is to His Father" (*ICAG*, 159). While this sounds a lot like Eckhart, Weil qualifies this remark by asserting that an identity of relations is not possible between humanity and God (*ICAG*, 159). "When Plato speaks of assimilation in God, it is no longer a question of resemblance, for no resemblance is possible, but one of proportion. No proportion is possible between men and God except by mediation. The divine model, the perfectly just man, is the mediator between just men and God" (*ICAG*, 141).[42] By defending language of "proportion" rather than "resemblance," Weil hopes to preserve the *viator* status of humanity. The difference between humanity and God is not collapsed into simple identity.

As suggested in the above quote, moreover, the incarnation of justice is a condition for our assimilation to God through justice. In Eckhart, too, justice has to become incarnated in order for us to have knowledge of it. "If justice did not justify, no one would have knowledge of it, but it would be known to itself alone, as in the text: 'No one has ever seen God; the Only-Begotten who is in the Father's heart has made him known' (John 1:18)."[43] For Eckhart and Weil the incarnation of justice occurs eternally through all just persons, insofar as they are just. Both would agree that knowledge of justice is possible only in the form of a participation in justice, by realizing justice in one's life. In contrast to Eckhart, however, Weil insists that the perfect example of justice is not merely in the incarnation, but in the crucifixion of the just person!

Thus, the afflicted just person is the model for decreation in Simone Weil. The decreated person is detached and naked from all idols, whether those of an experiential, imaginative/conceptual nature or of those that divert our gaze from human affliction and veil God's hiddenness. Decreation is the mystical consciousness that we are "equal to nothing." Weil relates this to humility: "Humility with the object of assimilation to God. . . . I cannot bear to be less than God; but in that case I have got to be nothing . . ." (*NB*, 120). Assimilation to justice thus occurs through a humble renunciation of the will-to-power and of the illusion that we are the center of all space, time, and values. It is through a just life that vision of God becomes a possibility.

ATTENTION, CONTEMPLATION, AND LOVE

Simone Weil's notion of attention certainly incorporates the themes we have discussed as detachment, void, and decreation, but it also corresponds to something else. For Weil, at its highest moment attention is an experience of ecstasy, an ecstasy that leads to vision and union with God. Through such a vision (*theoria*), a new consciousness of God, self, and cosmos happens. Attention, however, needs to be trained and exercised in order to discern God's presence in history and nature. In this section I hope to explore the meaning of attention in Weil in relation to spiritual exercises of an intellectual, aesthetical, and ethical nature (attention to truth, beauty, and the Good). The limitations of active exercises of the will, however, make obvious the requisite passivity, vigilance, and openness in attention. The passive character (negative effort) of attention owes much to the fact that in Weil attention is motivated and inspired by desire and love. Will power alone cannot compel a consciousness of God to emerge; grace is indispensable. The iconic manifestation of God as love brings about a transformation of consciousness and leads to a new way of life in the face of divine mystery.

As already mentioned, attention is prepared by a voiding of the mind, body, and spirit. True attention can emerge only when the idols of the senses, imagination, and intellect are detached and decreated.[44] "Attention consists of suspending our thought, leaving it detached, empty, and ready to be penetrated by the object . . ." (WFG, 111). If attention is not prepared in such a way, the possibility of idolatry emerges. "Those who are incapable of such an attention do not think of God, even if they give the name of God to what they are thinking of . . ." (NB, 515). Such idols block the manifestation of grace.

The emptying of attention, by facing the void, leads to decreation. Decreation is at the heart of attention for Weil. In this sense, Weil claims that attention is the "highest ecstasy" (NB, 515). True attention takes us outside of ourselves (ek-stasis) and makes accessible to us a wisdom beyond the grasp of the ego. The cross of Christ is a key model for this selfless act of attention. "There is not, there cannot be, any human activity in whatever sphere, of which Christ's Cross is not the supreme and secret truth" (SNLG, 195–96). The renunciation of the self is central to attention, including a renunciation of the illusory belief that we are the center of space or time or the center of all values. The decentering of the human person makes possible love of truth, love of the beauty of the world and love of neighbor (ICAG, 175). Attention to these spheres begins with the recognition that they are truly Other than the projections of my desires, wants, needs, and so forth. In relating this decreating and decentering to justice, Weil writes: "Justice. To be continually ready to admit that another person is something other than what we read when he is there (or when we think about him)" (NB, 43, 200). For Weil, this interpretation concerning ethics equally pertains to attention in the realms of truth and beauty.[45]

"Attention alone—that attention which is so full that the 'I' disappears—is required of me. I have to deprive all that I call 'I' of the light of my attention and turn it on to that which cannot be conceived" (*NB*, 179, 291). Thus, the voiding, emptying, and decreating of the self (ecstasy) is a necessary condition for the possibility of true attention. The idols must be deconstructed in order to prepare the way for the attentive reception of God.

It is clear that attention includes all the domains of truth, beauty, good, and, at the highest level, God. "Pure, intuitive attention is the only source of perfectly beautiful art, truly original and brilliant scientific discovery, of philosophy which really aspires to wisdom and of true, practical love of one's neighbor" (*MA*, 253). Attention cannot be isolated as any one realm of human experience. Indeed, the sin of polytheism is for her the separation of truth, beauty, and good (*NFR*, 241). What is extraordinary about genius, Weil contends, is its ability to shed light on all these spheres of human life. "There exists a focal point of greatness where the genius creating beauty, the genius revealing truth, heroism and holiness are indistinguishable" (*NFR*, 224). Thus, Weil can assert that all forms of true attention (whether in the sciences or humanities) are only debased forms of religious attention (i.e., contemplation and prayer) (*NB*, 515).

We must remember that love and desire are central to attention, not will power or pure intellectual activity. "We confer upon objects and upon persons around us all that we have of the fullness of reality when to this intellectual attention we add that attention of still higher degree which is acceptance, consent, love" (*ICAG*, 188). "What could be more stupid than to tighten up our muscles and set our jaws about virtue, or poetry, or the solution of a problem? Attention is something very different" (*NB*, 205). Anyone can attest to the difficulty, pain, and reluctance involved in paying attention to something or someone of little or no interest to us. Without desire and absent any interest, distraction and weariness easily defeats attention, even among those with the best of intentions. Plato knew well that the philosophical life would not find a following without evoking yearning and desire, without evoking *eros* in the potential disciple. Without falling in love with wisdom, no one would be willing to make the sacrifices demanded of a student of Socrates. For these reasons, attention, for Weil, is dependent upon inspiration and grace. The breath of the Spirit, as an expression of God's gift of love, resuscitates and invigorates attention. Attention becomes capable of a mystical consciousness.

Since decreation corresponds to loss of self, moreover, Weil argues that decreation must be dependent upon something other than the self. "I must necessarily turn to something other than myself since it is a question of being delivered from self. Any attempt to gain this deliverance by means of my own energy would be like the efforts of a cow which pulls at its hobble and so falls on its knees" (GG, 3). The sin of pride emulates the natural law of gravity and shuns the supernatural law of grace (GG, 105). In this case, pride scorns the need for an-Other, for something outside of the self. Obedience to gravity follows the dictates of self-interest and survival of the fittest.

The natural law of history ordains that the powerful rule the weak, Weil notes in reference to Thucydides (WFG, 141). The only force that is an exception to this natural law is the miraculous force of grace. Even when given the means and power to rule, compassion animated by grace refuses control and renounces the will-to-power (WFG, 148). Humility is inspired by grace and is indispensable to attention.

A sense of human belonging and participation in the cosmos is also an important part of the mystical life (leading to a vision of God) for Simone Weil. She gives an important role to the faculty of vision. Her deep love of art and the beauty of the world led her to insist that salvation occurs by looking (WFG, 193). Following Plato, Weil insists that a true understanding of vision makes clear the necessity of love in addition to intellectual comprehension. *Theoria* (vision of God or contemplation) is only possible when attention is illuminated by faith and love. "Human thought and the universe constitute the books of revelation *par excellence*, if the attention, lighted by love and faith, knows how to decipher them" (ICAG, 201). God's revelation is deciphered through loving attention. Such attention makes possible the ascent of the soul to God. At the highest level, then, attention is prayer, contemplation, and a graced vision of God.

Intellectual Attention

While a mystical consciousness of God is finally inspired by love, the intelligence has an important role to prepare for ascent to God (SL, 139). One of the major functions of intelligence in the mystical vision of Simone Weil is to check an illegitimate use of mystery. The intellect performs a critical function in clearing the ground of illusory and idiosyncratic mysteries (idols), in order to make possible a reception of legitimate mystery (icons).

The notion of mystery is legitimate when the most logical and most rigorous use of the intelligence leads to an impasse, to a contradiction which is inescapable. . . . Then, like a lever, the notion of mystery carries thought beyond the impasse, to the other side of the unopenable door, beyond the domain of the intelligence and above it. But to arrive beyond the domain of the intelligence one must have traveled all through it, to the end, and by a path traced with unimpeachable rigor. (*FLNB*, 131)

Central to the rigorous use of the intellect in Simone Weil is school studies, including geometry, philosophical dialectics, language studies, and recitation of poetry. Study is training in attention. "Since prayer is but attention in its pure form, and since studies constitute a gymnastic of the attention, it follows that every school exercise should be a refraction of spiritual life" (*NB*, 597). As with the Stoics, the gymnastics of attention is central to Weil's understanding of the philosophical life. The actual exercise of the attention is, for Weil, a preparation for attention to God.

The critique of the illegitimate use of mystery has a demand for blind assent as its target (whether the assent is to church dogma, nationalism, or social conventions). The demand for such an assent (fideism) results in the gagging of the intelligence, Weil claims (*LTP*, 39). Worse yet, the reduction of articles of faith and belief to perfunctory assent or denial is idolatrous to Simone Weil. "The dogmas of the faith are not things to be affirmed. They are things to be regarded from a certain distance, with attention, respect and love. . . . This attentive and loving gaze, by a shock on the rebound, causes a source of light to flash in the soul which illuminates all aspects of human life on this earth" (*LTP*, 48). The confessions of Christian belief become idols when they are reduced to objective and theoretical objects of predication. Idolatry in relation to mystery, therefore, is the reification of mystery in the form of perfunctory assent or denial. Faith is not equivalent to belief. The path to faith is, rather, through a loving attention that realizes the Christian mysteries by living them. Faith is orthopraxis before being the strict observance of orthodoxy.

Peter Winch makes an interesting comparison of this aspect of Weil to Ludwig Wittgenstein. Winch quotes Wittgenstein: "Actually I should like to say that . . . the *words* you utter or what you think as you utter them are not what matters, so much as the difference they make at various points in your life. . . . A theology which insists on the use of *certain particular* words and phrases, and outlaws others, does not make anything clearer. . . . *Practice* gives the words their sense."[46] Thus, for both Weil and Wittgenstein the utterance of particular words or phrases is not what constitutes Christian faith. When Christian orthodoxy is defined by such dogmatic assent, then the idolizing of what is fundamentally incomprehensible or ineffable naturally follows.

The intellect, however, is important in clearly and coherently stating what can be said. Again, to quote Wittgenstein: "What can be said at all can be said clearly; and whereof one cannot speak thereof one must be silent. . . . There is indeed the inexpressible. This *shows* itself; it is the mystical."[47] Weil always insists that matters within the powers of the human mind should be examined with rigor and thoroughness. Along these lines, then, meditation on doctrine and philosophical dialectics performs the function of training the attention. Regarding legitimate mystery beyond the limits of the human mind, however, the intellect is most iconic when it recognizes its limits and silences itself. Thus, intellectual exercises in Simone Weil perform an important function in preventing an appeal to mystery from becoming a cloak for careless and incoherent thought. When this idolatrous form of mystery is deconstructed, then a more divine iconic form of mystery will emerge.

A critical and thoughtful reflection, in short, is to make evident both the possibilities and limits of intellectual thought. In Weil, intellectual exercises train the attention and reveal the possibilities of human thought. Rigorous, critical reflection is a condition for the possibility of mysticism. By checking illusory and mindless appeals to mystery, a reception of true mystery might be credible. "Only the intelligence must recognize by those means which are proper to it, namely, verification and demonstration, the preeminence of love. It must only submit itself when it knows in a perfectly clear and precise manner why. Otherwise submission is an error, and that to which it submits itself, in spite of the label attached, is something other than supernatural love" (*NB*, 240). Such a submission in error is idolatry.

A legitimate exposure of the limits of the intellect, however, is equally the goal in the training of attention. An idea is most iconic when, through an exhaustive and coherent reflection, a self-negating methodology reveals the limits of intellect. When the intellect is exhausted, a transgression beyond the intellect is imaginable. This transgression of the intellect is love, faith, and justice in Simone Weil. "The consented subordination of all the natural faculties of the soul to supernatural love is faith. . . . In St. Paul faith and justice are constantly identified . . ." (*FLNB*, 131). Faith, love, and justice bring about a new consciousness of truth unavailable to the discursive intellect.

For Simone Weil such a subordination of the intellect to love is a transformation of the intellect to a higher level, not an annulment of intellectual knowledge. Love gives rise to a cognitive insight into reality. Love is not a mere experience of truth, then; rather, love educates the intellect in grasping truths that would have remained inaccessible to the discursive intellect. "When the intelligence, having become silent in order to let love invade the whole soul, begins once more to exercise itself, it finds it contains more light than before, a greater aptitude for grasping objects, truths that are proper to it. Better still, I believe that these silences constitute an education for it which cannot possibly have any other equivalent and enable it to grasp truths which otherwise would forever remain hidden from it" (LTP, 59).

Aesthetical Attention

Simone Weil considers love of beauty a form of the implicit love of God (WFG, 137). Her thought is deeply aesthetical. "For anyone who possesses artistic and poetic culture and a keen sense of beauty the least deceptive analogies for illustrating spiritual truths are aesthetic analogies" (FLNB, 361). Why is it that aesthetics provides the "least deceptive" analogies concerning spiritual truths? I believe that the answer to that question is similar to the way in which Weil interprets the meaning of the past. In regard to beauty or the past, the proper attitude is one of attentive openness, silence, waiting, and passivity. "The past—it forms part of the reality of this world . . . towards which we are unable to make a single step, towards which all we are able to do is to turn ourselves so that an emanation from it may come to us. For this reason it is the image *par excellence* of eternal, supernatural reality (Proust)" (NB, 335). The past or the perception of beauty is ravaged when our attitude is one of control and domination. Suspension of our controlling will is a condition for the reception of beauty. The metaphors that Weil contrasts, in this regard, are looking and eating.

"It may be that vice, depravity, and crime are nearly always, or even perhaps always, in their essence, attempts to eat beauty, to eat what we should only look at" (WFG, 166). Weil relates visual metaphors of looking to contemplation and, ultimately, to love. In the case of contemplation and love, the recognition of the autonomy and integrity of the Other should determine our attitude toward it (i.e., toward beauty, the past, another person, text, event, image, etc.). The renunciation of the will and ego is necessary for allowing the Other to manifest itself. With regard to the beauty of the world, the decreation of the self (as an illusory center of space) makes possible the reception of an iconic self-disclosure. In the case of St. Francis, Weil explains, "Vagabondage and poverty were poetry with him; he stripped himself naked in order to have immediate contact with the beauty of the world" (WFG, 166). The poverty and nakedness of the spirit (detachment, void, decreation) makes possible an immediate or direct contact with the beauty of the world. For Job, as well, the manifestation of beauty came only after an encounter with the void stripped him of all his possessions (WFG, 177).

The renunciation of the will in aesthetical attention implies that the reception of beauty is absent of intentions, motives, and utilitarian purposes. "Only beauty is not the means to anything else. It alone is good in itself, but without our finding any particular good or advantage in it" (WFG, 166). "The imitation of the beauty of the world, that which corresponds to the absence of finality, intention, and discrimination in it, is the absence of intention in ourselves, that is to say the renunciation of the will" (WFG, 178). When perfectly understood and realized, we are attracted toward beauty without a desire for possession. We are not in control of beauty; instead, "it offers us its own existence" (WFG, 166).

The ultimately passive character of aesthetical attention does not, however, preclude the need for training and for cultivating an aesthetical sensibility. The contemplation of the order and beauty of the universe trains one in the mystical life. Following Plato, Weil avers that such training is an imitation of the circular patterns of the heavenly stars, planets, seasons, days and hours.[48] Weil believes that the peasants are potentially the best situated to perceive the rhythms of nature. Through the fatigue, pain, and joy of work the seasons and days enter the body (NB, 21). Work restores both the kinship between the body and the soul, on the one hand, and the kinship between the human being and the cosmos, on the other.

An image of the circular patterns of the cosmos is the Divine Trinity, Weil writes (ICAG, 96). Dance and music are also images of the circular character of time. By this process of contemplation, the notion of history as progress is undermined, and along with it the desires, intentions, and motives of the will. "By contemplating this equivalence of the future and past we pierce through time right to eternity, and being delivered from desire oriented to the future, we are delivered also from the imagination which accompanies it and is the unique source of error and of untruth" (ICAG, 96). The harmonies of music, the rhyme of poetry, the rhythm of dance, the order of a religious ritual, the grandeur of a cathedral, or the contemplation of the patterns of the cosmos—all such experiences of beauty allow eternity to pierce through the banality of history and to transport our soul from profane to sacred space.

At the heart of these spiritual and aesthetical experiences is the idea of the Logos, says Weil. "Thus the Word is a model for man to imitate. Not in this case the Word incarnate in a human being, but the Word as the orderer of the world. . . . Here is the source of the idea of microcosm and macrocosm which so haunted the Middle Ages" (ICAG, 96). The human being as microcosm belongs and participates in the macrocosm. The awareness that we are part of the whole, that we belong to the universe, is a key factor that enables the soul to ascend to God. The horror of suffering and oppression is, in this light, the obliteration of this experience of beauty. "But to destroy cities, either materially or morally, or to exclude human beings from a city, thrusting them down to the state of social outcasts, this is to sever every bond of poetry and love between human beings and the universe. It is to plunge them forcibly into the horror of ugliness" (WFG, 181). Force and violence destroys human kinship with the cosmos.

Even if activity of the will is implied in Weil's notion of attention, we would be misguided in assuming that active effort constitutes attention per se. At best, attention is a negative effort, especially in regard to aesthetics. Beauty cannot be controlled by the self; beauty discloses itself. We can prepare for the manifestation of beauty, but the consciousness of beauty is pure gift. For this reason, Weil speaks of the seduction of beauty. The mystic is she or he who is seduced by the beauty of God. "The soul in quest of pleasure encounters the divine beauty which appears here below in the form of the beauty of the world, as a snare for the soul. By the power of this snare, God seizes the soul in spite of itself" (ICAG, 3). God captures and possesses the soul by beauty. This divine initiative becomes idolatrous when we seek to reverse this order and to capture and possess God by beauty—a form of rape. We must attentively wait for the icon to show itself. When it does so, God enraptures the soul and ecstatically carries her outside of herself.

Ethical-Political Attention

The third area in which Weil locates the manifestation of God is in the face of the neighbor, especially the afflicted neighbor. Attention to the afflicted is "a recognition that the sufferer exists, not only as a unit in a collection, or a specimen from the social category labeled 'unfortunate,' but as a person, exactly like us, who was one day stamped with a special mark by affliction" (WFG, 115). The face of an afflicted other can be an icon in the thought of Simone Weil.[49] In order for this to be possible, a miraculous kind of attention must exist. Attention to the afflicted is miraculous insofar as it resists the natural reaction of revulsion to the disfigured, unattractive, and naked face of the afflicted. "Thought is so revolted by affliction that it is as incapable of bringing itself voluntarily to conceive it as an animal, generally speaking, is incapable of suicide" (*SNLG*, 187). As an animalistic response, thought flees from attention to the afflicted. Thought seeks to evade confronting the truth of affliction by lies, consolations, and illusions.

Job's friends are guilty of such an evasion of affliction (*NB*, 287). The lies concocted by the self are evasive maneuvers that seek to conceal the fact of our own human fragility and susceptibility to suffering. Facing the truth of affliction in another person becomes possible when we begin to die to ourselves. In order for attention to the poor and oppressed to be possible, a self-renunciation must empty and detach attention. "The soul empties itself of all its own contents in order to receive into itself the being it is looking at, just as he is, in all his truth. Only he who is capable of attention can do this" (*WFG*, 115).

In Simone Weil, attention has a public function. The major task before public institutions, as well, is to heed the sigh of the oppressed creature (*MA*, 53). The complacency of inaction is almost as culpable as causing suffering. "It is clear that to bring the full light of the attention to bear upon a state of suffering, to know that we can come to the aid of it, and not to do so, is like causing it" (*NB*, 288). Reflection on social and political matters should be inspired by this kind of attention, argues Weil. "Meditation on the social mechanism is in this respect a purification of the greatest value. . . . *Contemplating* the social mechanism is as good a road to follow as withdrawing from the world" (*NB*, 311). We have already seen, as with Eckhart, that the mysticism of Weil is not confined within the boundaries of inward prayer. Insofar as contemplation on the social mechanism is inspired by an attentive openness to the afflicted, it is an important part of the mystical vision of Simone Weil.

Key to mystical consciousness, then, is attention to the poor and oppressed neighbor. Here Weil moves beyond the resources of the Greeks. In both intellectual and aesthetical attention, the Platonic and Stoic heritage is an important source for Weil. In regard to ethics, however, attention to God is more obviously related to the poor and afflicted neighbor. The Jewish and Christian prophetic heritages (and the conception of *agape*) enter the picture in Weil's thought. Thus, the site of the iconic gift of God's self-disclosure is clear: it is at the cross and in the face of those individuals and communities who risk crucifixion on a daily basis.

Loving Attention and Divine Mystery

While truth, beauty, and the good are sites of God's manifestation, God cannot be reduced to these three spheres of human experience. Attention has limits insofar as God cannot be reduced to a mere conceptual object of theoretical, aesthetical, or ethical attention. "Cases of true contradictories: God exists; God doesn't exist. Where lies the problem? No uncertainty whatever. I am absolutely certain that there is a God, in the sense that I am absolutely certain that my love is not illusory. I am absolutely certain that there is not a God, in the sense that I am absolutely certain that there is nothing real which bears a resemblance to what I am able to conceive when I pronounce that name ..." (*NB*, 127).[50] Since God ultimately transcends all concepts (including the concepts we have in mind when we assert God's existence), God is only present to human beings by love. God is a "nothingness" that is "without name or form" (*NB*, 232). Insofar as God is nothingness, knowledge of God is given to humanity only through contact with God. Along these lines, Andrew Louth insists that contemplation (*theoria*) is not simply knowledge *about*; "it implies identity with, participation in, that which is known."[51] Contemplation of God is nothing else than this contact and love of God (*GG*, 110). At this apophatic level of Weil's thought, the self-manifestation of God occurs through love.

While contemplation or vision of God involves actual intellectual, aesthetical and ethical spiritual exercises for Simone Weil, the process of purification then gives way to an attentive waiting. "When the limit of attention has been reached in this way, one should fix the soul's gaze on that limit with the longing for that which lies beyond. . . . Grace will accomplish the rest causing one to go up and emerge [from the cave]" (*NB*, 527). "Similarly, the true Good can only come from outside, never as the result of our own effort" (*NB*, 531). The Good is strictly impossible for human effort; it is beyond the being of the world (*NB*, 434). The centrality of grace surfaces conclusively here.

The Good is never apprehended as a result of effort. Grace in the form of desire and love motivates the search for the Good and makes possible union with God. Likewise, truth is never discovered without grace. "Love is the teacher of gods and men, for no one learns without desiring to learn. Truth is sought not because it is truth but because it is good" (*GG*, 107). In this prioritizing of good over truth, Weil maintains that knowledge of truth is dependent upon longing, yearning, and desire for truth. In the form of grace, the Good provokes in us desire for truth. If we are able to wait with attention and silence, God will come to us. "The notion of grace, as opposed to virtue depending on the will, and that of inspiration, as opposed to intellectual or artistic work, these two notions, if they are well understood, show the efficacy of desire and of waiting" (WFG, 197).

The significance of asserting that *theoria* is not simply a knowledge *about* God implies that God is inconceivable as a mere object of theory. "The object of my search is not the supernatural, but this world. The supernatural is the light. We must not presume to make an object of it, or else we degrade it" (NB, 173). Since God is not an object of my search, the most appropriate language with regard to the transcendent is denial—the *via negativa* (NB, 254, 357). The Good beyond being is, then, emptiness and void in relation to the being of the world. But it is an emptiness that "manifestly appears as the only reality that is truly real . . ."(NB, 545, 491). Divine emptiness is ultimate reality. Weil's thoughts on emptiness suggest the insufficiency of objective and predicative language about God. An engaged and participatory praxis in the world (love) is the only path to a consciousness of the reality of the emptiness or nothingness of God. Through love the contemplative knowledge of the Good beyond being is possible.

Simone Weil claims that the Good beyond being (God) is the only exception to the axiom that "love requires an object to exist." For God is not an object, nor does God exist "in our sense of existence" (FLNB, 324). Thus, we must love God insofar as God is pure good without having to first be. "The good certainly does not possess a reality to which the attribute 'good' is added. It has no being other than this attribute. Its only being consists in being the good. But it possesses in fullness the reality of that being. It makes no sense to say the good exists or the good does not exist; one can only say: the good" (FLNB, 316). Mystical *theoria* for Simone Weil is constituted and inspired by love. The iconic self-manifestation of God as love effects a transformation of one's attention and consciousness that brings about faith.

As we have seen in Weil, faith is not dogmatic assent to certain words or phrases. Faith is love. "All that I conceive of as true is less true than these things of which I cannot conceive the truth, but which I love" (NB, 238). Faith is the illumination of truth, beauty, and good by love. "Further, it is only insofar as the soul orients itself towards what ought to be loved, that is to say insofar as it loves God, that it is *qualified to know and understand*" (SNLG, 104). Simone argues that this is the proper understanding of Platonic vision.

The wisdom of Plato's philosophy is not, strictly speaking, a philosophical search for God by human reason, Weil asserts. In contrast to Aristotle, Plato's wisdom is nothing but the orientation of the eyes of the soul toward grace (ICAG, 85). "It is a question here of something very different from such an abstract conception of God as the human intelligence may achieve without grace . . ." (ICAG, 79). Knowledge of God, she continues, is at a different level altogether than intellectual (or aesthetical and ethical) achievement. Plato's wisdom makes evident that the basis for knowledge of God *(theoria)* is the manifestation of love, namely, grace. Thus, sight for Plato means nothing else but love. "The sun is the good. Sight is then the faculty which is in relationship with the good. Plato, in the *Symposium*, says as definitely as possible that this faculty is love" (ICAG, 134).

LIFE FOLLOWING MYSTICAL CONSCIOUSNESS

In this chapter we have seen that the mysticism of Simone Weil is a way of life that includes the critique of idols and the cultivation of attention. Her mysticism maintains that knowledge of God is only possible through an engaged life entailing spiritual exercises and an openness to God's gift of love. The praxis of justice and love is central to her version of the mystical life. Such practices are not merely ethical, however; instead, they involve an apophatic critique of idols and the self-negating function of mystical language. In other words, justice and love make apparent the limits of objective predicative language, indeed, of all language in the face of divine mystery. Justice and love are apophatic practices that indicate the nonobjective character of God and, thus, necessitate an approach to God that proceeds otherwise. This way of life that proceeds otherwise consists of the practice of justice as well as of love of truth, beauty, good, and ultimately, God. *Theoria* is prayerful contemplation that is not talk *about* God, but rather is an actual contact with God or, in other words, a consciousness of the presence of God.

The mystical way of life espoused by Simone Weil is one that is deeply in the world, but not of the world.[52] "The soul which has attained to seeing the light must lend its vision to God and turn it on the world" (FLNB, 269). The moment of redescent or reaction to the consciousness of God is an important part of Weil's mystical vision. Weil names this redescent the return to the cave (*LP*, 221). Central to this moment of Weil's mystical vision is the claim that "earthly things are the criterion of spiritual things" (*FLNB*, 147). Explicitly repudiated is the claim that attention to God leads to a life unconcerned with earthly things. "The value of a religious or, more generally, a spiritual way of life is appreciated by the amount of illumination thrown upon the things of the world" (*FLNB*, 147). Terms such as God, justice, love, and good, likewise, are only valid insofar as they illuminate our plight in history and nature, even if they are terms strictly inconceivable. "To use them legitimately one must avoid referring them to anything humanly conceivable and at the same time one must associate with them ideas and actions which are derived solely and directly from the light which they shed" (*MA*, 77).

For Simone Weil, then, the validity of mysticism is dependent upon the quality of one's life following upon the consciousness of God. In imaginative metaphors suggestive of Eckhart she explains this point with regard to a pregnant woman.

> The soul's attitude towards God is not a thing that can be verified, even by the soul itself, because God is elsewhere, in heaven, in secret. If one thinks to have verified it, there is really some earthly thing masquerading under the label of God. One can only verify whether the behavior of the soul as regards this world bears the mark of an experience of God. In the same way, a bride's friends do not go into the nuptial chamber; but when she is seen to be pregnant they know she has lost her virginity. . . . When a person's way of behaving towards things and men, or simply his way of regarding them, reveals supernatural virtues, one knows that his soul is no longer virgin, it has slept with God. . . . The only certain proof a young woman's friends have that she has lost her virginity is that she is pregnant. Otherwise there is no proof—not even if she should talk and behave lewdly. . . . In the same way, if a soul speaks of God with words of faith and love, either publicly or inwardly, this is no proof either for others or for itself. It may be that what it calls God is . . . a false God and that it has never slept with God. (*FLNB*, 145–46)

Central to these rich reflections is the claim that mysticism cannot be reduced to a verifiable experience or doctrine about God. There is no proof for others *or* for oneself that one has slept with God, save the character of one's life. When one gives birth to others (Plato, Eckhart) one can be assured that one's consciousness of God is of the iconic, not the idolatrous, God.

Talk about God does not in itself constitute the mystical life. As Weil says, one can speak confidently and lewdly of sleeping with God. This in itself does not validate mysticism. In a statement suggestive of Wittgenstein, Weil asserts: "One cannot know what is in a man's mind when he speaks a certain word (God, freedom, progress . . .). One can only judge the good in his soul by the good in his actions, or in the expression of his original thoughts. . . . It is not the way a man talks about God, but the way he talks about things of the world that best shows whether his soul has passed through the fire of the love of God. In this matter no deception is possible" (*FLNB*, 144-45).

While the experience of love eluded Simone Weil in actual life (as far as we know she never had a romantic relationship with another person), she did not hesitate to express her approval of the use of sensual metaphors to describe the relationship between God and the soul. Sensual love for another person, she claims, is a desire to embrace universal beauty in a concrete, particular form and is, moreover, a longing for the Incarnation (*FLNB*, 83-84; also *WFG*, 171). In this regard, the use of nuptial language by the mystics is not only legitimate, but manifests a yearning to be united with universal beauty.

In other instances, Weil is more explicit about the use of metaphors of erotic love. The Holy Spirit, she argues, is the breath of fire, the *pneuma*; it is the word of God (*FLNB*, 287). The word of God is the divine seed that impregnates the human soul. In order for the soul to receive the word of God, the soul must be passive and attentive (*FLNB*, 144-45). "How marvelously, therefore, this word applies both to the genital semen in carnal love and to the engendering of good by the love between God and a human soul!" (*FLNB*, 350). This results, Weil asserts, in the birth of Christ within the soul and the decreation of the "I."

> Then the seed becomes an embryo, and at last a child; Christ is born in the soul. . . . That is what it is to be born anew. . . . After this operation, "I no longer live, but Christ lives in me." It is a different being that has been engendered by God, a different "I," which is hardly "I," because it is the Son of God. . . . Our soul is shut off from all reality by an enclosing skin of egoism, subjectivity, and illusion; the germ of Christ, placed in our soul by God, feeds on this; when it has grown enough it breaks the soul, explodes it, and makes contact with reality. (*FLNB*, 287-88)

The birth of Christ in the soul brings a greater fullness of reality than the illusion of subjectivity and egoism. One now lives for the sake of others without motives, intentions, and will. As in the thought of Eckhart, one's self has been displaced by the Father's begetting of Christ within the depths of the soul.[53]

The new life following upon the birth of Christ in the soul is an existence for the good of others. "After that, there is a new creation, which the soul accepts—not for the sake of existing, since its desire is not to exist, but solely for the love of creatures . . ." (FLNB, 224). The understanding of virtue as an obligation performed for a particular purpose or motive, even for God, is nullified. One loves and is just without a why. "That is why expressions such as to love our neighbor in God, or for God, are misleading and equivocal. A man has all he can do, even if he concentrates all the attention of which he is capable, to look at this small inert thing of flesh, lying stripped of clothing by the roadside. It is not the time to turn his thought toward God. . . . There are times when thinking of God separates us from him" (WFG, 151).

Simone Weil would certainly have affirmed Eckhart's sentiment that "One should not accept or esteem God as being outside oneself, but as one's own and as what is within one; nor should one serve or labor for any recompense, not for God or for his honor or for anything that is outside oneself. . . ."[54] For Eckhart, this is exemplified most poignantly by the just person. "For just men, the pursuit of justice is so imperative that if God were not just, they would not give a fig for God; and they stand fast by justice, and they have gone out of themselves so completely that they have no regard for the pains of hell or the joys of heaven or for any other thing."[55] The just person has no will and lives without a why and gives without conscious intent.

In the vision of Simone Weil, this passion for justice is joined with an attentive love that inspires and forms the mystical life. It is a mystical vision deeply immersed in the world even while not being of the world. The spiritual passivity and waiting does not translate into inaction, but, on the contrary, into intense worldly activity. One acts in a manner freed from the egoistic will. "To remain motionless does not mean to abstain from action. It is a spiritual, not material[,] immobility. But one must not act, or indeed, abstain from acting, by one's own will. . . . Their model is the crucifixion of Christ" (SNLG, 154-55). Participation in the cross of Christ is at the heart of the mystical life of justice and attentive love.

Gustavo Gutiérrez's own formulation of mystical theology is, likewise, one that is deeply immersed in history and society and profoundly aware of violence and suffering in human life. Gutiérrez argues that this awareness and demand for action is incomplete, however, without the indispensable dimension of mystical thought and experience. Through Gutiérrez's development of mystical theology, the allure and beauty of God's love is made manifest in locations of God's seeming absence, in locations of oppression and cross. To that dimension of Gutiérrez's theology we now turn.

III ⟡

Mysticism and Love in the Theology of Gutiérrez

While liberation theology is regularly declared to lack a spiritual or mystical element, Gustavo Gutiérrez proves false such a claim by including a spiritual dimension at the heart of his theological project.[1] As early as his classic work *A Theology of Liberation*, Gutiérrez has insisted that theology and spirituality must not be estranged from each other. Poverty, oppression, and affliction may form crucial cornerstones of liberation theology, but Gutiérrez contends that such a vision is not exclusive of spirituality. Indeed, without a spiritual dimension the struggle against injustice and oppression is in danger of lapsing into bitterness, resentment, and revenge, he contends (*OJ*, 87–88). The spiritual dimension inspires the prophetic element by infusing the Christian life with the gratuitousness and beauty of God's love.

Certainly the understanding of mysticism and spirituality in liberation theology is deeply indebted to the Christian tradition. While there are moments that signal important departures from the tradition of Christian spirituality, the richness of classic Christian spirituality is preserved by Gutiérrez. For Gustavo Gutiérrez, the following of Jesus is at the heart of Christian spirituality, wherein meditation on the Scriptures and prayer play a central role (*WDOW*, 1–3). The central significance of the Bible in the thought of Gutiérrez should provide a hint about the place of spirituality in his theology. After all, much of the tradition of Christian spirituality and mysticism was, before anything else, a form of contemplative and meditative biblical exegesis *(lectio divina)*.[2]

Gutiérrez insists that terms such as "spirituality" and "mysticism" must be refined by a more careful and comprehensive examination of the terms in the Christian tradition. "It is important, therefore, to go back to the biblical sources as well as to the authors of the great spiritualities, and to refine our understandings of certain ideas" (*WDOW*, 54). While Gutiérrez provides us with a fruitful understanding of spirituality, he is less clear about the meaning of mysticism. The closest he comes to offering us a suggestion of its meaning is in saying, "While I do not offer this as a general definition of what we mean by mysticism, it is clear that it has something to do with an experience of God in a key of love, peace, and joy" (*MIC*, 81). Of course, it would be misguided to argue that since a definition of mysticism is lacking in the theology of Gutiérrez, it follows that mysticism is absent from his thought. The task of this book as a whole is to demonstrate the significance of mysticism in contemporary thought, including in the liberation theology of Gutiérrez and to contribute to refining and elaborating on the meaning of mysticism. By studying the traditional and novel elements of spirituality and mysticism in the thought of Gutiérrez, we will be in a position to better judge the interpretation of these terms by Gutiérrez.

TRADITIONAL ELEMENTS OF SPIRITUALITY IN GUTIÉRREZ

Challenging the Split between Theology and Spirituality

Gutiérrez notes that in the early Church, theology was seen as a form of wisdom that had spiritual training and the following of Christ at the core of its being. "As a matter of fact, in the early centuries every theology took the form of what we today call a 'spiritual theology'—that is, it was a reflection carried on in function of the following of the Lord, the 'imitation of Christ' . . . But toward the fourteenth century a divorce began to take place between theology and spirituality that was to be harmful to both" (*WDOW*, 36). The harm that ensued for both theology and spirituality concerned the mutual estrangement between thoughtful, attentive reflection, on the one hand, and participatory and loving praxis, on the other. The seeds of the split between theory and practice, between theology and spirituality, were planted by the Scholastics at this time. In the fourteenth century, theological Scholasticism centered in the universities increasingly became separated from the monastic context of traditional spiritual theology. In his work *A Theology of Liberation*, Gutiérrez laments the fact and consequences of this split (even if the move of theology beyond the walls of the monastery is to be encouraged) and insists that "the spiritual function of theology. . . . constitutes a permanent dimension of theology" (*TL*, 5).

What exactly is spiritual theology for Gutiérrez? It could be said that spiritual theology in Gutiérrez is guided by a *transformational* rather than an *informational* model of theology (though he himself does not use these exact terms). The central task of the theological enterprise is to inspire and provoke a new way of thinking, acting, and believing. Spiritual theology is form of reflection that seeks to inform, transform, and conform our lives to the example of Christ.[3] Spirituality is an all-embracing style of life that "gives a profound unity to our prayer, thought, and action" (*WDOW*, 88). Even questions regarding method in theology, Gutiérrez argues, should not be divorced from spirituality. In fact, he says, the Greek word for method comes from *hodos*, "way." It was by their particular lifestyle and manner of life that the early Christian community distinguished themselves from the surrounding world. Thus, the early Christians were known as followers of the "way" (*WDOW*, 80-81). For Gutiérrez, then, spiritual theology has its origins in the scriptural mandate to imitate the life of Christ. Theological reflection is impoverished when theory is isolated from this Christian praxis. "Reflection on the mystery of God (for that is what a theology is) is possible only in the context of the following of Jesus" (*WDOW*, 136; *TSMYF*, 5).

Gutiérrez understands spirituality as a conversion to a new way of life. An encounter with God's presence shocks and grips the recipient and brings about unforeseen and novel possibilities. The old mode-of-being-in-the-world is abandoned for a new manner of interpreting, experiencing, and acting. While Gutiérrez regards the ethical commitment to justice and compassion to be at the heart of this new way of life, it would be a mistake simply to reduce his reflections on spirituality to an issue of ethics. Instead, what is also involved is a reconsideration of what we mean by knowledge, truth, or faith. In the thought of Gutiérrez, knowledge is not simply a detached, cognitive representation of reality by an idea or concept. In the Bible, Gutiérrez avers, knowledge "is a very rich concept that is not limited to the intellectual realm but also connotes taste, fellow feeling, and love. Knowledge here is a direct and profound kind of knowledge that embraces all dimensions of the person who is known and loved" (*GL*, xiv). With the prophets, for instance, truth is more of an event or happening that is disclosed in the history and struggles of the prophet and Israel as a whole (*PPH*, 60). Thus, for Gutiérrez, we come to knowledge of truth only by a process of participation, engagement, and involvement. Truth comes by way of manifestation and gift.[4]

This vision of truth shapes Gutiérrez's understanding of faith as well. Far from being a detached intellectual assent to certain propositions and doctrines, faith is, rather, an attitude of commitment (*PPH*, 20).[5] Faith is not merely an affirmation that God exists or an affirmation of particular ecclesial dogmas; instead, faith is the "vital acceptance of the gift of the word, heard in the community of the church as encounter with the Lord and love for one's fellow human beings. Faith pervades Christian existence in its entirety" (*PPH*, 55; *TSMYF*, 6). Gutiérrez also describes the commitment of faith as a kind of ecstatic love (*PPH*, 20, 59). It is ecstatic in that faith demands a movement outside of oneself into an-other, whether that other be God or one's neighbor. Faith is a knowledge born of love.

Gutiérrez's employment of the term "orthopraxis" should be seen in light of this interpretation of faith. The goal, Gutiérrez says, "is to balance and even to reject the primacy and almost exclusiveness which doctrine has enjoyed in Christian life and above all to modify the emphasis, often obsessive, upon the attainment of an orthodoxy. . . . In a more positive vein, the intention is to recognize the work and importance of concrete behavior, of deeds, and action, of praxis in the Christian life" (*TL*, 10). Gutiérrez interprets the famous definition of faith by Anselm along these lines.

In his *Proslogion* Anselm prays: "I have no wish, my Lord, to plunge into your depth, for my intelligence could never exhaust it. I desire only to grasp in some measure that truth of yours that my heart already believes and loves. I seek not to understand in order to believe. I believe in order to understand. For I am certain that if I did not believe, I would not understand" (*PPH*, 56). Gutiérrez interprets this monastic understanding of faith to mean that theological reflection is sterile without both a spiritual and ethical commitment. Objective and detached talk *about* God is in danger of becoming stagnant and trite if theology is not primarily concerned with talk *to* and *with* God. Prayer reminds us of the irreducible mystery of God and the limits of an intellectual comprehension of the Divine. Gutiérrez concludes his reading of Anselm by reiterating that faith means "feeling, acting, and thinking" as Christ (*PPH*, 56).[6]

The example of Christ allows Gutiérrez to insist that the Christian way of life (Christian orthopraxis) is not simply any form of action, however. Indeed, action in itself is ambiguous. There must be some norms or standards by which to judge human action. In this sense, Gutiérrez certainly does not shun the need for theory or doctrinal standards. The revelation of truth in the life, death, and resurrection of Christ is *the* norm of praxis in the theology of Gutiérrez. "The ultimate criteria come from revealed truth, which we accept in faith and not from praxis itself" (*TSMYF*, 101). This returns us to the importance of Scripture for Gutiérrez. As he is fully aware, the tradition of Christian spirituality was "essentially meditation on the Bible, geared toward spiritual growth" (*TL*, 4). The Bible was *the* sacred text by which all manner of thinking, acting, and believing was evaluated. An imitation of Christ was to be the fruit of all theological reflection. Knowledge of God came about through the encounter and discovery of truth in the example and life of Jesus of Nazareth. It is an experiential knowledge "that springs from the everyday sufferings, struggles, and hopes of the people; not an 'orthodoxy' that exhausts itself within itself, but the affirmation of a vital, extremely intimate, and yet conscious and reflective truth" (*PPH*, 143).

Gutiérrez also wants to make clear that spirituality in the Christian tradition is a communal affair. Only with the modern world did Christianity begin to take on a more individualistic meaning associated with bourgeois freedoms and rights (*TSMYF*, 110-11). A more accurate understanding of spirituality, Gutiérrez claims, is to see it as a communal journey of an entire people. Gutiérrez relates the communal way of life to Israel's journey from oppression to freedom narrated in the book of Exodus. "The Bible in fact depicts it [the spiritual journey of Exodus] as a collective venture: under the prior action of the God who liberates, a people breaks out of exploitation and death, crosses the desert, and reaches the promised land. Or, if you will, it is the venture of a 'messianic people' itself called *the way*. . . . These biblical paradigms have inspired Christian experience and reflection on this theme down through the history of spirituality" (*WDOW*, 3-4).

Gutiérrez is certainly right to insist on this collective dimension of Christian spirituality. In spite of popular New Age understanding of spirituality today, spirituality and mysticism were phenomena deeply imbedded in the religious beliefs, practices, and communities of the Christian tradition. Bernard McGinn's understanding of mysticism as a part or element of a concrete religion ratifies this interpretation of Gutiérrez.[7] Spirituality is, for Gutiérrez, a communal journey located within particular historical and religious communities and traditions.

The Moment of Silence in Theology

Gutiérrez contends that the split between theology and spirituality is related to a lack of modesty in modern theological reflection. The failure to incorporate a moment of silence marks much modern God-talk. This failure has resulted in an idolatrous neglect of the limits of language in the face of divine mystery. The moment of silence in the face of divine incomprehensibility is thus a crucial element in the theological method of Gutiérrez. Central to his entire work has been the insistence that talk about God is only possible within the prior horizon of contemplating God and doing God's will. Contemplation and ethical-political commitment are conditions for the possibility of theology.

He has frequently referred to these moments as the first and second act of theology.[8] "Contemplation and commitment combine to form what may be called the phase of *silence* before God. Theological discourse, on the other hand, is a *speaking* about God. Silence is a condition for any loving encounter with God in prayer and commitment. Experience of the inadequacy of words to express what we live out in our depths will make our speech both more fruitful and more unpretentious. Theology is talk that is constantly enriched by silence" (TSMYF, 3; OJ, xiii).[9] Reflection on the mystery of God, therefore, can only take place following spiritual and ethical-political praxis.

Gutiérrez associates mysticism and prophecy with this moment of silence in the face of divine ineffability. Both of these forms of religious belief and practice suggest that God cannot be approached apart from an entire way of life. Mystical and prophetic languages indicate the insufficiency of detached, scientific talk about God. Mysticism and prophecy are concerned with fostering an attention to where God is revealed. "The mystery that is God reveals itself in contemplation and in solidarity with the poor" (TSMYF, 56).

Prophetic language makes evident the barren character of God-talk that fails to inspire solidarity with the neighbor. Love of neighbor is not merely an ethical demand, however; rather, the love that is expressed in compassion for the poor and oppressed, Gutiérrez argues, is the path to knowledge of the truth and goodness of God. Mystical language serves to foster an awareness of the manifest presence of God in our lives, and yet it does so without relinquishing the unmanifest mystery of God.[10] Contemplation provides an avenue for contact with God and for a greater comprehension of the God who is immanent in the world and within the core of our being. The greater the comprehension, however, the more we are struck by the overwhelming incomprehensibility of God. In this light (or darkness), Gutiérrez perspicaciously interprets the meaning and necessity of silence and contemplation in theological reflection.

In interpreting the historical roots of the term contemplation (*theoria*), Gutiérrez mentions the original, Platonic connotation. "Plotinus, for example, would place the emphasis on theory insofar as this means union with God to the disparagement of political praxis. This position in turn would influence theology, where theory would be thought of as contemplation and union with God, and practice would be seen primarily as work for the neighbor, or the active life" (TSMYF, 91-92). While, it is clear that Gutiérrez does not wish to contribute to this disparagement of political and ethical praxis, he also does not want to deprecate the importance of contemplation and spirituality. For *theoria*, in the contemplative sense, has vision of and union with God as its final end. In the thought of the Christian Platonists, and Gutiérrez, at the heart of this contemplation and prayer lies the love of God. Contemplation is a participatory and loving form of knowledge. Knowledge about God is only possible through a life that embodies love and beauty. Contemplation plays a crucial role for Gutiérrez in fostering and inspiring a life that is fully aware of the gratuitous love of God (WDOW, 110-11). In this sense, "theory" (as a form of spirituality) is indispensable for theology.

The Mystery of God

As we have seen, the theological form of knowledge that Gutiérrez advances is nonobjective. Silent and contemplative praxis may make knowledge of God possible in a way in which neutral and objective speech about God fails. The major reason for this is simple: God is no object of human knowledge. "It is important to be clear on this point at the very beginning of any discourse on the faith, for God is truly more an object of hope (which respects mystery) than of knowledge" (TSMYF, 55). Gutiérrez often mentions the following statement of Aquinas in this regard: "We know more of what God is not than of what God is" (TSMYF, 55).[11] The fact that we cannot know the essence of God implies for Gutiérrez the limitations of rational language. Faith, hope, and love are Christian forms of experience and practice that give birth to knowledge of "things unseen" (St. Paul).

The sense of divine incomprehensibility is a central feature of Gutiérrez's work and warns us of limitations of ideas, images, metaphors, and so forth in speaking of God. In the view of Gutiérrez, when such ideas or symbols are employed they point not only to the object to which they refer, but to their own insufficiency. Symbols belong to the realm of silence, as does the experience of human love. "As the experience of human love shows us, in this kind of encounter [when] we enter depths incapable of communicating what is experienced at the affective level, then we are fully engaged in loving. And when words are incapable of showing forth our experience, we fall back on symbols, which are another way of remaining silent. For when we use a symbol, we do not speak; we let an object or gesture speak for us. This is precisely how we proceed in the liturgy; symbolic language is the language of a love that transcends words" (OJ, xiv). The affirmation and denial of language and symbols are thus held in a dialectical tension.

In Gutiérrez's reading of the book of Job, Job discovers a God that confounds our expectations and that eludes all rational systems that we construct to understand God. The Otherness of God interrupts all human attempts to fully comprehend God, whether in the form of explanations for suffering by Job's friends, or by Job's temptations to repudiate God altogether. On the one hand, Job's friends profane the mystery of God by reducing God's actions in history and nature to rational norms of reward-punishment. All of human life is interpreted vis-à-vis this punitive understanding of suffering. In this framework, good works are performed in expectation of reward. Gutiérrez contends that this version of self-seeking religion constructs an idol in lieu of the true God (OJ, 5).

This idolatrous framework is utterly cruel to Job. His friends are incapable of listening to him attentively and silently. Their coarse words desecrate a wisdom demanding silence. "Will no one teach you to be quiet—the only wisdom that becomes you. Kindly listen to my accusation and give your attention to the way I shall plead" (Job 13:5-6). Their inability to be silent impedes their ability to empathize with the suffering of others. It also, however, impedes them from coming to know the mystery of God. As much as Job's friends claim to be defending and representing God, they in fact are doing so dishonestly. "Do you mean to defend God," Job asks, "by prevarication and by dishonest argument?" (Job 13:7). The "divine consolations" that Job's friends offer are no more than false opiates that these sorry comforters offer in defense of God.

For Gutiérrez, this text reveals the idolatry of any form of theism that fails to keep silent when appropriate. In order to preserve both the mystery of God, on the one hand, and to express our solidarity with the afflicted, a silent contemplation and praxis is indispensable. Job's friends fail to recognize this. "The self-sufficient talk of these men," Gutiérrez remarks, "is the real blasphemy: their words veil and disfigure the face of a God who loves freely and gratuitously" (OJ, 29).

The opposite idolatry is the simple and outright repudiation of God. No doubt, Job is tempted by this option. The idolatry of some forms of theism (Job's friends) is thus not the only mistake that the book of Job calls to mind. Another desecration of the mystery of God is a confident repudiation of God. Job's encounter with God makes possible reconciliation with God and, consequently, a renewed hope. The anger, bitterness, and despair that Job naturally feels are prevented from dominating the rest of his life. He arrives at knowledge of God that ends his resignation and leads to a new life. Gutiérrez suggests here that a bold repudiation of God, as in modern atheism, is as idolatrous as the explanatory words of Job's friends. Ultimately, such a rejection of God may lapse into a replacement of God by the human person. God is domesticated and fabricated as an idol in this act. "Yet, in simple truth, the logic at work in a knowledge that claims to know everything about the Lord [even in a negative manner] . . . leads in the final analysis to the replacement of God with self and to the usurpation of God's place. It leads, in other words, to the denial of God" (*OJ,* 79).

The knowledge born of Job's suffering conveys to him a point significant in understanding mysticism in the thought of Gutiérrez: consciousness of the finitude and littleness of human nature. Human life is fleeting and human nature is like a shadow, as the prayer of Psalm 39 has it: "Lord, let me know my end, and what is the measure of my days; let me know how fleeting life is. . . . Surely everyone stands as a mere breath. Surely everyone goes about like a shadow." The suffering of Job teaches him humility, but not, notice, a recognition of his sinfulness. Job never comes to believe that he has been deserving of his suffering [as punishment for sin]. "He acknowledges his littleness but does not admit he has sinned; he expresses humility but not resignation. Job feels himself to be little [literally: trivial, of little weight]—that is, unimportant, of little value. . . . The speeches of God have brought home the fact that human beings are not the center of the universe and that not everything has been made for their service. Acknowledgement of his littleness may thus be an important step toward the abandonment of his anthropocentrism" (*OJ,* 76). This recognition of Job's littleness, that humanity is not at the center of the universe, is an important step in the face-to-face vision of God.

Love and Mysticism

The significance of love in the Christian mystical tradition can scarcely be overestimated. The confession from Scripture that "God is love" provides the entire Christian tradition with the decisive clue as to who God is (1 John 4:7ff.). The importance of love certainly has been maintained by Christian mystics, even those mystics we have traditionally come to see as "intellectual mystics."[12] For Christian mystics, love brings an awareness and consciousness of God, the self, and the cosmos that is unobtainable by pure discursive rationality. Of course, that does not mean that love in Christian mysticism is simply an emotional, romantic, anti-intellectual experience. Instead, Christian mystics often maintain that love itself is a form of knowing.[13] Gustavo Gutiérrez shares this understanding of mysticism. That love of God leads to knowledge of God is a central theme of his theology (PPH, 8; TL, 198, 194).

To place love at the heart of mysticism makes apparent the falsity of reducing mysticism to extraordinary states, visions, locutions, powers, and so on. In this way, love is a norm by which to judge the authenticity of mysticism. In reading the letters of St. Paul, Gutiérrez notes the importance of Paul's claim that while all spiritual gifts will pass away, love alone will remain (WDOW, 62; 1 Cor. 13). Greater than the power of tongues, the working of miracles, and prophesying is the power of love. "The power of the Spirit," Gutiérrez states, "leads to love of God and others and not to the working of miracles" (WDOW, 63). It is through this love, he continues, that we are united to God and become one with God (WDOW, 63).

Of course, the fact that love is a dominant presence in the thought of Gutiérrez does not prove that mysticism is necessarily an important element in his thought. To speak of mysticism proper there needs to be a more explicit articulation of the immediate or direct presence of God.[14] Bernard McGinn has shown the plurality and diversity of Christian understanding of the nature of mysticism. Such models include "contemplation or vision of God, rapture or ecstasy, deification, living in Christ, the birth of the Word in the soul, radical obedience to the will of God, and especially union with God."[15] In spite of such diversity, all these models of mysticism attempt to express, in finite human language, the direct or immediate presence of God. While Gustavo Gutiérrez has not dwelt at length on the history of Christian mysticism, the presence of mystical themes plays an important role in his thought. In Gutiérrez's reading of Job, for example, an expression of an immediate, face-to-face encounter with God comes to the forefront and lends credibility to the attribution of a mystical element to the thought of Gustavo Gutiérrez.

"I once knew you by hearsay, now my eyes have seen you . . ." (Job 42:5). Job speaks of an immediate and direct presence of God in his life, a presence that had been lacking hitherto. This experience of God in his life instigates a transformation in his understanding of himself, God, and the cosmos. From a mood of dejection, bitterness, and despair he learns to trust anew in the God he had previously known only by hearsay. He learns to appreciate and cherish the wonder and beauty of the cosmos.

He learns that, while there is chaos and disorder in the world, it is not all chaos (*OJ*, 80). Most of all, Gutiérrez maintains, Job learns that God is his redeemer and that God is love.

> Job now perceives that there is another way of knowing and speaking about God. His previous contact with God had been indirect, "by hearsay" through others (his friends!); now it is direct, unmediated. Job is now beginning to savor the Pauline "face-to-face" encounter with God in which faith, hope, and love abide, 'but the greatest of these is love' (1 Cor. 13:13). . . . Job therefore surrenders to God and can say with Jeremiah in time of crisis: "The Lord in with me" (Jer. 20:11), and with the psalmist: "I shall behold thy face in righteousness; when I awake, I shall be satisfied with beholding thy form" (Ps. 17:15). He can repeat here, after this meeting with God, what he had earlier said in hope: "My heart is bursting within my breast" (Job 19:27). . . . Job has previously addressed God on various occasions in protest; now he does so in acceptance and a submission that is inspired not by resignation but by contemplative love. (*OJ*, 85)

Job's direct contact with God literally saves his life. The emotions he tries to describe as a bursting, overflowing heart are far removed from his earlier despair and even temptations of suicide. Job's encounter with God pronounces a different, mystical way of "knowing and speaking about God." Objective language about God, language of hearsay, is replaced by a knowledge that is born of contemplative love. The vision of God by Job brings a knowledge that causes his heart to burst within him, a knowledge that eschews rational explanations whether in the form of the arguments of Job's friends or as the outright repudiation of God as the cause of evil.

For Gutiérrez, the presence of grace is what consumes the life of Job and is at the heart of mysticism. The language of mysticism is animated by pure grace and love. Mystical language heightens our consciousness of the mystery and gratuitousness of God, contends Gutiérrez. It reminds us of the limits not only of the human mind but also of human works. While the building of the kingdom of God demands the pursuit of justice, for example, ultimately the kingdom of God is pure gift. "Entrance into the kingdom of God is not a right to be won, not even by the practice of justice; it is always a freely given gift" (*OJ*, 89). This recognition of the freedom and gratuitousness of God enables us, Gutiérrez avers, to avoid the idolatry of reducing God to human ideas, categories, works, and so on. Contemplation disposes us to recognize that everything is gift (*WDOW*, 111). The nature of love is *the* decisive clue in the regard. Why? Because "true love is always a gift, something that transcends motives and merits" (*WDOW*, 110). When we love, we give without a why, without counting the costs, and without seeking reward (unlike Job's friends). Love silences all motives and (without words) contemplates God both in the form of prayer and in the form of our neighbor.

NOVEL ELEMENTS OF SPIRITUALITY IN GUTIÉRREZ

While we are going to consider some elements under the designation of novel elements of spirituality and mysticism, it would be wise to begin by mentioning that in some ways they are, in fact, quite traditional. First, while the insistence on the accessibility of mysticism to whole groups of marginalized, uneducated, and poor peoples is a novel element of liberation spirituality, it is not without its forerunners. In chapter 1 I briefly mentioned how trends in late medieval spirituality were inviting the participation of the laypeople, women, and the uneducated. Jean Gerson, for example, exclaimed that even young girls and simple people (*idiotae*) can become mystical theologians.[16]

Second, the claim that liberation spirituality and mysticism locates the most profound contact with God in the face of the neighbor is certainly not without precedent. Indeed, this may be obvious, since *agape* is crucial to the entire Christian tradition. The early Christian fathers, for example, were unanimous in their refusal to disparage the importance of praxis for the Christian life, even if they conceded with many of the Greek philosophers (and especially Neoplatonists), the superiority of *theoria* over praxis. This disagreement with pagan thinkers is a crucial element for the later mystical tradition. Concerning the early church fathers Bernard McGinn remarks: "Where they do not agree with late pagan philosophers is in their refusal to reject *praxis*, because they had come to understand it not as politics but as the practice of the Christian love for the neighbor (*agape*) enjoined by Jesus. . . ."[17] As we will see, the novel element of liberation spirituality insists that agape has political implications as well.

Another issue at stake concerns the necessarily public character of the Christian message in opposition to the private, esoteric teachings of gnosticism. Christian mysticism runs the risk of becoming gnostic rather than mystical when it is no longer accessible to the masses, and when it fails to locate Divine Otherness in the otherness of the neighbor. Finally, the centrality of the issue of suffering and affliction in the thought of liberation theology is not a novel element per se. As we have seen, the "dark night" of John of the Cross articulates an experience of affliction and abandonment by God in a way that is congenial to liberation spirituality and mysticism. In Gutiérrez's reading, this aspect of John's mysticism will be pushed further to include the agony of oppression, widespread poverty, racism, and exploitation. Struggle and combat will become as necessary to mysticism as are moments of stillness and silence. Now that we have briefly mentioned some of the traditional elements implicit in liberation spirituality and mysticism, we can turn to consider the novel elements.

History and the Eruption of the Poor

The rise of historical consciousness in the modern, western world has dramatic implications for all philosophy and theology, but also for the study of mysticism. Even though mysticism attempts to express the timeless mystery of God, it unavoidably does so through the historical, sociocultural, and linguistic paradigms of any age and place. Mysticism, no less than religion as a whole, is finitely situated in time and space.[18] Gutiérrez explains that such a fact accounts for the tremendous diversity of Christian spiritualities. "The reason for this diversity is that the nucleus around which a spiritual way is built is not exactly the same in every case. . . . The starting point in each instance bears the mark of the historical context in which the experience of encounter with the Lord took place" (*WDOW*, 88–89, 26–27). The mark of an authentic spirituality and mysticism is, consequently, a hermeneutical creativity animated by a rereading of the treasures of the past in light of present questions and struggles (*WDOW*, 31). This creativity seeks to bring into dialogue the resources of the past with the contemporary situation and worldview. In the thought of Gutiérrez, the reappropriation of past spiritual traditions (warranted by both the tradition itself and our contemporary, historical situation) is joined with an engagement in the issues and experiences of poor and oppressed groups in the context of the third world.

The large scale of injustice, poverty, exploitation, and premature death experienced by many in third world countries forces us to reconsider the significance of spirituality, and religion in general, in the face of such events. In what manner, if at all, do spirituality and mysticism contribute to enriching human life in such a context? What contributions can spirituality offer given the common portrayals of it as a sentimental and self-affirming product of a bored consumer? Is spirituality a credible expression of Christian life if it fails to confront the nocturnal face of history? Gutiérrez maintains that spirituality must be willing to reflect on these questions of suffering and injustice if it professes to be following in the footsteps of Christ crucified.

What is new to liberation spirituality is not exactly the awareness of suffering, however. More accurately, it is a consciousness of the roots of suffering caused by man. "Our increasingly clear awareness of the harsh situation in Latin America and the sufferings of the poor must not make us overlook the fact that the harshness and suffering are not what is truly new in the present age. . . . What is new is that the people are beginning to grasp the causes of their situation of injustice and are seeking to release themselves from it" (WDOW, 20). For historical change to be possible, freedom and a critical awareness must pervade the consciousness of the marginalized groups.

The contemporary situation in which spirituality finds itself, Gutiérrez continues, includes the emergence of global issues and struggles. More than class analysis is needed. In his work Sobre el trabajo humano Gutiérrez explains: "The question of injustice today is not solely [limited to] the perspective of social class, but also has transcended national borders and demands an account of the global dimension of injustice. In this dimension the relations between rich and poor countries are involved, as with the actions of multinational corporations in the international economy" (STH, 17; my translation). We are faced with issues and questions that extend beyond our borders and include political and economic systems, colonial policies, the distribution of wealth and power in parts of the world, and so on. Gutiérrez demonstrates that many of these issues have become part of the social teachings of the Catholic Church. In particular, the encyclicals Laborem exercens and Populorum progressio differ from past social encyclicals, he maintains, in that they reflect on non-European historical issues and problems (STH, 19). Within these two encyclicals, conflict is seen to exist not merely between individual countries and nations, but also between entire parts of the world, that is, between the first world and the third world.

There is an escalating awareness of the poor and marginalized throughout the globe. This awareness seeks to counter the absence of representation on behalf of the powerless and afflicted. The fact that such voices are now declared to have been absent voices in modernity signals the importance of their eruptive presence. With liberation theology there emerges a concerted effort to incorporate the suffering and struggles of these subjugated groups into its theological reflections. Modernity is faulted for having obscured from view, and even subjugated, the voices of the poor and oppressed. Retrieval of their insights and traditions is at the heart of liberation theology.

Gutiérrez argues that liberation spirituality challenges the monopoly of spirituality by the educated and clerical. While he fails to mention the historical roots of trends and movements opposing such a clerical spirituality, he offers trenchant remarks on the implications of a more democratic spirituality. Central to this transformation of spirituality is an openness to the spiritual experiences of the dispossessed and uneducated (*WDOW*, 14). Those who live on the margins of the privileged political, economic, and cultural worlds are invited to participate and contribute to our understanding of Christian spirituality. Insofar as spirituality is a following of Jesus, in the view of Gutiérrez, the Gospel is clear in its invitation of discipleship to all, including the poor, the sick, the blind and lame, the oppressed, sinners, and so on. In the vision of St. Paul, Jesus invites those foolish in the eyes of the world and those of low birth (1 Cor. 1:26). Gutiérrez contends that this openness must accompany any spirituality and mysticism that operates under the name Christian.

Solidarity with the poor and oppressed is a crucial moment of Gutiérrez's understanding of spirituality. Without attention to these powerless voices and persons, conversion to God is hindered; for at the heart of the ethical relationship with the poor is a turning of one's soul from oneself to an other. Sin is precisely that reality which fails to attend to God in others. "When we accept the divine message, we are converted to the Other in others. It is with them that we live out the message. Faith cannot be live in pure privacy with the self; it is the negation of every turning in upon the self" (*TSMYF*, 13). In the view of Augustine, conversion is the graced transformation of the will curved upon itself. This conversion is, for Gutiérrez, the starting point of any spiritual journey (*WDOW*, 95).

The recognition of political, economic, and military causes of suffering and oppression has brought about, concomitantly, a greater consideration of sin at the level of structural and material realities (*WDOW*, 99). In this form, sin is those actions, structures, and policies which lead to the degradation of human life. Poverty and material lack can be sinful realities that spirituality has the task of challenging. A spirituality that neglects the material dimension of human reality in interest of a purely "spiritual" reality not only neglects the concrete struggles of the poor and hungry, but from a theological standpoint is heretical. Such a spirituality is Gnostic insofar as it establishes a strong opposition between the life of the spirit and that of the body by elevating the former and denigrating or neglecting the needs of the latter.

According to Gutiérrez, then, spirituality is a way of life that confronts and opposes all the forces that destroy the life of body and spirit. For this reason, spirituality must be involved with the realms of life usually consigned to the secular and profane, including the realm of politics (*PPH*, 52). In a Christian perspective, spirituality becomes heretical when the material needs of bread, water, medicine, housing, and so forth are ignored.

Premature Death as an Obstacle to Spirituality and Mysticism

At the heart of Gutiérrez's spiritual theology lies the troubling question: "How can we thank God for the gift of life when the reality around us is one of premature and unjustly inflicted death? . . . How can we sing when the suffering of an entire people chokes the sound in our throats?" (*WDOW*, 7). Extreme forms of affliction and oppression, bodily and spiritual death, are obstacles to the mystical life in the thought of Gutiérrez. The violence of conquest, exploitative and servile labor, and the harshness of poverty all prevent the cultivation of a mystical consciousness of God. Reflections on these death-dealing obstacles play an important role in the spirituality of Gutiérrez. The significance of these issues calls into question the exclusive relegation of spirituality to either a purely sacred or religious realm, a private or interior realm or a nonmaterial, "spiritual" realm. The claim that spirituality involves the whole of human life leads Gutiérrez to defy the limitation of spirituality to any one of the above realms (*WDOW*, 88). Spirituality demands attention to the manifestation of the Divine in areas of human life that we consider profane, such as politics; to public locations outside of ourselves, such as the neighbor; to the material and physical corporeality of human nature (*WDOW*, 15; *PPH*, 52). This broad reading of the character of spirituality leads Gutiérrez to consider the forces that threaten the Christian life. "Every obstacle that degrades or alienates the work of men and women in building a humane society is an obstacle to the work of salvation" (*PPH*, 32).

The analysis of poverty in the theology of Gutiérrez has always been at odds with a romantic reading of the poor. The situation of poverty is not simply interpreted as a location where humility, simplicity, and worldly detachment thrive. Even if some of these characteristics of spiritual poverty are present, Gutiérrez condemns the situation of material poverty.

Indeed, he will argue that poverty means death (*WDOW*, 9). "In a word, the existence of poverty represents a sundering both of solidarity among humanity and also of communion with God" (*TL*, 295). The prophets repudiated poverty, he contends, because to accept poverty and injustice is to fall back into the conditions of servitude that existed prior to the liberation from Egypt (*TL*, 295). The servile conditions of poverty mean more than death of persons and communities, however. The death of entire cultures and traditions may accompany the harsh situation of poverty (*WDOW*, 10). Oppression in all its forms is a violent adversary of the God of life (*GL*, 3, 8).

In a novel fashion, Gutiérrez demonstrates this claim through his reading of the Spanish conquest of the Indies in his book *Las Casas: In Search of the Poor of Jesus Christ*. The Dominican missionary Las Casas was tireless in asserting that the Indians were being "stripped of their lives before their time" and therefore despoiled of "space for their conversion" (*LC*, 4). No doubt, the rapacious plundering of the lands and communities of the Indians was an obstacle to the possibility of conversion. The premature spiritual and bodily deaths of the Indians prevented them from living a complete and dignified life. In addition to the vicious violence of the initial conquest, the servitude and poverty perpetuated by the colonial system extended the violence in new directions. The exploitative and servile work of the *encomienda* system was a major culprit in the oppression of the Indians. In the words of Las Casas, the Indians suffered "servitude, than which, except for death, there is no greater evil" (*LC*, 75).

Las Casas directs a concentrated and sustained attack against the evils of the *encomienda* system. This system was the structural root of the injustices of colonial society. The lives and labors of the Indians were exploited for the sake of the spoils of gold and silver mines. The *encomienda* system created an entire republic that reduced labor "to the most vile and lowest exercise that can be imagined, which is to dig and turn over the dirt" (*LC*, 275). The meaningless character of this labor was clearly not the most nefarious aspect of this system, however. The expropriation of the life and liberty of the Indians was, in fact, the great evil. Indeed, the exploitative labor directly caused death and destruction on a massive scale.

It is this system, Las Casas writes, that has been the cause of the extermination of the Indian populations. The *encomienda* is the "true and effective cause . . . of the annihilation and decimation of all of these peoples, almost since their discovery" (*LC*, 287). Even when it did not kill the Indians, this system humiliated and degraded them. Exploitation had transformed their mode of existence into something altogether different from their precolonial life. Las Casas perceptively notes that both the kings and masses of the Indians have been reduced to a state of the most oppressed and unfortunate and that, consequently, they are "humiliated, belittled, afflicted, and tormented" (LC, 290). The impact of their suffering extends beyond mere physical death and includes spiritual death.

Las Casas is clear in his denunciation of the *encomienda* system. It is by establishing a "moral and political edifice" in the most "consummate state of evil" that this system is to be condemned (LC, 119). The Indians were employed as mere instruments serving the colonizer's pursuit of gold. "Thus," Las Casas writes, "the Spaniards use the Indians as no more than means and instruments to acquire the gold and wealth they desire and hold for their end" (LC, 442). The effect of this reversal of means and ends was the devaluation of the Indians' humanity and, conversely, an exaltation of the gold and wealth sought—the latter became the god of the Spaniards.

In the eyes of some of the Spaniards, the Indians were no more than animals. The humiliation and degradation of the Indians were justified by their ostensible inferiority. Taking his starting point with Aristotle, the Spanish theologian Sepulveda exclaimed that "in prudence, invention, and every manner of virtue and human sentiment, they are as inferior to Spaniards as children to adults, women to men, the cruel and inhumane to the gentle . . . finally, I might almost say, as monkeys to human beings" (LC, 293). The system of the *encomienda* fostered this mentality and servitude even when not expressed in Sepulveda's manner. Gutiérrez reads this, to be sure, as an oppressive and destructive obstacle to Christian spirituality.

An analysis of alienating labor in the modern world is at the heart of Gutiérrez's commentary on the papal encyclical *Laborem exercens* as well. In *Sobre el trabajo humano* Gutiérrez follows the pope in castigating modern forms of economic production. The perversion of labor, Gutiérrez says, is at the heart of this encyclical. This perversion consists in the reversal of means and ends; that is, the well-being and dignity of the human person is sacrificed in the interest of material production and capital (STH, 21, 29). The human person becomes an instrumental means to the demands for accelerated and mass production. Workers are made to serve material things and, in the process, the worker is made into a thing. Gutiérrez refers to this as alienation: one is made a slave of the fruits of one's labor. "Thus, what should be an expression of one's dominion over the earth, by the fruits of one's work, is made alien and hostile to the human person" (STH, 30; my translation). The effect of alienation is to destroy the possibility of the worker creatively assuming initiative as the subject and author of her or his work (*STH*, 40). Following the pope, Gutiérrez contends that such initiative is granted by the mandate of Genesis that humanity, being created in the image of God, is to subdue the earth. Industrial modes of production, on the contrary, only exacerbate the subjugation of humanity by earth, so to speak, by adding the more brutal subjugation of humanity by history and society in the form of oppression.

The Deconstruction of Idols as a Condition for Mysticism

At the origin of premature death caused by violence, servitude, and oppression, Gutiérrez contends, lies the worship of idols. The idolatry at work here is more than the idolatrous concealment of divine incomprehensibility by human images and ideas, the profanation of the transcendence of God. The idolatry that Gutiérrez confronts concerns those idols that legitimate and advance exploitation and death.[19] Nor is Gutiérrez primarily concerned with an idolatrous denial of God's existence. Gutiérrez maintains that death-dealing idolatry is a greater threat to Christian faith than the modern threat of atheism. Idolatry leads to the placing of one's trust in what is other than God: in power, wealth, one's ego, and so on.

In the Scriptures, he notes, idolatry is seen not merely in terms of one's denial of God, but rather as a way of behavior that violently and unjustly mistreats others. In Ps. 53:1, for example, the fools who say "There is no God" are corrupt by their "abominable acts." Their idolatry is less their words than their rapacious actions; they who "eat up my people as they eat up bread" deny God by their vicious ways of life (Ps. 53:4). "Idolatry is first and foremost a behavior, a practice. . . . This view of idolatry," Gutiérrez explains, "has special validity in Latin America. A tragic characteristic of this continent—the only continent in which the majority are at the same time Christian and poor—is the danger of claiming to be able to straddle the issue: to declare oneself in words for the God of Jesus Christ while in practice serving mammon by mistreating and murdering God's favorites, the poor. . . . This attempt, rather than the pure and simple denial of God's existence, is the great challenge to the proclamation of the gospel on our continent" (*GL*, 48–49; *TSMYF*, 32).

The interpretation of idolatry by the prophets, Gutiérrez argues, deepens our understanding of these issues and enriches the critique of idolatry in the mystical traditions. The pursuit of one's own gain leads to a blind disregard of suffering. Jeremiah says: "But your eyes and heart are set on nothing except your own gain; On shedding innocent blood, on practicing oppression and extortion" (Jer. 22:17). In the description of Ezekiel, the Jewish leaders have turned Israel into a "bloody city" by act-ing "like wolves that tear prey, shedding blood and destroying lives to get unjust gain" (Ezek. 22:27). The sacrifices of the unjust will not be ac-cepted by God, Sirach maintains: "The Most High approves not the gifts of the godless, nor for their many sacrifices does he forgive their sins. Like the man who slays a son in his father's presence is he who offers sacrifices from the possessions of the poor" (Sir. 34:19–20). The sacrifices offered by the wicked, Gutiérrez concludes, are no more than the lives of the poor offered on the altar of an idol (GL, 54). The culprit of this violence is avarice and the pursuit of power and glory. Las Casas concludes that "there is less veneration and worship of God than money" (GL, 61). Greed for gold is the sacrilegious passion of the Spanish conquistadors.

It is important to note that the reading of idolatry by Gutiérrez is not a condemnation of all non-Christians as pagan idol-worshippers. We would seriously misunderstand Gutiérrez if his critique of idolatry was read as a denunciation of "paganism" or of "primitive" religious traditions. Instead, Gutiérrez insists that idolatry is a permanent temptation "lying in wait for every religious person" (GL, 48). The brilliant vision of Las Casas ratifies this interpretation. The stunning claim of Las Casas is simply that the Christians, not the Indians, are the true idolaters. The human sacrifices of the Indians are eclipsed in severity by the human sacrifices of the Span-ish. Against the theologian Sepulveda, Las Casas argues: "The Doctor has reckoned ill. In all truth, it would be far more accurate to say that the Spaniards have sacrificed more to their beloved adored goddess Codicia ["greed," "covetousness"] every single year that they have been in the Indies after entering each province than the Indians have sacrificed to their gods throughout the Indies in a hundred years" (LC, 178). The Spaniards wor-ship the god gold, to whom they sacrifice innocent blood. The insatiable lust for gold is at the heart of the idolatrous actions of the Spanish con-quistadors. They have become "captives and slaves of money," writes Las Casas, "and must do what their lord commands . . ." (LC, 439). Accord-ing to St. Paul, this greed is idolatry (Col. 3:5). Las Casas will then dare to say the salvation of the Christian is more in question than that of the Indian (LC, 224).

In addition to the need to deconstruct the idolatry of greed, Las Casas argues that certain words and terms are in the need of a critical unmask-ing. The term "conquest" itself was one such term. The use of this term, he contends, attempts to justify the murder and enslavement of the Indian populations. The acceptance of this term by the Church would amount to a blessing of the violence and, in his words, a "baptizing" of the wars (*LC*, 106). "This term or name, 'conquest,' used with regard to all of the lands and realms of the Indies discovered and to be discovered, is a tyrannical, abusive, improper, and hellish term" (*LC*, 108). Related to the critique of the term "conquest," Las Casas, following in part Francisco de Vitoria, takes issue with illegitimate titles. Some of these include the claim that the emperor is the sovereign of the whole world; that the pope is temporal sovereign of the world; that the right to sovereignty came with the discovery; that the barbarians sin against nature; that the Indians have made a free choice in consenting to the conquest; and that God has made a special concession to the Spaniards (*LC*, 335).

Gutiérrez reads the criticism of these titles by Vitoria as a task of "intellectual hygiene. His conclusion is crisp and clear: none of the titles listed is capable of legitimating the European presence in the Indies" (*LC*, 335). When such intellectual hygiene is lacking, the threat of idolatry is insidiously present. When not resisted, idolatry leads to more than intellectual error: it leads to the consecration of violence and death.

Gutiérrez has long claimed that theology has been inadequately concerned with this kind of death-dealing idolatry. Instead of solidarity with the nonpersons of history and society (the victims of idolatry), modern theology has been concerned with apologetics directed toward nonbelievers. Liberation theology seeks to reverse this emphasis and attend to those whom the prevailing social order has scarcely regarded as human, namely, the poor and oppressed, despised cultures, ethnicities, and classes. "This challenge, then, unlike that of the nonbeliever, is a call for a revolutionary transformation of the very bases of a dehumanizing society" (*PPH*, 57, 193).

Freedom and Justice as Soil for Spirituality

The violent intrusion of the Spanish, and the dehumanizing servitude and poverty that ensued, was depriving the Indians, Las Casas maintained, of one of the most precious gifts of human nature—freedom. "No power on earth is competent to curtail or cripple the status of the free, as long as the key of justice is maintained, for freedom is the most precious and paramount of all the goods of this temporal world and so beloved and befriended by all creatures sentient and nonsentient, and especially by rational ones" (*LC*, 82). Throughout the writings of Las Casas, the insistence on the essential possession of freedom rings out loud (*LC*, 75, 80–84).

The indispensable requirement of any culture and people is freedom (*LC,* 83).

With unflagging consistency Las Casas asserts that the Indians are being deprived of this fragile gift and, thus, are prevented from knowing the God of freedom and justice. For Las Casas, and this is the heart of the matter, the God of Jesus Christ brings freedom to all, especially the mistreated and oppressed. "By all of which they shall know and appreciate the great value attached by our mighty God and merciful Father to the deliverance of the oppressed, the succor of the anguished, and the salvation and redemption of souls, for whose remedy the Son of God came upon earth, fasted and hungered here, took his repose and preached, and at last, died, together with the other merciful exploits he accomplished" (*LC,* 81). The bold claim of Las Casas is that God brings deliverance and freedom to *all* people, not simply Christians. The fact that human beings are created in the image of God warrants treatment of all persons with dignity and respect.[20]

In Gutiérrez's theology, the significance of liberty is grounded in his vision of spirituality. No doubt, there is much that he has learned from the insights of the modern traditions stemming from the Enlightenment. Still, at its core, freedom is a biblical and spiritual notion, he contends. Liberation from oppression and injustice has roots in Scripture, most poignantly illustrated by the story of Exodus, but also by the New Testament. We have seen that at the heart of Gutiérrez's reading of spirituality is love. A crucial companion to love is freedom, he maintains. Spirituality is characterized by a bold love that is free from the law (*WDOW,* 91). According to St. James we are to "speak and act as those who are to be judged under the law of liberty" (James 2:12). Gutiérrez interprets the portrayal of Jesus by the Gospel of John along the lines of freedom. Jesus "*freely* decides to give his life in *solidarity* with those who are under the power of death" (*WDOW,* 92).

Most clearly, Paul presents us with a picture of a life liberated by Christ. The distinction between "freedom from" and "freedom for" expresses well the heart of Christian spirituality. For Gutiérrez, this distinction calls to mind freedom from sin, selfishness, injustice, and oppression, on the one hand, and freedom for love and service to others, on the other (*WDOW,* 92). In this reading, freedom is neither bondage nor libertinism. Las Casas, for example, insists that at the heart of justice is consent (*LC,* 14). Since the Indian peoples have not consented to the European presence, it is illegitimate and unjust. The insistence on the demand for justice prevents freedom from being reduced to mere libertinism or, in modern terms, to "rights." As Gutiérrez says: "Human rights, to be sure. But not in a laissez-faire, liberal, merely formally egalitarian perspective; rather, along the lines of the rights of the poor, who are condemned to death and destruction by the oppressor whose quest is for gold" (*LC*, 44). Christian spirituality must operate, Gutiérrez implies, between the extremes of bondage and libertinism.

Therefore, Christian spirituality and mysticism have before them the task of instilling a spirit of love and freedom into conditions of oppression and injustice. Any form of social and political analysis, Gutiérrez holds, must operate under the guidance of spiritual discernment and training. Spirituality has the task of enriching, not obstructing, our analysis of the situation of the poor and oppressed. Social analysis has the task of studying the concrete conditions required for a historical transformation (*LC*, 288). "The structural causes of injustice should not be concealed, but on the contrary they must be analyzed and transformed" (*STH*, 53; my translation). Social analysis plays a part in preparing the soil so that human beings can grow and thrive. Among other things, what Gutiérrez finds so admirable about Las Casas is the Dominican's concrete insights into the causes of the poverty and oppression of the Indians. "Bartolome's conviction prevents him from simply protesting against particular injustices and leads him to add to that protest what in contemporary terms we would call a social analysis" (*LC*, 288). In the case of both Las Casas and Gutiérrez, this type of social analysis is, at its roots, spirituality.

Memory and Cultural Traditions as Soil for Spirituality

Against a modern, liberal notion of freedom Gutiérrez insists that without memory of the past, freedom is a truncated and impoverished notion (*PPH*, 12). An important element in Gutiérrez's interpretation of spirituality concerns the memory of the past and, in particular, of non-European cultures and traditions. The popular religious beliefs and practices of indigenous peoples augment and enrich the Western spiritual tradition. The nurturing of rootedness, thus, includes both the presence of freedom and justice as well as the memory and preservation of the resources of the dead. Using a very traditional metaphor (from Plato), Gutiérrez claims that "the human being is like a plant: to stay alive, the human being, too, needs to sink his or her roots in the earth" (*LC*, 79). The violence perpetrated against the Indians uproots their communities by preventing their participation in their natural and cultural contexts. Las Casas charges that the displacement of persons from the place of their birth to unfamiliar locations of servitude (i.e., the mines) has wreaked havoc in the lives and cultures of the Indians (*LC*, 79). Oppression divests the victims of injustice of memory, culture, and tradition. "A people afflicted with amnesia are an unstable people . . . ," Gutiérrez writes; "Conquerors always try to erase or block the memory of those whose necks they have bent" (*LC*, 413). The obliteration of memory, or amnesia, renders impotent the ability of a people to resist. It is an effective instrument of subjugation (*LC*, 415).

The task of liberation spirituality, then, is to retrieve marginalized and subjugated voices. Rereading history from the perspective of the vanquished (the underside of history) is a crucial step in the remaking of history. The recovery of the "scourged Christs of America" lends spirituality a subversive character (*PPH*, 20–21). This subversive character of spirituality is, nonetheless, one grounded in a traditional theological position, namely, that God embraces the most afflicted and abandoned of history. In the words of Las Casas, "God has a very fresh and living memory of the smallest and most forgotten" (*LC*, 194). While the dominant social and political orders forget the dignity of the least of society, God's memory is unflagging. Gutiérrez appeals to the Old Testament to substantiate this point. At the heart of the history of Israel is the demand to remember—to remember that they were once an enslaved people and, subsequently, that God heard their cries and liberated them from oppression (*LC*, 221; Exod. 13:3; Deut. 15:15). For Las Casas, the forgetfulness of the Spaniards is most reprehensible in failing to observe the central Christian precept: love of neighbor. "What memory must there be of that precept of charity, 'You shall love your neighbor as yourself,' among persons so oblivious of being Christians, or even human, that they have dealt with humanity in these human beings?" (*LC*, 221).

The retrieval of forgotten voices and persons (or nonpersons) comprises the heart of the liberation spirituality of Gutiérrez. Gutiérrez argues that this is an essential aspect of any spirituality and mysticism. "The vigorous existence of local churches in places geographically and culturally far removed from Europe, the force of their voices, containing accents of pain and hope, the contribution of their theological reflection and the new challenges this brings represent the most important event for the Christian faith in these last years of the second millennium of its history. This is the context in which we must discuss the subject of mysticism and oppression" (*MIC*, 82). These global issues, thus, constitute an original contribution to the study of Christian spirituality and mysticism.

While demanding a refinement of popular beliefs and practices (insofar as mysticism includes an element of idolatry-critique), the mystical element of Gutiérrez's theology insists that the language of contemplation is enriched by the popular faith of indigenous and non-European cultures (*OJ*, 95). The mystical element of Gutiérrez's work is grounded in an affirmation of the gratuitous love of God, a gratuity that is manifested as an option for the outcasts and poor of history and society (*MIC*, 89). Attention to despised cultures, ethnicities, and classes is a key element in Gutiérrez's understanding of mysticism (insofar as God is revealed in the midst of such groups). Such attention has the establishment of justice as its primary aim, and justice, Gutiérrez says, is a "condition for attaining the face-to-face vision of God" (*LC*, 10).

Insofar as mysticism is associated with the love of God in a key of peace, hope, and joy, mysticism is faith in the risen Christ. This faith in resurrection is never complete, however, without heeding the voices of those who bear the cross. "Faith in the risen Christ is nourished by the experience of suffering, death and also of hope among the poor and oppressed, by their way of relating to each other and to nature, by their cultural and religious expressions. . . . Going to the roots ensures creativity, renews the tree. At the heart of a situation that excludes them and strips them of everything, and from which they seek to free themselves, the poor and oppressed believe in the God of life. Rilke was right when he said that God is in the roots" (*MIC*, 89).

Spirituality of Work

With the cultivation of freedom, justice, and memory there emerges the realistic possibility of work becoming a spiritual exercise. Gutiérrez quotes Isaiah that "they shall not build and another inhabit; they shall not plant and another eat. . . . They shall not labor in vain . . ." (*PPH*, 32; Isa. 65:21, 23). Against a romantic version of such an image of work, Gutiérrez insists that in every act of work there is pain and struggle. Gutiérrez maintains that it is social oppression and exploitation that pulverizes the human spirit, not the natural experience of fatigue. Gutiérrez quotes Pope John Paul II's words: "In relation to the reality of work, the life of each society and even all of humanity is ruined not merely with the effort involved and personal fatigue, but in the midst of much tension, conflict, and crisis" (*STH*, 32–33; my translation). Social conflict and crisis are a more dangerous threat to the human spirit than natural suffering. With the cultivation of the conditions of life for the human person, however, work can become a spiritual training. By participating in both creation and cross, work takes on a mystical dimension for Gutiérrez.

Insofar as work is involved in creation, it takes part in the transformation of the world. Gutiérrez follows Marx, and parallels Simone Weil, in maintaining that change occurs through the material forces of history and society. An important material force of history is the economic mode of production and the requisite laborers. Analysis of these factors plays an important role in changing the world (rather than merely interpreting the world in a purely philosophical mode) (TL, 29-30). Concerning these matters, however, the foundation of Gutiérrez's position is less the work of Marx than the theological vision of creation (STH, 25).

For Gutiérrez, the significance of work is articulated, even if implicitly, in Genesis. Here humanity is seen as the center of the work of creation and is, thereby, called to continue the act of creation by labor (TL, 158; Gen. 1:28). The mandate of Genesis (to subdue the earth) is read by Gutiérrez as the dignified call of humanity to transform nature and to enter into relationships with others. "Only in this way does he come to a full consciousness of himself as the subject of creative freedom which is realized through work" (TL, 295). Through work, humanity freely exercises a power over nature and history. Conditions of servitude and oppression militate against the mandate of Genesis and, furthermore, seek to return humanity to the condition of preliberated Israel. By working for a just society, humanity exercises its autonomy and self-determining dignity. "By working, transforming the world, breaking out of servitude, building a just society, and assuming his destiny in history, man forges himself" (TL, 159).

In addition to taking part in creation, work is a bearing of the cross, for Gutiérrez. If we simply read work in terms of creation, we may potentially overestimate and overvalue the freedom of the human being vis-à-vis nature. The cross makes this impossible. The cross manifests the vulnerability and dependency of human nature, Gutiérrez contends. It makes evident the conditional character of human "lordship" over creation. "Lordship yes, but dependence as well, in respect to God and others" (STH, 59; my translation). Human freedom is never a libertinism that disregards our dependency on and obligations toward God and others. The experience of suffering in work brings us into contact with our finitude and fragility. It is a participation in the cross. "In human work the Christian discovers a small part of the cross of Christ and she accepts it with the same spirit of surrender" (STH, 60; my translation).

Through the cross, we are brought into contact with God and others. "In this case, work is the location of distinctive human action; work places us in relation to God and contributes to the creation of a global brotherhood. By being the location of encounter with God and others, by having a place in the work of salvation, work has—beyond others—a spiritual dimension in the sense that we have recalled" (*STH*, 58; my translation). Thus, work is a spiritual exercise that participates in both creation and cross. The tension between human freedom and dependency is at the heart of Gutiérrez's spirituality of work.

The spirituality of work is an expression of the richness of Christian truth, Gutiérrez contends. "These basic affirmations pertaining to labor have arisen precisely from the richness of Christian truth, especially from the message of the 'Gospel of work,' creating the foundations of a new way of thinking, valuing, and acting" (*STH*, 36; my translation). This new way of life inspired by a spirituality of work brings the human person into contact with both suffering and creative freedom. At the heart of Christian spirituality and mysticism, contends Gutiérrez, lies this encounter with God through both cross and creative, liberating love.

IV ⌁

The Prophetic-Tragic Thought of Simone Weil: Reflections on the Hidden God

In light of the disturbing presence of affliction and evil in human affairs, the question of God's absence or hiddenness confronts theology with an unavoidable urgency. While we have already begun to address this theme in relation to mysticism, it is now necessary to examine the question of evil and divine hiddenness in a more comprehensive manner. To be sure, insofar as theology is a form of critical reflection on God, it must attempt to confront the question of evil in relation to the goodness and omnipotence of God (theodicy) in an honest and courageous manner. The reality of evil can only be evaded at the price of theological dishonesty or complacency in the face of unjust suffering. Religion becomes no more than a consoling opiate when the dark face of existence is disregarded. Perhaps even more damaging in this regard, however, would be the suspicion of a failure of theology to adequately interpret a central symbol of Christianity, namely, the cross. Such a theological failure would hold for the interpretation of the Hebrew bible as well, especially the Psalms, Job, Lamentations, and the prophets. In these texts, an interpretation of the God who hides himself irrepressibly emerges from the experience of Israel's oppression and suffering. God appears to be absent from the struggles and cries of the afflicted.[1] A reading of God's hiddenness arises, then, both from the experiences of affliction and evil in human life, on the one hand, and from the Scriptures of Jews and Christians themselves, on the other.

Liberation theology is one form of contemporary thought that creatively and honestly faces the reality of global suffering and oppression in relation to the hiddenness of God. Reflection on God is interpreted in light of the struggles of excluded, marginalized, and colonized peoples, especially of the third world. The impact of power and violence in history and society, as in colonialism, receives thoughtful attention by liberationist thinkers. For Christian liberation theologians, the manifestation of God in history and society is located where God is most seemingly absent: in the faces of whole crucified peoples. God is manifested in hiddenness, in locations of poverty, death, and suffering. According to Gustavo Gutiérrez, theology must be nourished by an attention to the presence of God in the weakness and scandal of the cross. "But, again like Job, we cannot keep quiet; we must humbly allow the cry of Jesus on the cross to echo through history and nourish our theological efforts" (*OJ*, 103).

Central to many liberation theologians is the intimation that in order to most persuasively speak of the living and liberating God, the reality of death-dealing evil must be confronted. In the face of evil, God seems to be absent from, or indifferent to, suffering in history and nature. The reality of affliction, thus, makes reflection on the hiddenness or absence of God a necessity in our contemporary context.

In the liberation theologians, the confrontation with a "presence of absence"[2] is not reduced to a struggle with suffering at a personal, existential level. The abyss or horror of suffering is most threatening in historical and natural events, such as global imperialism and colonialism, the Holocaust, and countless other violent events. Simone Weil notes that "relentless necessity, misery, distress, the crushing burden of poverty and of exhausting labor, cruelty, torture, violent death, constraint, terror, disease" are all effects of the hiddenness of God in history and nature (*NB*, 401). We have seen in chapter 1 that Weil names this presence of God's absence "void." In this chapter I hope to develop Weil's thought on the void or absence in relation to the hiddenness of God.

Far from generating an apathetic philosophy, sensitivity to the void or hiddenness of God by both Weil and the liberationists gives birth to a creative attention to where God is most truly revealed: in cross, negativity, conflict, suffering. Unlike certain forms of theism, Weil insists that the struggle with the hiddenness of God resists the temptation to find a theoretical explanation to the problem of evil or concomitantly to rationally justify God's existence. In succumbing to this temptation, modern forms of theism too often evade the reality of affliction in spite of (or perhaps because of) the creation of modern, argumentative solutions to the problem of evil or "theodicy."[3] Philosophical atheism and agnosticism certainly are no more thoughtful on the question of evil than modern theism. God's existence is often denied or ignored on explicitly rational grounds. Missing from their accounts is a creative reflection that seeks to confront and inspire resistance against the crescendo of evil in our time.

In this vein, Simone Weil argues that modern forms of theodicy are often idolatrous subterfuges that distract and avert our gaze from human affliction. The destruction of such idols makes a struggle with evil in history and nature, and even with God, a necessary moment of theological and philosophical thought. The prophetic-tragic element of Simone Weil demonstrates an exceptional sensitivity to conflict in human life: from conflict between a person and society; between humanity and God; and, in the most intense instances, between God and God.

Thus, for Simone Weil the struggle with the hiddenness of God is anything but an apathy and indifference toward either the afflicted or God, as in much of atheism and agnosticism. Indeed, she insists that only those who know God's presence can cogently speak of God's absence (*NB*, 343). Struggle with God's hiddenness in the thought of Weil is the path to contact with God. "For it seemed to me certain, and I still think so today, that one can never wrestle enough with God if one does so out of pure regard for the truth. Christ likes us to prefer truth to him because, before being Christ, he is truth. If one turns aside from him to go toward the truth, one will not go far before falling into his arms" (*WFG*, 69). In her reading of Greek tragedy, she will claim that wisdom is born only of suffering, pain, struggle; grace comes violently (*NB*, 390).

Struggle with God and the concrete experience of human suffering are necessary encounters for shedding light on the conflict between God and human suffering. In Weil's thought, reflection on the question of evil cannot be isolated from the existential confrontation with suffering. The question of evil resists theoretical solutions and brings the intellect to its knees (as a koan). For Simone Weil, thus, glimpses of the meaning of suffering will only be detectable through the concrete encounter with suffering. "I feel an ever increasing sense of devastation, both in my intellect and in the center of my heart, at my inability to think with truth at the same time about the affliction of men, the perfection of God, and the link between the two. I have the inner certainty that this truth, if it is ever granted to me, will only be revealed when I myself am physically in affliction . . ." (*SL*, 178). In such a vision, wisdom is born of suffering.[4]

Simone Weil insists that rational speculation alone is futile in shedding light on the question of evil. The separation of theory and practice only exacerbates the thoughtlessness on the question of evil fostered by modern forms of theodicy. For Weil, therefore, attention to the hiddenness of God proceeds by spiritual exercises and the painful struggle to endure and transform suffering itself. For her, contact with the afflicted (living and dead) is the most significant avenue for contact with God. It is here that God's seeming absence manifests a hidden presence. It is in the faces of afflicted that we discover that the void of God is a greater plenitude than the presence of all worldly entities.[5] Contact with God is given to us through the hiddenness of God. "Contact with human creatures is given to us through the sense of presence. Contact with God is given to us through the sense of absence. Compared with this absence, presence becomes more absent than absence" (NB, 239-40).

THE RELATIONSHIP OF PROPHECY AND TRAGEDY

Prophecy

I am arguing that the prophetic and tragic have certain affinities, but it does not follow that they mean the same thing. Such terms are only confused and obscured when they are conflated. The distinctions between these terms is, in fact, as important as any affinities.

I fully recognize that the terms "prophetic," "prophet," or "prophecy" are diverse and complicated terms, especially in the broad context of the ancient Near East. Nevertheless, I have been persuaded that it is with the classic Hebrew prophets of the eighth to fifth centuries B.C.E. that the unique and distinctive Jewish form of prophecy emerges.[6] The task of prophecy in this context is to proclaim the word of God in history and society in the form of rebuke, exhortation, warning, or counsel to the people. Breaches in the covenant provoke the ire of God and the fury of God's spokesperson, the prophet. While the apathy of others produces blindness and deafness, the prophet is acutely aware of the suffering and affliction of the poor and forgotten. In this case, the target of the prophet's denunciation is the sins of the people. The suffering and oppression that Israel endures is related to the disobedience of the nation.

In spite of this covenantal theology, however, the prophets often intimate that the suffering of Israel is not simply a matter of sin. In the book of Deuteronomy, for example, Yahweh tells Moses (the archetypal prophet): "I shall hide my face from them. I shall see what their end will be" (Deut. 31:17, 18; 32:20). With this sense of God's hiddenness, Jeremiah complains of his plight in life, of his undeserved suffering. "Why did I come forth from the womb, to see sorrow and pain, to end my days in shame?" (Jer. 20:18). In the figure of the suffering servant, Isaiah expresses the cries and woes of one who is innocent, one who is despised and rejected by all, a man of suffering (Isa. 53). His suffering is *not* seen as punishment for sin and disobedience. Elsewhere Isaiah laments what appears to be God's absence. "Where is He who brought them up from the sea with the shepherd of His flock? . . . Oh that you would rend the heavens, that you would come down . . ." (Isa. 63:11–64:2). Isaiah then concludes that God has hidden his face from us (64:6).

In the classic prophets, then, suffering is seen in terms of both sin and God's inscrutable providence. The prophets, as with Amos for example, are sensitive to the hiddenness of God in the conflict and injustices of society. The prophets express an exceptional sensitivity to the abyss of suffering and evil in history. An awareness of the presence of power, violence, conquest, and oppression in history is central to their extraordinary visions. In this light, the suffering of the poor and dispossessed is more than a matter of the people's sin. For the prophets, an acute awareness of God's hiddenness leads them to suggest that the ravaging of terror and violence in history is not simply intelligible within the reward-punishment framework of covenantal theology, even if the sins of the people clearly play an important role.

Central to the Christian preservation and augmentation of the prophetic tradition is the claim that the Word of God is manifested within a historical event. In the Jewish prophets, the word of God comes to a human mediator, whereas the Christian tradition confesses that the Word of God is incarnate in the life, death, and resurrection of Jesus of Nazareth. Whereas the Jewish prophets are messengers of a divine word to the nation Israel, Jesus the Christ is interpreted as the Word of God to all nations and peoples. The Apostle Paul, for example, preaches "Christ crucified" as the Word of God to all people, gentile or Jew, slave or free, woman or man. If the Hebrew prophet is a spokesman of God on behalf of the covenant, then for Christians the prophet is the spokesman of God on behalf of the new covenant established by Christ.

The prophetic character of Christianity is most evident in the tradition of theology of the cross. In this tradition, as with the Jewish prophets, the manifestation of God occurs in hiddenness. The historical event of the suffering and death of Christ is the central location of God's self-disclosure. God is not primarily revealed in the beauty of nature—indeed, for the prophets an aesthetical religion of nature frequently leads to idolatry. Instead, God is revealed in the midst of history, including the conflict, negativity, and suffering in history. God seems to be visibly absent and only discernible to those who look to the underside of history, to locations of poverty and suffering. In the theological tradition, the Protestant Reformers emphasized this aspect of Christianity. Luther and Calvin insist that if one only follows the guidance of human reason, one will conclude that either there is no God or that God is unjust.[7] In order for the worship of the true God to be possible, one must turn to God's Word disclosed in Scripture. For Luther, this self-disclosure of God's Word occurs most fully in the filth and darkness of the world (i.e., at the *cloaca*).[8]

Tragedy

While there are key differences between the prophetic traditions of Judaism and Christianity and Greek tragedy, there are also points of contact often overlooked by much of the history of Christian theology. From the time of Justin Martyr, the influence of Greek philosophy on the contours and substance of Christian theology is an evident and incontrovertible fact. In our discussions of mysticism, for instance, we have seen how significant Plato's philosophy has been for the development of Christian spirituality. Why is it, however, that it was usually the philosophers and almost never the tragedians that Christian thinkers engaged and incorporated into their theology? Some of the reasons for this neglect of tragedy are clear, especially in light of the less than flattering depiction of the Greek gods. Ambiguity, capriciousness, amorality, violence, jealousy—these human, all too human traits were characteristics of divine behavior in many Greek poets. Certainly the improper and impure behavior of these gods contrasts sharply with Plato's vision of the Good or the One. It is Simone Weil's original contention, however, that there is much wisdom among the tragedians that might find a congenial ally in Christian theology, especially in light of the passion narratives of the Scriptures.

What exactly is tragedy? From the outset it is important to challenge the common assumption that tragedy is necessarily fatalistic and despairing. In the plays of the great tragedian Aeschylus, for example, a portrayal of the bitter role of violence and force in human life does not preclude him from ending his works, in the *Oresteia* for example, with a hopeful resolution. The founding of the courts of justice at the end of the *Eumenides* gives us hope that the cycle of revenge and violence will be broken by the strong, yet gentle presence of persuasion.[9]

Simone Weil claims that an awareness of the presence of misery and suffering in human life is the genius of the "bitterness" of the Greeks. Such bitterness cannot be equated with a despairing fatalism or sadness, she insists. In reference to Greek poetry she maintains that "no matter how painful they are, these dramas never leave us with an impression of sadness" (*ICAG*, 19). Indeed, she will insist that it is with the moderns that a despairing sadness dominates the interpretation of tragedy. "I cannot accept any catastrophic interpretation of Greece and its history. . . . True, their conception of existence was a bitter one, as it is for all whose eyes are open; but their bitterness had a motive; it had meaning *in relation to* the happiness for which man is made and of which he is deprived by the harsh constraints of this world. . . .Whereas there are so many modern people . . . in whom sadness is connected with a loss of the very instinct for happiness; they feel a need to annihilate themselves" (*SL*, 122–23). In short, Greek tragedy was not nihilistic; nor is Weil's tragic vision.[10] Indeed, for Weil, the genius of Greek tragedy is the beauty of the poetry. In an honest and artistic fashion it illuminates the truth of the human condition in a way that refuses to ignore the dark and brutal forces in history and nature.[11] It opens our eyes to the weight of suffering in human experience. And, for those who suffer, artistic expressions of tragedy—in poetry, art, or music, e.g. the blues—just possibly makes life endurable and even beautiful.

Paul Ricoeur contributes much to the understanding of the theology of tragedy. Ricoeur insists that a tragic vision of humanity is the other side of a tragic vision of the divine.[12] Tragic theology is inseparable from the tragic vision of human history and nature. Central to this tragic theology, he maintains, is the ambiguity of the gods, "the non-distinction between the divine and the diabolical."[13] In this vision, humanity is led to destruction through a blindness that is conceived of as the fault of divine initiative. In tragedy, such a divine malevolence has two poles, Ricoeur continues, an impersonal one in fate and a personal one in the will of the gods. In the case of the former, necessity reveals a blindness and indifference to human values; the sun shines on the good and bad alike. Anyone is vulnerable to the blows of fate. With regard to the will of the gods, tragedy shields the hero from moral condemnation and offers him or her as an object of pity. The initiative of the gods is held culpable. Compassion is thereby invoked in the hearts of the spectators, who are called to empathize with the plight of the person crushed by the gods.[14]

Ricoeur concludes that tragedy properly emerges only when the theme of predestination to evil comes up against the theme of heroic freedom and greatness. The conflict between fate and freedom, between the will of the gods and the protests of the hero is displayed in tragedy proper.[15] The complexity and unruliness of tragic theology demands expression in nonrational forms such as myth, narrative, and drama. The ambiguity of the gods or the unresolvable tension between fate and freedom make evident the *unthinkable* character of tragedy for Ricoeur. At the level of rational thought it is unthinkable (and thus for Plato unacceptable), but in terms of the human experience of evil in history and nature the tragic vision is also "invincible."[16]

It is important to emphasize that in contrast to the prophetic tradition in Judaism and Christianity, tragedy avoids the suggestion that human suffering and evil are the result of sin. In Judaism and Christianity the idea of redemption is related (even if not exclusively) to the forgiveness of sin. In Greek tragedy, the presence of suffering and violence is not moralized in the same manner. An important part of Weil's reading of tragedy is the claim that evil and suffering occur to human beings often as the result of chance. A seemingly chaotic, impersonal force metes out pain and suffering to some and well-being to others. Weil insists that the mystery of suffering is debased when reduced to a matter of sin. As with Ricoeur's emphasis on the unthinkable character of tragedy, Weil's reading of the tragic vision will insist that the problem of evil is an inexplicable mystery. Along these lines, Lucien Goldmann also claims that tragedy is a "universe of agonizing questions to which man has no reply."[17]

Prophetic-Tragic Thought

In confronting the absence or hiddenness of God in history and nature, Simone Weil articulates both a prophetic and tragic vision of Christianity. With regard to the prophetic, however, a persuasive case could be made to disqualify Weil from such a title. After all, her reflections on the Jewish prophetic tradition are not only tendentious, but more often shallow and closed-minded. While her criticisms of the traditions of conquest in the Old Testament (e.g., Exodus, Joshua, Numbers) are legitimate and even necessary, she is surprising in her lack of attention to the beauty and complexity of the Jewish Scriptures. Indeed the greatest flaw in her extraordinary thought is her narrow reading of the Old Testament.

If, however, we understand the prophetic to involve a Christian theology of the cross in which the self-disclosure of God's Word is located in historical conflict, struggle, suffering, and cross, then the title of "prophetic" is not inappropriately imputed to Weil's thought. In Weil, this prophetic element is clearly related to a tragic sensibility. Her reading of the passion narratives is an attempt to reconcile the prophetic element of Christianity and the tragic element of the Greeks. Her reading of the crucifixion of Christ maintains that the death of God at the cross represents not merely the redemption of human sin but also the divine response to the question of suffering and evil. The mystery of evil still eludes rational understanding, but in the example of Christ the Christian is inspired to respond to suffering by thoughtful action. I believe that this prophetic-tragic vision is a creative and important project.

THE HIDDENNESS OF GOD IN SIMONE WEIL

An interpretation of void and absence of God in the thought of Simone Weil may be fruitfully illumined by studying this central element of her thought in relation to the prophetic-tragic hiddenness of God. One of the major points of convergence between prophetic and tragic traditions concerns attention to conflict, violence, and suffering in history and nature. While the tragic vision displays a greater pessimism regarding history than the prophetic, the attention to conflict and force is shared by these traditions. One way of reading these two different traditions in the thought of Weil is to associate them with the categories of hiddenness 1 and 2, as developed in the work of B. A. Gerrish and David Tracy.

Gerrish claims that in the thought of Luther, there is an uneasy tension between the hidden knowledge of God manifested in the historical, incarnate, and crucified Word of Jesus Christ, on the one hand, and a hidden knowledge of God outside of Jesus Christ, on the other. He has helpfully referred to these as hiddenness 1 and 2, respectively.[18] Hiddenness 1 articulates a classic theology of the cross, championed in a creative way by Luther. In this tradition, God is disclosed in hiddenness: in the folly and scandal of cross and death. The glory of Christ is not recognizable in visibly dramatic nor beautiful ways. Far from being the object of adoration, Christ is the object of scorn, revulsion, and disgust. Christ's glory is hidden beneath affliction.

Hiddenness 2 is more disturbing and problematic. In his most troubled moments, Luther suggests that even after the historical manifestation of God in Christ, there is much that remains unknown about God. The "concealed and dreadful will of God," Luther says, remains "the most awesome secret of the divine majesty."[19] Why is the hidden will of God dreadful for Luther? One aspect of that answer concerns the question of predestination. The dreadful will of God is none other than the decision of God to consign a portion of humanity to perdition. While the incarnate God does not desire the death of the sinner, the *deus absconditus* damns a majority of the human race. Luther: "He does not will the death of the sinner—in his Word, that is. But he does will it by that inscrutable will."[20] Is there a struggle within God himself between contradictory elements of mercy and wrath? Does the death of Christ on the cross reveal a God struggling on behalf of humanity against the wrath of an unknown God?

David Tracy sums up the importance of the issue of hiddenness 2 very well: "At the very least, this literally awe-ful and ambivalent sense of God's hiddenness is so overwhelming, so powerful that God is sometimes experienced as purely frightening not tender: sometimes as an impersonal reality of sheer power and energy signified by such metaphors as abyss, chasm, chaos, even horror, sometimes as a violent personal reality. . . . It is Luther (here quite different from even Augustine and Pascal) who will speak of what the ancient Greek tragedians named 'fate' in ways Aeschylus and Sophocles if not Euripides would have understood."[21] In this manner, the question of the hiddenness of God 2 is an agonizing effort to confront the unthinkable, to face the awe-ful and frightening experiences in history. The admiration Weil felt for the Greeks was precisely in their honest struggle with the problem of evil, whether in terms of their conception of "fate" or with their mystical reflections on divine ambiguity.

While for Luther the experience of the ambiguity of God and of the ostensible conflict within God is related to the issue of predestination (which he relates to the tragic notion of fate!), for Simone Weil the conflict is most clearly apparent in the issue of evil and affliction. The seeming chaotic rule of force and violence in history and nature is the source for her reflections on the hiddenness of God. Why God allows affliction and force to destroy human life is the troubling source of her thoughts on the apparent conflict within God. "The great enigma of human life is not suffering but affliction. . . . It is not surprising that disease is the cause of long sufferings, which paralyze life and make it into an image of death, since nature is at the mercy of the blind play of mechanical necessities. But it *is* surprising that God should have given affliction the power to seize the very souls of the innocent and to possess them as sovereign master" (SNLG, 171–72). It is not surprising that Weil notes the fact that the Scriptures speak of a God who both manifests and hides himself. In reference to Isa. 45:15 she writes, "'*Vere tu es Deus Absconditus.*' . . . The universe both manifests and hides God" (NB, 149, FLNB, 161).

As we have seen, void in Simone Weil is one way she interprets the hiddenness of God. More terrifying than the absence of God, however, is the experience of the anger and violence of God toward God's own creation. In the book of Job, for example, Job interprets his suffering as the unjust violence of God against him. Daringly Job reads the actions of God in history as seeming chaos and violence. "I was at ease, and he broke me in two; he seized me by the neck and dashed me to pieces; he set me up as his target; his archers surround me. He slashes open my kidneys, and shows no mercy; he pours out me gall on the ground. He bursts upon me again; he rushes upon me like a warrior" (16:12-14). It is precisely such a text, along with expressions of divine ambiguity in Greek tragedy, that is the source for her reflections on the hiddenness of God. She dares to say that even the ambiguity of the Greek gods has something to teach us. "The Greek gods—capricious, neither good nor evil, good and evil in turn, more readily evil than good, worse than man and more powerful. One cannot do without them either" (NB, 243). Why can we not do without the Greek gods? After all, are we not repulsed by their bizarre and strange behavior? What could the myths of conflict and war among the divine realm contribute to the Christian interpretation of God?

Simone Weil clearly suggests that the seeming ambiguity of the Greek gods is not entirely unlike the tension in the Jewish and Christian Scriptures between the unpredictable anger and wrath of God, on the one hand, and the mercy and forgiveness of God, on the other. As I have suggested, this apparent conflict within God is also detectable in the thought of Luther, though most clearly as related to predestination. Lucien Goldmann claims that such a conflict within God is the mark of the tragic vision.[22]

In Weil's interpretation of the conflict between Zeus and Prometheus, for example, the outlines of her thoughts on the conflict within God are clear. In the Aeschylean version, Zeus reveals his wish to destroy the human species and to sow a new race. In Weil's translation Prometheus says: "And to that [plan to destroy the human race] none made opposition, but only I have dared. I have delivered mortals from the damnation that would have flung them into Hades" (ICAG, 62).[23] For that defiant act, however, Prometheus suffers. Prometheus says, "Against me the tempest from Zeus, bringing terror advances visible" (ICAG, 65). Prometheus confronts the wrath of God. In Weil's reading, "Prometheus suffers because he has loved men too well. He suffers in man's stead. The wrath of God against the human species is entirely carried by him . . ." (ICAG, 67).

The split that occurs between God, Weil avers, is between the power and wisdom/love of God. The dilemma is between the omnipotent God who is the author of all and the powerless God who is only author of good. "God is the author of all; God is only the author of good: we cannot escape from this dilemma" (NB, 207). For Weil, this estrangement between God and God is anguish. "In God, at the point where the two opposites, Power and Love, are separated a supreme anguish exists. . . . How are the Most-High God and this crucified corpse going to set about becoming reunited?" (NB, 539). Thus, Weil also relates this split to the experience of Christ at the cross confronting the harsh will of God the Father. "The idea of a situation where God would be separated from his Wisdom is very strange. But it appears also, although less insistently, in the story of Christ. The Christ accuses His Father of having abandoned Him; and Saint Paul says that Christ has become a curse before God in our stead. At the supreme moment of the Passion, there is an instant where there appears a thing which to human eyes seems a separation, an opposition between the Father and the Son" (ICAG, 68).

Weil is right. This is strange and troubling for our understanding of God. It certainly brought Luther much pain and anguish. In Weil, this sense of divine ambiguity is explicitly related to the issue of evil and afflic-tion. The idea of the hiddenness of God 1 and 2 is neither an attempt to explain the presence of evil nor to reject God. It is, rather, a painful at-tempt to confront the inscrutable presence of evil in relation to the love and goodness of God. It is one way of interpreting and grappling with the real ambiguity of human experience: the contradictory realities of vio-lence and peace, death and life, suffering and joy, evil and good, and so on. For Simone Weil, sentimental or nice portrayals of the divine often obscure the more terrifying experiences of history. Only when the tragic face of God is confronted does faith in the tenderness and love of God become a realistic hope for history and nature. The possibility of recon-ciliation between the prophetic and tragic elements (hiddenness of God 1 and 2) is not precluded by Weil. The possibility of a reunion between God and God is an important part of Weil's reading of the crucified God in Jesus Christ.

I propose to study this issue in greater depth by relating the prophetic element of Simone Weil to hiddenness 1, and the tragic element of her thought to hiddenness 2.

The Hiddenness of God 1

The hiddenness of God 1 in Simone Weil reveals itself in attention to the revelatory presence of God in locations of God's seeming absence. For Weil, this prophetic understanding is primarily determined by the mani-festation of God in Jesus Christ. Christ has been, is, and will be present wherever affliction occurs. Weil quotes Pascal in this regard: "Jesus will be in agony until the end of the world" (*ICAG*, 70).[24] "Through redemptive suffering God is present in extreme evil. For God's absence is the divine form of presence which corresponds to evil—an absence that is felt" (*NB*, 343). For Weil, it would be unpardonable for God to be absent from the affliction and terror of human experience. "If the Redemption, with the sensible signs and means corresponding to it, had not been present on this earth from the very beginning, it would not be possible to pardon God . . . for the affliction of so many innocent people, so many people uprooted, enslaved, tortured, and put to death in the course of centuries preceding the Christian era. Christ is present on this earth . . . wherever there is crime and affliction" (*LTP*, 17; also *WFG*, 192).[25]

For Weil, then, God's hidden love is most fully disclosed in locations of suffering and conflict. There is a "plenitude of God's presence in what seems absence, void, silence" (*SNLG*, 90). In order to detect God's presence in the void, however, we must first destroy the idols that obscure God's hiddenness. "Our effort has been the means of destroying part of the false plenitude which exists in us; and the divine emptiness, fuller than any plenitude, has come to dwell in us" (*NB*, 531). One example of an idol of false plenitude (which obscures attention to the hidden God) is the worship of the glory and power of Christ by society and culture. Society as the "Great Beast" (Plato) disregards the humiliated beggar in Christ and adores a mighty god instead.[26] "After the Resurrection the infamous character of his ordeal was effaced by glory, and today, across twenty centuries of adoration, the degradation which is the very essence of the Passion is hardly felt by us. . . . We no longer imagine the dying Christ as a common criminal. . . . Today the glorious Christ veils from us the Christ who was made a malediction . . ." (*ICAG*, 142–43). The depiction of God as a glorious king leads us away from contact with the Christ who was made a malediction for humanity.

Simone Weil maintains, moreover, that those who themselves participate in the cross of Christ are most able to recognize God's presence in hiddenness. Aeschylus expresses this well by suggesting that "wisdom is born of suffering" (*ICAG*, 57; *NB*, 439). For Weil this means that those who have the harsh privilege of knowing suffering are in the best position to recognize God's hiddenness.[27] One example of this, Weil says, is African American slaves. "To accept God as a common convict, shamefully tortured and put to death, is truly to overcome the world . . . but who thinks of Christ today as a common convict . . ? People worship the historic grandeur of the Church. The black slaves overcame the world by faith in Christ: 'They crucified my Lord'" (*FLNB*, 144–45). The interpretation of Christianity by the slave narratives, songs, and laments, Weil intimates, is potentially more profound and accurate than the readings of Scripture by cultural elites.

Weil contends that the figure of the fool in Shakespeare is also a brilliant attempt to convey the wisdom implicit in all the ostracized and subjugated groups of humanity. The fools of Shakespeare reveal a wisdom that is inaccessible to pure intellectual prowess. They speak the truth of the human condition in a way that is overlooked and repressed by others. "There is a class of people in this world who have fallen into the lowest degree of humiliation, far below beggary, and who are deprived not only of all social consideration but also, in everybody's opinion, of the specific human dignity, reason itself—and these are the only people who, in fact, are able to tell the truth. . . . And not satirically or humorously true, but simply the truth. Pure unadulterated truth—luminous, profound, essential" (*SL*, 200).[28] In a similar way, the village idiot expressed the truth by dwelling in a subjugated, humiliating state (*MA*, 67, 70).

The insight into the human condition conveyed by such slaves or fools is actual cognitive truth. It is not simply the case that their experiences are ethically inspiring. They are able to pierce the truth of reality in a way ignored by the powerful and wealthy. Indeed, in the New Testament it is the blind, lame, poor, and marginal who recognize the truth of Christ. Thus, St. Paul exclaims that God chooses what is foolish in the world to shame the wise (1 Cor. 1:26–31). What is this truth or wisdom that the outcasts of society potentially bear?

Martin Luther suggests that an aspect of this truth (wisdom born of suffering) is the recognition that we are all beggars.[29] Weil explains this as the awareness of human fragility, finitude, transience. "Man must learn to think of himself as a limited and dependent being, suffering alone can teach him this" (*ICAG*, 57). Suffering brings recognition of human misery and of the precarious and ephemeral character of life (*NB*, 236; *NFR*, 169). Suffering deconstructs the illusion of autonomy, of the belief that we are complete masters of our life. It makes evident our vulnerability to forces and events beyond our control. For Weil, this recognition is a bearing of the cross (leading toward decreation). "When everything is going more or less well, we do not think about this almost infinite fragility" (*SNLG*, 185). "Unless constrained by experience, it is impossible to believe that everything in the soul—all its thoughts and feelings, its every attitude towards ideas, people, and the universe, and, above all, the most intimate attitude of the being towards itself—that all this is entirely at the mercy of circumstances" (*SNLG*, 187). Attention to the presence of afflic-

tion in human life—recognition of the hidden God—is central to the wisdom born of suffering.

Theology of the cross in Simone Weil, therefore, inspires an attentiveness to God's hidden presence that the adoration of power, wealth,
and worldly beauty veils. It seeks to inspire solidarity with the victims and
dispossessed of history as a prerequisite for contact with the crucified
Christ. The marginalized and oppressed people of history and society are
those in the best positions to detect this hidden God. For Simone Weil,
society and church too often worship a different god.

What if, however, the suffering is so oppressive and destructive that,
far from wisdom, what is engendered is the death of truth, love, wisdom,
God-consciousness? This brings me to a tragic consideration of the
hiddenness of God 2 and the mystery of evil in the thought of Simone
Weil.

The Hiddenness of God 2

No doubt, there are experiences of affliction in history that one cannot
but name evil. Far from ennobling, such suffering and violence often
pulverizes whatever is in its path. Simone Weil's interpretation of the
hiddenness of God 2 should be seen in light of the destructive presence
of force in human life. The domination of violence in social oppression,
war, and conquest often irreparably damages its victims. Tragic experiences of violence and suffering arouse responses of lament and protest.
Even the hidden God revealed in Jesus Christ is altered by the anguish
and pain of his destiny. In the intense moment of Christ's cry of abandonment on the cross, the understanding of hiddenness 1 gives way to
the more troubling question of hiddenness 2.

With her broad awareness of the destructive presence of force in human life, Weil's reading of the hiddenness of God can be reduced to
neither the issue of predestination with Luther or Calvin, on the one
hand, nor to the personal feeling of anxiety and estrangement among the
modern existentialists, on the other. For Simone Weil (and the liberation
theologians) the hiddenness of God is most powerfully apparent in the
faces of whole groups and histories of marginalized and oppressed peoples.
David Tracy eloquently interprets the hiddenness of God along these lines.
He insists that the hidden God is revealed in "cross and negativity, above
all in the suffering of all those others whom the grand narrative of modernity has too often set aside as non-peoples, non-events, non-memories, in
a word, non-history."[30]

In her life and thought Weil expresses an extraordinary sensitivity to the afflicted of history and society. "Let us suppose a man whose entire family has perished amidst tortures, and who himself was long exposed to torture in a concentration camp; or an American Indian of the sixteenth century who was the sole survivor of the massacre of his people. . . . I myself have not gone through such things. But I know they exist . . ." (NB, 432). Confronting the harsh existence of evil is a central mandate in the prophetic-tragic vision of Simone Weil. Greek tragedy, the vision of Job, and the cry of Jesus on the cross permeate her thought on the issue of evil. Like Job, Weil complains of the violence on the earth and God's apparent indifference. Job says, "Why are times not kept by the Almighty, and why do those who know him never see their days? The wicked remove landmarks; they seize flocks and pasture them. They drive away the donkey of the orphan; they take the widow's ox for a pledge. They thrust the needy off the road; the poor of the earth all hide themselves. . . . They lie all night naked, without clothing, and have no covering in the cold. . . . From the city the dying groan, and the throat of the wounded cries for help; yet God pays no attention to their prayer" (Job 24:1–12). Faced with this void and abyss of affliction Weil turns to consider the hiddenness of God.

As mentioned, affliction is most apparent through the destructive presence of force in history and nature. War and conquest make evident in an obvious and blatant manner the impact of violence in human affairs. In chapter 1 we considered the destructive impact of force in the form of social oppression, especially exploitative work. In the present context, we need to consider force in relation to war and conquest as another face of the hiddenness of God in history.

The greatness of the Greeks, Weil claims, should be seen in light of their genius to illuminate the destructive presence of force in human life, as in war, and yet to despise it (ICAG, 116). Their tragic vision is a lucid construal of the terror of history, of the harsh realities of suffering and violence. Greek tragedy, and Homer in particular, shows how force turns all subject to it into a "thing" (MA, 163). In Weil's essay on the Iliad, she cogently explains that force destroys all roots of memory as well as the inclination to rebel. "Curses, feelings of rebellion, comparisons, reflections on the future and the past, are obliterated from the mind of the captive; and memory itself barely lingers on" (MA, 169). As in the "dark night" of John of the Cross, memory is lost and emptied when confronted with affliction.[31]

In The Need for Roots Weil interprets this loss of memory at the hands

of force in light of concrete instances of historical violence such as conquest. Human communities and traditions are uprooted and destroyed
when violence seizes their lives and identities. "Uprootedness occurs whenever there is a military conquest. . . . It reaches its most acute stage when
there are deportations on a massive scale, as in Europe under the German
occupation, or along the upper loop of the Niger, or where there is any
brutal suppression of all local traditions . . ." (NFR, 42). Far from proving
ennobling of such countries or traditions, conquest brings a destruction
from which the conquered may never recover (NFR, 152). "For several
centuries now, men of the white race have everywhere destroyed the past,
stupidly, blindly, both at home and abroad. . . . The past once destroyed
never returns. The destruction of the past is perhaps the greatest of all
crimes. . . . We must put an end to the terrible uprootedness which European colonial methods always produce, even under their least cruel aspects" (NFR, 49).

In her lifetime, Weil directed her attention against many instances of
colonization in the modern world. She was tireless in reproaching the
French government and people for their cruelty and indifference to the
people of Algeria. Weil harshly reproached Europeans for their oppression and exploitation of African people (NFR, 77). On the issue of the
colonization of the Americas, she showed contempt for those who sought
to justify or mitigate the offense in any way (NFR, 268). Weil was particularly upset at an article written in a Catholic review in New York on the
anniversary of the "discovery" of America by Columbus. The article apparently suggested that Columbus had been sent to America in order to
give rise in the future to a nation capable of defeating Hitler. In Weil's
satirical words: "God, apparently, also despises colored races: the whole-
sale extermination of native American peoples in the sixteenth century
seemed to him a small price to pay if it meant the salvation of Europeans
in the twentieth . . ." (NFR, 268).

Prior to the beginning of World War II Simone Weil even dared to
suggest that a world war, while certainly not desirable, might prove to be
punishment for the cruelty of modern European nations toward colonized peoples. "When I think of a possible war, I must admit that the
dismay and horror such a prospect evokes in me is mingled with a rather
comforting thought. It is that a European war can serve as the signal for
the great revenge of the colonial peoples, which will punish our uncon-
cern, our indifference, and our cruelty."[32]

The issues of colonization and war in the modern world were, indeed, major reasons Weil repudiated so harshly the idea of progress. Honest

attention to the presence of violence and suffering in modernity belied, for Weil, any optimistic faith in reason and progress. "For those dreamers who considered that force, thanks to progress, would soon be a thing of the past, the *Iliad* could appear as an historical document; for others, whose powers of recognition are more acute and who perceive force, to-day as yesterday, at the very center of human history, the *Iliad* is the purest and the loveliest of mirrors" (MA, 163). There is a dark underside to the ostensible progress of the Western modern world. The histories (or rather nonhistories) of whole groups of oppressed and subjugated peoples challenge modernity's confident celebration in enlightenment and evolution.

In the cases of war and conquest, Weil explains, force exercises a destructive influence upon all in its path. Affliction brands the human spirit with the mark of a slave and makes a "thing" of the human person. Conquest uproots its victims and devastates their traditions, communities, even their hope in God. To Simone Weil (and Job) it seems as if God is complicit in such affliction, if God is not the cause. Accusing God for the affliction of the world seems unavoidable in the face of evil. "Just as God, through the mouth of Christ, accused himself of the Passion, so we should accuse God for every human affliction" (*FLNB*, 95).

Simone Weil notes a very important text in the book of Job. "This recalls an extraordinary passage in the Book of Job (16:19–21): 'Also now, behold, my witness is in heaven, and my record is on high. My friends scorn me: but mine eye poureth out tears unto God. O that one might plead for a man with God, as a man pleadeth for his neighbor. O that God himself might be the arbiter between man and God . . .'" (*ICAG*, 60; *NB*, 525). Job calls upon a mediator to act as a witness to and against God. Weil defends the protest of Job as a legitimate cry of anguish and sense of abandonment (*SNLG*, 172). In the midst of affliction or through compassion for the affliction of others, a struggle with God is not only valid but necessary for a more complete faith.

Indeed, Weil reluctantly admits that there are times when the love of God is painfully difficult. "It is when I am in contact with the affliction of other people, those who are indifferent or unknown to me as much as the others, perhaps even more, including those of the most remote ages of antiquity. This contact causes me such atrocious pain and so utterly rends my soul that as a result the love of God becomes almost impossible for me for a while. . . . I hope he will forgive me my compassion" (*WFG*, 91). Indeed, Weil avers that compassion for others often appears to be at odds with love of God. "For in view of the host of terrible sufferings—and so often such undeserved ones—inflicted upon mankind, one might think that the love of one's neighbor leads to a rebellion against God" (NB, 281). Weil insists that this is not blasphemy but a painful grappling with the issue of evil and God. It is a dark night of the soul.

Weil wants to make clear that a struggle with God can be a deeply religious act. As with Prometheus struggling against Zeus or Jesus' cry of abandonment on the cross, the disobedience of Job is divine. "Is there a secret version in which, corresponding to human disobedience through lack of love, there is divine disobedience through excess of love?" (FLNB, 344).

The struggle with and against God is nothing else than the struggle with the hiddenness of God. Central to the experience of affliction in history and nature, in the tragic vision of Simone Weil, is the insistence that evil and affliction often strike innocent and undeserving victims in a haphazard manner. Affliction is not distributed according to a rational process of reward and punishment; affliction is not the result of sin.[33] It is rare to encounter, Weil says, a depiction of suffering that does not reduce affliction to either sin or to the suggestion that affliction is a natural vocation of the afflicted (MA, 193). When misfortune is seen in this way, then the afflicted become a "legitimate object of contempt. . . . This is a view which makes cruelty permissible and indeed indispensable" (MA, 193).

Margaret Farley contends that this kind of radical evil (i.e., conquest) cannot be understood within the traditional categories of redemption. "If the disease that crippled human life were only the guilt of sin, then the atoning death of the Christ would be a revelation of such love, mercy, and redemptive power that it would wipe away all the evil of history. . . . The suffering that ravages the innocent, the young, and the persecuted is not relieved by atonement. . . . Radical suffering is outside the bounds of justice and cannot be returned to the harmony of justice by consolation, vindication, or retribution. It cannot be *justified*."[34] In contrast to the prophetic tradition (hiddenness 1), the tragic vision (hiddenness 2) maintains that radical evil is interruptive of all simple explanations. The Christian model of redemption is challenged. In the thought of Weil this gives rise to a sustained reflection on tragedy in relation to the passion of Christ. In contrast to some of the beliefs of the Jewish and Christian traditions, Greek tragedy depicts the cause of affliction to be the product of haphazard and chaotic force.

Weil explains that affliction often strikes as a blind mechanism. "A blind mechanism, heedless of degrees of spiritual perfection, continually buffets men hither and thither and flings some of them at the very foot of the Cross. . . . Affliction is above all anonymous. . . . It is indifferent, and it is the chill of this indifference—a metallic chill—which freezes all those it touches, down to the depth of their soul" (SNLG, 175; NFR, 232). For Weil affliction is not a rational mechanism distributing punishment in a just fashion, nor is affliction the punishment by a personal God. The influence of tragedy on her thought leads her to suggest that affliction is an inevitable aspect of a world in which chance and chaos are stubborn realities in perpetual struggle with order and beauty. In a more theological sense, Weil intimates that the indifferent face of necessity is an aspect of the impersonal, hidden face of God, the face of God that rains on the just and unjust alike. It is this impersonal providence of God that allows blind and indifferent necessity to have dominion (WFG, 125; NB, 542).[35]

Weil's theory of creation is certainly beyond the scope of this chapter. In this context, however, we should note that the presence of indifferent necessity and force in creation is the result of God's self-sacrificial act. In creation, God renounced God's omnipotence in order to allow creation to be truly autonomous and other from God.[36] Thus the powerless God is not only revealed at the cross, for Weil, but also in the very act of creation. As an act of love, creation is the limitation of God's power (NB, 541). Creation is, therefore, an act of God in which the possibility for chaos and evil exists (NB, 191–93, 213; FLNB, 100, 120, 164; GG, 97–98).

This understanding of creation does not act as an explanation for the existence of evil, however. Why did God have to allow chaos and evil to thrive? There is no solution to this question. Weil does not conclude that evil exists because creation must involve freedom, for example. For Weil, the unruly presence of force and evil in creation resists any conclusive explanations. While we must attempt to understand the causes of suffering, especially to ascertain human guilt and responsibility, the why of suffering is pure mystery (SNLG, 196). In her view, explanations often mask a quest for false consolation and a disregard for innocent sufferers.

Theodicies, in this light, are often imaginary attempts that avert our gaze from attention to affliction and contact with the hidden God. Certainly Job's friends avert their gaze from affliction by their confident explanations for suffering (NB, 287). Thought is so revolted by affliction that it takes refuge in lies (SNLG, 188). Indeed, Weil is quite suspicious of all language on the question of evil (and the mystery of God!). More often than not, attempts to understand evil in the form of argument lead to theoretical solutions and rational explanations that inevitably reduce the mystery to idols of language and thought. "As a rule our imagination puts words into sounds in the same way as we idly play at making out shapes in rumpled linen or in smoke wreaths. But when we are too exhausted . . . then we must have real words. . . . All we get is silence" (*NB*, 627). We yearn for explanations and solutions, but we only hear silence.

In Weil's view, this silence echoes the Father's (non)reply to Christ. "God allowed God to send up a cry to him and did not answer. It is when from the innermost depths of our being we need a sound which does mean something—when we cry out for an answer and it is not granted us— it is then that we touch the silence of God" (*NB*, 627). The ability to hear the silence of God and to resist consoling theodicies is to participate in the cross. By attention to misery and affliction we ascend to God. "The attentive contemplation of misery, without compensation or consolation, drives us on into the supernatural . . ." (*NB*, 287).

Suffering, thus, is completely resistant to theory and abstract specula-tion. It interrupts and deconstructs all rational thought. "The thought of suffering is not of the discursive kind. The mind comes slap up against physical suffering, affliction, like a fly against a pane of glass, without being able to make the slightest progress or discover anything new, and yet unable to prevent itself from returning to the attack" (*NB*, 483; *FLNB*, 292). The idols of thought (theodicies) continue returning to "the attack." When it is understood that theoretical solutions are impossible, then suf-fering becomes a koan to the mind. The only way of making progress is through contemplation, but a contemplation without a why. "To con-template what cannot be contemplated (the affliction of another), with-out running away . . . that is what is beautiful" (*FLNB*, 71). When we are able to remain silent, then the possibility of hearing the silence of God emerges. "Our soul is constantly clamorous with noise, but there is one point in it which is silence, and which we never hear. . . . For, if he re-mains constant, what he will discover buried deep under the sound of his own lamentations is the pearl of the silence of God" (*SNLG*, 197–98).

The refusal to explain the mystery of evil equally pertains to the con-flict within God that I have been discussing. While Weil may have been tempted by a Manichaean solution to the problem of evil by positing two gods, she explicitly rejects that temptation. A simple positing of an evil, creator God as the cause of affliction is, no less than some theodicies, a debasing of the mystery of suffering. This reduction of the mystery to a confident separation of good and evil gods is the mistake of Manichaeism, Weil claims. "As regards the question of good and evil, one may perhaps reproach the Manichaeans with having diminished the impenetrability of the mystery of evil by their manner of enunciating it" (*NB*, 352). Any confident rational solution is to be shunned for Weil. A struggle with and against God does not lead to the positing of two gods in Weil anymore than the struggle with God does for Job.

As we have seen, then, the hiddenness of God 2 in Simone Weil is an honest attempt to confront the devastating presence of violence and oppression in history and nature. In a haphazard and indiscriminate manner force strikes whole communities and histories of innocent persons (or nonpersons). Theodicies become idols when force and suffering are reduced to the punishment of sin and the chaotic rule of force is neglected. By attention to such unjust force in history and nature, Weil confronts the hiddenness of God and God's seeming complicity in the face of destructive violence. As Job exclaims, "If not he, then who else?" (Job 9:24). God as Power is seen to be, if not the cause, at least complicit in the affliction of human beings. God appears to be impersonal and indifferent to human well-being; the hidden God works life and death in the righteous and wicked alike. Finally, however, for Weil the presence of evil is resistant to all explanations, including the simple and outright repudiation of God.

Reconciliation of the Hiddenness 1 and 2:
   The Prophetic-Tragic Thought of Simone Weil

"Thus do the gods justify the life of man: they themselves live it—the only satisfactory theodicy!"[37] Simone Weil would agree with this quote of Nietzsche; the only satisfactory theodicy is through a divine solidarity with the affliction of the world. "The Cross of Christ is the only source of light that is bright enough to illumine affliction" (SNLG, 194). This does not suggest that the mystery of evil has a theoretical solution, even in the cross of Christ. The cross is, rather, a divine *response* to evil and the model for our response to the presence of affliction. It is a response that is marked by a solidarity without a why for suffering. It remains silent, void of explanatory whys.

For there to be a reconciliation between the hiddenness of God 1 and 2, Weil proposes that the cross of Christ is not merely a redemption of sin, but includes as its central meaning the embrace of affliction and the transformation of radical evil. Thus, in Weil's view, the passion of Christ cannot be reduced to a consequence of the Fall. "Thus it is true to say that the Incarnation and the Passion are and are not consequences of Adam's disobedience" (NB, 236). Human misery, she claims in this context, is misunderstood if reduced simply to a matter of sin. The suffering of God at the cross is more than a response to a moralizing reading of the Fall. Instead, it is a response to the question of evil by God living it.

For Weil, the reconciliation of the prophetic and tragic vision occurs with the struggle of Christ at the cross. Contrary to the martyrs, Jesus approaches his death with fear and trembling. He is shaken and disturbed by the prospect of affliction. "The accounts of the Passion show that a divine spirit, incarnate, is changed by misfortune, trembles before suffering and death, feels itself, in the depths of its agony, to be cut off from man and God" (MA, 192). Christ did not die as a martyr; he died as a common criminal (WFG, 125; NB, 26). Thus, the most supernatural aspect of Christ's life, Weil avers, is not to be found in the power and glory of Christ. "The supernatural part is the sweat of blood, the unsatisfied longing for human consolation, the supplication that he might be spared, the sense of being abandoned by God. . . . 'My God, my God, why has thou forsaken me?' There we have the real proof that Christianity is something divine" (NB, 263; GG, 79). Affliction compelled Christ to cry out against God. As with Job, affliction thrusts Christ into a dark night of desperation and anguish. Affliction causes God to be absent.

In this light, the affliction of Christ is more than the redemption of the sin of humanity; it is a tragic event. The affliction Jesus endures brings a sense of loss and abandonment to his spirit and body. The torment of Christ is distorted when the glory and power of God in Christ is viewed as immunizing Christ from affliction. In the event approaching his death (Garden of Gethsemane) and at the cross, Christ is stripped of glory and power. Indeed, the Gospels portray a human-divine figure who is subject to the limitations, fragility, and dependency of human nature. Unlike the figure of Socrates, Christ reveals a tragic vulnerability.[38]

In addition to this fragility, Simone Weil reads a tragic element in the actual destiny of Christ. Christ is not a master of his own will. He empties himself of his will in order to make room for the will of God (decreation for Weil). "The mystery of the Cross of Christ lies in a contradiction, for it is at the same time an offering freely consented to and a punishment undergone entirely against his will. . . . Those who only conceive the crucifixion under the aspect of an offering take away from it its salutary mystery and its salutary bitterness. To desire martyrdom is to desire far too little. The Cross is something infinitely greater than martyrdom" (NB, 415). The bitterness of Christ's destiny should not be mitigated by an appeal to the divine freedom of God incarnate. Christ endures his destiny in the form of dependent and vulnerable human nature. The practical implication of this view is that affliction is not something one seeks, contends Weil. When it comes to one, it is often beyond the control of the autonomous agent.

In Weil's reading of the passion narratives, the fusion of a prophetic sense with a tragic vision of the brutality of affliction is accomplished. To a large degree, the latter sensibility dominates in Weil, even if the former is clearly not absent. By incorporating the prophetic vision in her thought Weil avoids the mistake of absolving human beings of responsibility and guilt for much human suffering. While her tragic sensibility does indeed highlight the impersonal rule of force and necessity in human history and nature, she also does not hesitate to speak of awareness of human sin reminiscent of the prophets. An important characteristic of sin, for example, is the consent and obedience to force and, related to this, the refusal to recognize the fragile and limited character of human life (GG, 43). Obedience to force as lust for power distorts a true self-understanding of our human nature. Feelings of invulnerability and omnipotence pervert our humanity and prohibit compassion for the weak and oppressed. Acceptance of human fragility and ethical attention to our neighbor lay the foundation for decreation and compassion in Simone Weil. The pride that clings to our own ego is the sinful obstacle to decreation and compassion.

The passion narratives disclose a God, thus, who illuminates both hiddenness 1 and 2. This God is disclosed in a hiddenness that reveals God's presence in suffering and conflict, and a hiddenness that confronts God's absence vis-à-vis the brutal and destructive impact of force in history and nature. In the lamentations and trembles of Jesus, the mystery of evil is confronted with a loving passion that defies and silences theoretical solutions. It is this powerless God who is the only model for Christians to imitate. "Obviously, we can only see with our eyes and can only imitate God-in-his-powerlessness, and not God-in-his-power" (NB, 542).[39]

The imitation of God-in-his-powerlessness is love and justice. In the loving, decreative act of Christ on the cross the separation between God and God is reconciled. "God is so essentially love that the unity, which in a sense is his actual definition, is a pure effect of love. And corresponding to the infinite virtue of unification belonging to this love there is the infinite separation over which it triumphs, which is the whole creation spread throughout the totality of space and time, consisting of mechanically brutal matter and interposed between Christ and his Father" (SNLG, 177). God is separated from God where chaotic force gives rise to affliction. Wherever and whenever in history and nature this occurs, God is estranged from God's self. We participate in the separation of God from

God in every act of suffering. Yet, in Christ's loving perseverance at the cross, we are given a hint of God's reconciling love, which triumphs over estrangement and alienation.

If tragedy is a key element in the thought of Simone Weil—and I am arguing that it is—it is because Weil was convinced that an understanding of tragedy would deepen our awareness of the realities of violence, war, and affliction in human affairs. Weil, however, never believed that such an awareness was enough: she never implies that resistance to violence and force is futile. Besides fostering this awareness, Weil suggests that an accurate understanding of tragedy is the basis for compassion. In understanding that all humans—friends or enemies—are vulnerable to unjust suffering, she hoped that the human response to the afflicted would defeat the temptation to judge or accuse the afflicted. Study of tragedy makes possible a compassion that recognizes oneself in the plight of another.

The prophetic-tragic vision of Weil ends hopeful. As she insists, a Christian reflection on affliction is not a "morbid preoccupation with suffering and grief" (*SNLG*, 192). As with tragedy, the cross of Christ is the path to an insight and awareness of the presence of evil in history and nature. When this awareness is joined with a loving attention to the affliction of others, participation in the cross becomes the location of God's reconciliation with humanity and with God's very self. In order for this to be possible, the mystery of evil must be posed as insoluble and rational explanations eschewed. The example of God disclosed in Christ is the inspiration for a response to evil that loves and is just without a why.

> In this condition, the praxis of justice and love are performed without a "why." The benefactor of Christ, when he meets an afflicted man, does not feel any distance between himself and the other. He projects all his own being into him. It follows that the impulse to give him food is as instinctive and immediate as it is for oneself to eat when one is hungry. Such a man would not think of saying that he takes care of the afflicted for the Lord's sake; it would seem as absurd to him as it would be to say that he eats for the Lord's sake. One eats because one can't help it. . . . The supernatural process of charity . . . does not need to be completely conscious. Those whom Christ thanks reply: "Lord when . . . ?" They did not know whom they were feeding. (*SNLG*, 190-92)

The union of justice and love in this conception of the Christian life is a key dimension of the mystical-prophetic thought of Simone Weil.

V ⚮

Liberation Theology and the Hiddenness of God in the Thought of Gutiérrez

The thought of Gustavo Gutiérrez is exemplary in its exposure of human responsibility and guilt for much suffering and evil in history. His prophetic vision disturbs and rouses the conscience of the modern person. As with the great Israelite prophets, his message is one of rebuke and denunciation in the face of injustice, exploitation, and oppression. Whether the part we play in the presence of such suffering is one of direct cause or of complicity and neutrality, there is no doubt, Gutiérrez argues, that we are all responsible agents. The contribution of liberation theology is, in part, the single-minded attention to the ethical demands and responsibilities of the Christian life, especially in relation to the weakest and most forgotten people of history and society. This prophetic vision in liberation theology has given birth to more than an ethical imperative concerning love of neighbor, however. It has led to an embrace of social scientific methods that seek to illuminate and pinpoint the causes and roots of suffering. In this manner, liberation theology is concerned with ascertaining and analyzing those agents (classes, groups, races, individuals, etc.) responsible for injustice and oppression. The target of this kind of analysis is sin, both at personal and structural levels.

Without disregarding this element of liberation theology, it is the central contention of this chapter that there is a significant shift in the later work of Gustavo Gutiérrez (from A *Theology of Liberation* to *On Job* and *Las Casas*). Without losing his prophetic passion and vision, Gutiérrez turns to consider the more troubling and unsettling question of evil in a manner not unlike the reflections of Weil on tragedy and the hiddenness of God that we have seen in the previous chapter. Here the issue turns from an exclusive concentration on sin as the cause of suffering toward a reflection on the impersonal and mysterious reality of evil. Reflection on theodicy comes to the forefront of his theology. There emerges in his thought a reading of suffering and affliction that has affinities with tragedy in addition to prophecy. Struggle with the question of God and evil now occupies center stage in his reading of Scripture. He dares to suggest that theology must be willing to confront the question of God in a way that honestly and bravely faces the horrors of history and nature. "Human suffering, involvement with it, and the questions it raises about God are in fact one point of departure and one central theme in the theology of liberation. But the first concern in this context is not with the 'evil of guilt' but rather with the 'evil of misfortune', the evil suffered by the innocent" (*OJ*, xv).

A central theme of liberation theology, he contends, is innocent suffering and the implications of such a fact for our understanding of God. Gutiérrez cogently presents us with a theological vision that heeds the cries, laments, and protests of the poor and afflicted. The question of God's absence or silence in the face of evil is an unavoidable issue in this theological understanding.

How can we speak of God amid the unjust suffering and oppression in the world? Gutiérrez claims that this is the principal question of his theology (*OJ*, xiv). For Gutiérrez, modern philosophies and theologies are too often preoccupied with providing apologetic arguments to nonbelievers to face the question of affliction (*TSMYF*, 7, 23–24; *OJ*, 16). If the question of affliction emerges at all in modern thought, it is often in the form of personal anguish and anxiety rather than affliction at communal and global levels. The willingness to disturb the complacency of modern thought on the question of God is at the heart of Gutiérrez's project.[1] He insists that the struggle with God may even be terrifying. "Some will feel genuine terror. And all of us will a disquiet, as we are deprived of our age-old securities" (*PPH*, 22).

This interruption of our confident securities leads us into unknown ground, toward new horizons for speaking of God. When theology is able to take such a risk it will begin to heed the voices of those persons and groups whom it has frequently ignored and overlooked. With Job, it will begin to learn of a wisdom born of suffering and complaint. "That is why I cannot keep quiet: in my anguish of spirit I shall speak, in my bitterness of soul I shall complain" (Job 7:11). "Nor can the poor and oppressed of Latin America remain silent," remarks Gutiérrez. "What the poor and oppressed have to say may sound harsh and unpleasant to some. It is possible that they may be scandalized at hearing a frank avowal of the human and religious experience of the poor . . ." (*OJ*, 102). The words and laments of the afflicted do, indeed, sound scandalous. What Gutiérrez makes clear is that these voices and cries cannot be avoided in any form of theological thought that professes to be an heir of the Jewish and Christian traditions. "Withdrawal and evasion in the face of these questions," he writes, "can end in an acceptance of evil and injustice, and even resignation to it, which are in the final analysis contrary to faith in the God who liberates" (*GL*, 155).

While Gutiérrez's context of the third world is an important source for his reflections on divine hiddenness, the history of Israel (as a history of suffering, exile, and oppression) plays a key role as well. The classic texts of biblical Israel articulate not only joy, song, and trust in God, but also complaint, terror, and confusion. Where is God when the wicked are permitted to trample the poor into the dust of the earth? Why does God hide his face in the times of trouble and distress? Johann Baptist Metz explains well the tragic beauty of this aspect of biblical Israel: "This language of prayer is itself a language of suffering, a language of crisis, a language of doubt and of radical danger, a language of complaint and accusation, a language of crying out and, quite literally, of the grumbling of the children of Israel."[2]

As Metz and Gutiérrez make clear, the problem of theodicy only emerges within this context of Israel's suffering *and* trust and faith in the goodness of God. With Marcion, for example, the issue of theodicy disappears altogether when the God of the Old Testament is repudiated as an evil Demiurge. When this position is condemned as heretical by orthodox Christianity, we are left with another possibility that attempts to account for evil: human freedom. For Augustine (who was a Manichaean for a period of time), the conversion to Christianity made the theodicy solution of two Gods, an evil and a good one, impossible. If we are not to find fault with God, then the fault must lie entirely with human nature. Human nature freely turned away from God, and evil is the consequence of this original sin. Salvation, in this Augustinian picture, is redemption from sin and guilt.[3] Invisible from this perspective is the history of affliction endured by the innocent, a suffering that cannot be reduced to guilt and sin.

I would like to study these aspects of Gutiérrez—as I did with Simone Weil—by relating them to both prophecy and tragedy. The hiddenness of God 1 will be employed to consider the prophetic manifestation of God in locations of poverty and cross. The hiddenness of God 2 will allow us to examine the elements of Gutiérrez that, in my view, have affinities with

tragedy. Central to this aspect of Gutiérrez is a confrontation with innocent suffering and a struggle with God in the face of evil.

THE HIDDENNESS OF GOD IN GUTIÉRREZ

While Gutiérrez does not develop his reflections on the problem of God
and suffering in terms of the hiddenness of God 1 and 2, the issues involved are implicit in his thought. Through his reading of the Old Testament, Gutiérrez often mentions the significance of God's hiddenness. In
the prophets, for example, God withdraws his presence and hides himself
when and where injustice and wickedness thrive. Yahweh leaves the temple
when it becomes a den of thieves. "This prompts me to reflect on a dialectic often found in the Bible: the tension between God's visibility and
invisibility, between God's obviousness and hiddenness" (GL, 69).

The hiddenness in this case expresses the absence of God when the
will of God is rejected. "But all these absences have a single theological
meaning: God is not there because the reign of God is not accepted;
because God's will is not carried out" (GL, 75). Sin is the target of this
prophetic reading of the hiddenness of God. In another manner, Gutiérrez
interprets the hidden God as the Lord who dwells in the underside of
history and society. This God will not be found in the glory and wealth of
the world; instead "God's presence is often hidden; God is present in
what is insignificant and anonymous. On many occasions God brings a
work of justice or salvation to completion in a hidden manner. God's
dwelling in history is not simple and obvious, so that it may be found
quickly, directly, and unmistakably" (GL, 80). I am referring to these aspects of the theology of Gutiérrez as the hiddenness of God 1.

Hiddenness of God 2 in Gutiérrez is the more disturbing struggle
with God's absence in the face of evil. Here, with Job, Jeremiah, or the
suffering servant of Isaiah, God seems to be absent from the afflicted and
oppressed. Order, beauty, and meaning seem to be absent and hidden.
"Job's suffering causes him to see the universe as chaotic, as lacking the
presence of God; from it God is absent as the one who creates it and
shapes it into a cosmos" (OJ, 8). Most relevant to these two senses of
Divine hiddenness is Gutiérrez's interpretation of the struggle of Job. Recall
that in Job's case, his suffering leads him to conclude that God is his
enemy. Job reproaches God. He dares to say that God laughs at the plight
of the innocent and destroys the innocent and guilty alike (Job 9:15-24).
Job sees himself as more than a victim of God's absence; instead he is,

more terrifyingly, a victim of God's direct violence. On the verge of resignation and despair, however, Job makes an odd appeal. He calls out for a divine mediator, a defender or avenger of his innocence. "I know that I have a living Avenger (*Go'el*) and that at the end he will rise up above the dust. After they pull my flesh from me, and I am without my flesh, I shall see God" (Job 19:25–26). Job appeals to God against God. The remarks of Gutiérrez are very significant.

> It might almost be said that Job, as it were, splits God in two and produces a God who is judge and a God who will defend him at that supreme moment; a God whom he experiences as almost an enemy but whom he knows at the same time to be truly a friend. He has just now accused God of persecuting him, but at the same he knows God is just and does not want human beings to suffer. These are two sides of the one God. This painful, dialectical approach to God is one of the most profound messages of the Book of Job. (*OJ*, 65)

I believe it is helpful to associate these two sides of the one God as hiddenness 1 and 2. However idiosyncratic this approach may seem, Gutiérrez insists that it is necessary. "The seeming lack of logic in this way of looking at God is simply a sign that any approach to the mystery of God must be complex" (*OJ*, 66).

The Hiddenness of God 1

The Hiddenness of God in the Prophets

Gutiérrez locates the decisive contribution of the Israelite prophets in their vision of God's revelation through the events and vicissitudes of history. The covenantal relationship with God is established through the hopes, expectations, and sufferings of history. Unlike the pagan religious traditions, the prophets insist that God is disclosed primarily through a salvific word in history, rather than through the regularity and beauty of nature. "Other religions think in terms of cosmos and nature; Christianity, rooted in Biblical sources, thinks in terms of history. And in this history, injustice and oppression, divisions and confrontations exist" (*TL*, 174). In Gutiérrez's later work, he qualifies this interpretation by maintaining that Judaism and Christianity also think in terms of cosmos and nature.[4] Nevertheless, his major point is still valid: the prophets interpret God's actions vis-à-vis the historical struggles of the nation Israel. In particular, the

event of Exodus becomes a central and foundational narrative for Israelite identity (Deut. 6:20–25). The alienation, exile, and oppression that
Israel endures at the hands of Egypt leaves an indelible mark on the
memory of this people. To remain faithful to God is to remember the
history of the people, that they were once slaves in Egypt.

To be sure, this narrative of oppression and suffering and, consequently, of liberation and freedom is central to the theology of Gutiérrez.
Salvation is an intrahistorical reality (*TL*, 152). Here God is revealed not
in the power and glory of the masters, but instead in the wretchedness
and poverty of the slaves. God hears the cries of the poor and vanquished
and intervenes to deliver them. Redemption occurs through the liberating acts of God in history. Thus, we can suggest that not only is the God
of Israel revealed in history, but he is revealed more specifically in the
underside of history. Gutiérrez says the sixteenth-century Dominican
Bartolome de Las Casas was able to discover as much when he went seeking God not in the mines of gold but rather in the faces of the exploited
Indians. For Las Casas, this was nothing less than a remembering of the
Exodus. The oppression and the brutality of the Spaniards was akin to
the Egyptian oppression of Israel, he argued, but worse: not even "Pha-
raoh and the Egyptians themselves committed such cruelties" (*LC*, 39).
The memory of suffering inspired the task of Las Casas and provided a
horizon for interpreting the suffering in his own time.

The reading of the prophetic tradition by Gutiérrez is also profoundly
animated by hope. After all, the story of Exodus is a story of liberation
and journey to the promised land. Gutiérrez shares the same hope in
history as the prophets. "In the face of skepticism and of the possible
discouragement of those who see themselves being crushed by the forces
of injustice, the Lord says that his will to life for all can indeed take flesh
in history" (*GL*, 93). Gutiérrez suggests that the eschatological dimension
of the prophets is a word that brings life and hope to history. In spite of
the catastrophes of history, Jeremiah and Ezekiel, for instance, hold that
God will renew Israel and bring a new everlasting covenant to Israel (Jer.
31:31–34; Ezek. 36:22–32). "A new heart I will give you, and a new spirit
I will put within you; and I will remove from your body the heart of stone
and give you a heart of flesh" (Ezek. 36:26). Gutiérrez claims that this
hopeful posture toward the future is a key characteristic of the Israelite
prophets (*TL*, 163). The promise of what is to come lends meaning and
purpose to the present.

Gutiérrez maintains, moreover, that the prophets embody an ethical
vision that leads them to criticize an exclusive focus on cultic worship. It

is not fasting and sacrifices that the Lord wants: to loose the fetters of injustice, to feed the hungry, and to clothe the naked, this is what the Lord desires (*TL*, 196; Isa. 1:10-17, 58:6-7; Hos. 6:4-6). When Jeremiah reproaches the Israelites for turning the temple of the Lord into a den of thieves, he makes it clear that God will consequently depart from that holy space. "Put not your trust in the deceitful words: 'This is the temple of the Lord! The temple of the Lord! The temple of the Lord!' Only if you thoroughly reform your ways and your deeds; if each of you deals justly with his neighbor; if you no longer oppress the resident alien, the orphan, and the widow. . . . will I remain with you in this place. . . ." (*GL*, 70; Jer. 1:1-7). God will hide his face when the poor and weak are exploited and abused.

The figure of Las Casas prophetically incorporates this ethical sensitivity. Indeed, Gutiérrez demonstrates how a passage from Sirach was crucial in awakening Las Casas from his slumber (*LC*, 47). "The Most High is not pleased with the offerings of the ungodly, nor for a multitude of sacrifices does he forgive sins. Like one who kills a son before his father's eyes is the person who offers a sacrifice from the property of the poor. The bread of the needy is the life of the poor; whoever deprives them of it is a murderer" (Sir. 23-25). Las Casas consequently associates the poor of Scripture with the Indians of the New World, by no means an obvious move (*LC*, 313). The Indians are those poor whose "belly cleaves to their backbone from pure hunger" (*LC*, 313-14). The Spaniards not only deprive them of their daily bread, but more viciously they devour them as wild animals devour their prey (*LC*, 447). In the face of these injustices, blindness and slumber can only be partners in crime. As Las Casas puts it, "God sleeps not when these injustices occur"; so too must we be roused from our slumber.

The reality of sin is, in this light, a glaring and blatant force. Gutiérrez claims that awareness of sin is central to liberation theology (*TSMYF*, 31, 138). This sin manifests itself in a self-serving lifestyle that leads to want, injustice, and oppression (*TSMYF*, 15). In *A Theology of Liberation* he insists that there are particular responsible agents for sin; it does not happen by chance (*TL*, 175). These actions contrary to God's will result in God's withdrawal. The presence or absence of God, he argues, is an effect of human freedom and actions (*ELC*, 82). As Jeremiah puts it, the sins of the people have provoked God's wrath and hiddenness. "The Chaldeans are coming in to fight and to fill them [Israelite houses] with the dead bodies of those whom I shall strike down in my anger and my wrath, for I have hidden my face from this city because of all their wickedness" (Jer. 33:5).[5]

The focus on history and the experiences of injustice, oppression, and violence leads us to highlight another important aspect of the theology of Gutiérrez, namely, the reality of conflict in history and society.[6] While not seeking or advocating conflict, the classic prophets announced a word of judgment and rebuke that often conflicted with the ruling groups of society. Far from being the intended outcome of their vocation, conflict was often the effect of the prophet's faithful witness to the covenant with God. The reluctance and resistance of the prophet in the face of God's overwhelming call should recall to us the harsh and unhappy vocation of the prophet. Certainly the laments of the prophets (Jeremiah, Jonah, the suffering servant of Isaiah) express the anguish of being ostracized and ridiculed by others; the pain of conflict and suffering is transparent in their lives.

For Gutiérrez, the conflict that we cannot avoid is simply the result of a prophetic faithfulness, of solidarity with the poor and oppressed. "The proclamation of this liberating love in the midst of a society characterized by injustice and the exploitation of one social class by another social class is what will make this emergent history something challenging and filled with conflict. This is how we bring to pass the truth of God at the very heart of a society in which social classes confront one another with hostility. For we shall be taking sides with the poor, with the populous classes, with the ethnic groups others scorn, with cultures that are marginalized" (PPH, 18). Taking sides with the dispossessed frequently will demand confrontation and clash. The hunger for justice and righteousness involves a willingness to resist, challenge, struggle. For Gutiérrez, this inevitable presence of conflict attests to the reality of power and politics in human life. Politics embraces the entire dimension of human endeavors. "Politics is the global condition, and the collective field, of human accomplishment" (PPH, 47). An apolitical way of life is implausible, he contends. To be human at all means to be historically and socially incarnate, to be implicated in the field of power interests and political conflict. Neutrality in the face of injustice and exploitation is nothing more than a false peace.

The appeal to conciliation and peace can be, in this case, a subterfuge for the preservation of unjust conditions. "Such a conciliation can be only a justifying ideology for a profound disorder, a device for the few to keep living off the poverty of the many" (TL, 48). Against a false optimism Gutiérrez reminds us of the dark, destructive and violent facets of history. There is tragic conflict between entire races, cultures, classes, nations, parts of the world, and so forth (TL, 36). In this vein, the prophet Jeremiah excoriated the dishonesty and self-deluding claims of those whose indifference and apathy prevented them from recognizing the injustice and suffering. "They have treated the wound of my people carelessly, saying, 'Peace, peace,' when there is no peace" (Jer. 6:14). Far from celebrating or advocating conflict, Gutiérrez laments the fact of conflict in human life. To ignore it, nevertheless, is to deceive oneself and to undermine efforts to transform violence into true peace (*TL*, 274). We must be willing to face the realities of oppression, exploitation, suffering, cross.

As Christians, he continues, we must equally avoid the debasement of justice into revenge and hatred. For Gutiérrez, recognition of conflict "cannot be allowed to justify a denial of, or exception to, the universality of Christian love" (*TSMYF*, 39). Love animates justice with a spirit of gratuity and tenderness without subverting the harsh demands of justice in the midst of inequality and violence.

In the new introduction to the second edition of *A Theology of Liberation*, he explains that such love and such struggle were central to the prayer of Jesus in the Garden of Gethsemane. The prayers of Jesus involved agony and combat. "Luke tells us that he was 'in an agony' as he struggled for his life, so that his sweat 'became like great drops of blood' (Luke 22:44–45). Our communion with the prayer of Jesus must reach this point of 'agony'— that is, of combat (that is what the Greek word *agonia* means). But this requirement is not difficult for those to understand who are putting their own lives on the line as they share the lot of the stripped and impoverished of Latin America" (*TL*, xxxi–xxxii). The agony of the defeated of history inspires the theological task of Gutiérrez. As the above quote suggests, God is revealed in the anguish and suffering of Jesus Christ.

The Hidden God in Jesus Christ: Theology of the Cross

Without a doubt, a theology of the cross is central to Gutiérrez. Indeed, Gutiérrez maintains that both Exodus and cross are central to his work (*PPH*, 16; *TSMYF*, 20). The Eucharist embraces both elements insofar as it is a remembrance of the death of Christ and at the same time a celebration originally instituted as the Passover meal. For Gutiérrez, then, we must carefully look to the experiences of cross and oppression in history to discern God's truth, justice, and love. The person of Jesus Christ is unrecognizable to those who look elsewhere for divine reality. Jesus is a hidden God. "God's presence in history makes itself known only in an unobtrusive way that necessitates spiritual discernment. The Bible often refers to God as a hidden God. . . . Christ makes himself present precisely through those who are 'absent' from history, those who are not invited to the banquet (see Luke 14:15–24), those who are not the great ones of the world, the respected, 'the wise and understanding' (Matthew 11:25)" (*TSMYF*, 157; also *GL*, 80).

The absent ones of history are those persons and groups ostracized and shunned by the community; they are those nonpersons virtually regarded as dead. Jesus himself, Gutiérrez remarks, was one of those absent ones. He was born on the margins of an insignificant nation. There was nothing in his form or appearance that would intimate greatness, as with the suffering servant of Isaiah.[7] "That is why many have trouble recognizing him. The God who became flesh in Jesus is the hidden God of whom the prophets speak to us. Jesus shows himself to be such precisely in the measure that he is present via those who are the absent, anonymous people of history–those who are not the controllers of history . . ." (*GL*, 86). If Jesus is a king, he is not a king in the eyes of the world. His kingship is of service, powerlessness, and compassion (*GL*, 87).

In the figure of Jesus, the hidden God identifies with the poor and afflicted, with the stranger and alien (Matt. 25). In the extraordinary vision of Las Casas, the suffering features of Christ are discovered in the scarred faces of an entire oppressed people. God is revealed in those persons whom the "civilized" peoples call savage and primitive.

> "Supposing, Sir," Las Casas interrogatingly asks, "that you were to see Our Lord Jesus Christ abused–someone laying hands on him, afflicting him, and insulting him with all manner of vituperation– would you not beg with the greatest urgency and with all your strength that he be handed over to you instead, that you might worship and serve and please him and do everything with him that, as a true Christian, you ought to do? "I surely would," replied the other. . . . "Indeed, Sir," Las Casas responds, "I have but acted in that very manner. *For I leave, in the Indies, Jesus Christ, our God, scourged and afflicted and buffeted and crucified, not once but millions of times. . . .*" (*LC*, 62; my emphasis)

The crime of the Spaniards is, Las Casas concludes, nothing short of blasphemy. They are, however, completely oblivious to this desecration of God's presence. They are blind to the hidden God; they only see and adore the visible god of gold and might. In fact, the Spaniards contend that Las Casas is misreading the Gospels and lying about God's compassion for the wretched of the earth. "When we preach to the Indians the humility and poverty of Jesus Christ, and how he suffered for us, and how God rejoices in the poor and in those the world despises, they think we are lying to them" (*LC*, 18). They are, no doubt, scandalized by the disturbing message of the cross.

Not surprisingly, Gutiérrez's thought is informed by St. Paul's reading of the scandalous Word of the cross. Paul's theology of the cross provocatively suggests that God has, first and foremost, called those of ignoble birth, the weak and ignorant in the world (*GL*, 105). "Not many of you were wise by human standards," Paul remarks, "not many were powerful, not many were of noble birth. Rather, God chose the foolish of the world to shame the wise, and God chose the weak of the world to shame the strong, and God chose the lowly and despised of the world, those who count for nothing, to reduce to nothing those who are something" (1 Cor. 1:26–28). The wisdom that God showers on these persons and groups is a wisdom born of suffering. Such wisdom is often a stumbling block and folly to comfortable intellectuals, Gutiérrez contends (*PPH*, 103). The folly of the cross eschews strictly rational attempts to explain life. It charges such projects with a failure to face death, conflict, and suffering. Participation in the cross, on the contrary, may yield an insight imperceptible to those in other existential situations (*TL*, 49). Job's friends do not accurately speak of God, Gutiérrez claims, because "they have not experienced the abandonment, poverty, and pain that Job has" (*OJ*, 29). It is the conditions of the poor, the blind, and the lame that lead them to speak of God correctly, that is, to recognize God's presence in the ignominious and base life of Jesus Christ. This wisdom is revealed to babes and hidden from the wise (Matt. 11:25–26).

Surely the cry of Jesus on the cross, "My God, my God, why have you abandoned me?" is folly for those who expect God to be displayed by manifestations of power, domination, and glory. The anguish of divine abandonment expressed by Psalm 22, which Jesus quotes, is all too common in the lives of millions throughout the globe. In Latin America, this experience of affliction is often represented by the images and symbols of Christ and the saints. In his essay on José María Arguedas, Gutiérrez mentions one of the Peruvian figures of Christ in Latin America known as the "Lord of the Terrified." Gutiérrez quotes the following description of "El Señor de los Temblores" from the pages of Arguedas. "The face of the crucified Christ was dark and gaunt, like that of the *pongo*. . . . Blackened, suffering, the Christ maintained a silence that did not set one at ease. He made one suffer; in such a vast cathedral, in the midst of the candle flames and the daylight that filtered down dimly, the face of the

Christ caused suffering, extending it to the walls, to the arches and columns, from which I expected to see tears flow" (*ELC*, 76; my translation). The dark face of Christ: silent, dislocated, fragile, suffering emanating from his form. Indeed, such an image is born of the plight of the Latin American people.

For Gutiérrez, though, such an interpretation of the suffering God is also central to the God revealed in the Scriptures. Echoes of this sense of tragic suffering are by no means limited to the Christian passion narratives. The suffering servant of Isaiah, for instance, is an innocent one who is despised and rejected by all, a person of suffering from whom society averts its eyes in revulsion (Isa. 53:3). Perhaps even more interesting is the interpretive possibility that the suffering servant represents the entire nation of Israel during the time of Babylonian exile and oppression. The suffering servant, then, is not merely an individual, but rather an anguished expression of lament by Israel (as is the case of the book of Lamentations as well). The history of this nation's suffering continues down through the centuries.

This kind of a tragic vision cannot solely be understood within the prophetic tradition, that is, within the paradigm of redemption and sin. The suffering servant of Isaiah, many of the psalms, Jesus's cry of abandonment, Job, the history of suffering persons and groups, all such expressions of pain are mistreated when reduced to a consequence of the fall of Adam.

The Hiddenness of God 2:
    Theodicy

While the hiddenness of God 1 reads God's *presence* as disclosed in locations of cross, the sense of hiddenness of God 2 raises the more troubling issue of God's *absence*—or violence—in the face of evil in history and nature. The question of theodicy is confronted in a way that eschews the explanation of evil in relation to human sin and guilt. The problem of evil is explicitly faced in the book of Job. Not only in this text is the cry of suffering audible, however. The texts of Psalms, Lamentations, and the prophets express the agony of unjust affliction. They often do so in reference to the hiddenness of God. Consider Psalm 44, where the author laments a humiliating and crushing defeat at the hands of an enemy: "All of this has come upon us, yet we have not forgotten you, or been false to your covenant. Our heart has not turned back, nor have our steps departed from your way, yet you have broken us in the haunt of jackals, and covered us with a deep darkness.... Rouse yourself! Why do you sleep, O Lord? Awake, do not cast us off forever! Why do you hide your face?" (Ps. 44:17–19, 23–24). It seems here that it is God not the people who has forgotten the covenant! This divine forgetfulness and hiddenness is restated many times, as in Psalm 13: "How long, O Lord? Will you forget me forever? How long will you hide your face from me?" (Ps. 13:1; also Pss. 22, 69, 88, 89, 102). The psalms utter words of complaint in the face of experiences in which God has forgotten his mercy and forgotten the life of the poor (Pss. 74, 77). Clearly, the book of Lamentations also expresses this grief in the midst of God's hiddenness. The people who yearn to see God's face are afflicted by the absence of God's face.[8]

Indeed, Gutiérrez provocatively suggests that divine hiddenness or silence is particularly disturbing to those who seek God's face and believe that God is loving and merciful. They are the ones who have the problem of theodicy. Does the silence of God in the face of unjust affliction lead us to conclude that God is, not unlike the pagan gods, mute and deaf? "The silence of God is hardest to bear," Gutiérrez explains, "for those who believe that the God of our faith is a living God and not like the 'gods' of whom the psalmist says: 'They have mouths, but do not speak' (Ps 115:5)" (*OJ*, xv). Is the God of Abraham, Isaac, and Jacob, then, just like the pagan gods who stand silent in the face of injustice and suffering? The book of Joel pleads with God to remember his kindness in order to disprove the enemies of Israel who mock Yahweh. "Why should it be said among the peoples, 'Where is their God'?" (Joel 2:17). Is God's hiddenness a piercing silence that hears not the cries of Israel, that disregards the laments of the poor and oppressed? These tough questions are not as blasphemous as one might think. The struggle with and against God is at the heart of the Scriptures and, as we have seen with Simone Weil, the road to a more sincere and authentic faith.

Abraham, Jacob, and Moses all illustrate not only faith and hope in God but also a willingness to contest God. Their lives represent a dispute or contest with God (*agonia*). In Genesis, for instance, Abraham takes issue with God's intention to destroy Sodom and Gomorrah (as God had already done with the entire world by means of the great flood). Abraham asks God critically, "Will you indeed sweep away the righteous with the wicked? . . . Far be it from you to do such a thing, to slay the righteous with the wicked, so that the righteous fare as the wicked!" (Gen. 18:23, 25). Abraham pleads with God not to forget his mercy.[9]

The archetypal prophet himself, Moses, also challenges the decisions of God. In the incident of the golden calf in Exodus, God is tempted to destroy all of Israel. Moses implores God not to allow his wrath to annul his promises and mercy. "Now let me alone," God angrily utters, "so that my wrath may burn hot against them and I may consume them. . . . But Moses implored the Lord his God, and said, O Lord, why does your wrath burn hot against your people, whom you brought out of the land of Egypt with great power and with a mighty hand? . . . Turn from your fierce wrath; change your mind and do not bring disaster on the people. Remember Abraham, Isaac, and Israel, your servants, how you swore to them . . ." (Exod. 32:10-14). By appealing to the covenant and God's promises, Moses successfully gets God to repent of his harsh intentions. Finally, the story of Jacob wrestling with God will have a decisive significance for the naming of the nation as Israel (Gen. 32:22-32). The name Israel will come to mean he who wrestles with God (see Hos. 12:3-4).[10]

In a sense these stories are related to the sins of the nation Israel. Yet, the complaints of Abraham and Moses are more precisely directed against the anger of God that would destroy the righteous and wicked together and, consequently, cause God to forget his promises of old. God's merciful face is hidden.

Especially in Gutiérrez's reading of the book of Job, these issues irrepressibly surface. Gutiérrez insists that reflection on the nature of suffering and evil in history cannot be contained within the paradigm of sin and guilt. While appearing to be piously defending God, the friends of Job speak incorrectly of God; they defend God by "dishonest argument" (OJ, 29; Job 13:7). In Gutiérrez's view, the position of Job's friends is all too common among experts in theology; such theologians do not take account of concrete situations and the suffering of human beings. Job's friends contend that Job is condemning God, and "Job, put on the defensive, answers that God is not to be justified by condemning the innocent" (OJ, 30). Indeed, the book of Job maintains that it is Job who has spoken correctly of God, not his friends (OJ, 11; Job 42:7-8).

Job's laments and protests are not, then, sinful: they are tortuous expressions in the face of terrible affliction. Job is led to curse the day of his birth: "Perish the day on which I was born and the night that told of a boy conceived. Why was I not still-born, or why did I not perish as I left the womb?" (Job 3:1-3, 11). Jeremiah cries out in a similar manner: "Why did I come forth from the womb to see toil and sorrow, and spend my days in shame?" (Jer. 14:18). In the case of Job, the problem is not exactly related to God's absence, but rather to the apparent violence of God in his life.

Like Abraham, Job deplores the fact that God seems to destroy the innocent and guilty alike: "It is all one, and hence I boldly say: he destroys innocent and guilty alike. . . . If not he, who else?" (Job 9:22, 24; *OJ*, 57). Job seeks to bring a lawsuit against these actions of God. In order to proceed with the lawsuit he asks God to "remove your hand, which lies so heavily on me, no longer make me cower from your terror" (Job 13:21; *OJ*, 61). Gutiérrez notes all the metaphors of divine violence in the book of Job. The terror that God's hand brings is God's inscrutable wrath. "He has torn me in his wrath, and hated me; he has gnashed his teeth at me; my adversary sharpens his eyes against me. . . . I was at ease, and he broke me in two; he seized me by the neck and dashed me to pieces; he set me up as his target; his archers surround me. He slashes open my kidneys, and shows no mercy; he pours out my gall on the ground. He bursts upon me again and again; he rushes at me like a warrior" (Job 16:12–14; *OJ*, 63). Elsewhere Job complains, "Even when I cry out, 'Violence!' I am not answered; I call aloud, but there is no justice. . . . His troops come on together; they have thrown up siegeworks against me, and encamp around my tent. . . . My bones cling to my skin and to my flesh, and I have escaped by the skin of my teeth" (Job 19:7, 12, 20). God is portrayed in less than flattering terms: he is like a ruthless warrior or a military commander sending his troops out to kill. As shocking as such images are, they are not unique to the book of Job.

The psalms cry out in a similar way: "O Lord, do not rebuke me in your anger, or discipline me in your wrath. For your arrows have sunk into me, and your hand has come down on me" (Ps. 38:1–2). It is God who feeds Israel the bread of tears, another psalm has it (80:5–6). Lamentations, moreover, compares God to a vicious animal. "He is a bear lying in wait for me, a lion in hiding; he led me off my way and tore me to pieces; he had made me desolate; he bent his bow and set me as a mark for his arrow" (Lam. 10–12). The book of Lamentations maintains that both good and evil come from God (Lam. 3:38). Of course, in the prophets lamentations and protests unto God are definitely present, even if they are most often related to the sin and guilt of the nation Israel (see Jer. 14:19). Confronted both with his own experiences and his reading of the Scriptures, Luther concludes that in the Scriptures God rebukes and threatens by using arrows.[11]

The sense of divine wrath or violence in Scripture is interpreted by Gutiérrez as most disturbing in relation to experiences of communal and historical suffering. In Gutiérrez's opinion, a crucial insight of the classic text of Job is the broadening of Job's horizons to include all who suffer innocently. Job moves from a position of lament concerning his own fate to a tragic awareness of the suffering of other innocent persons and groups. Gutiérrez quotes the following passage from Job: "The wicked move boundary-marks away, they carry off flock and shepherd. They drive away the orphan's donkey, as security, they seize the widow's ox. The needy have to keep out of the way, poor country people have to keep out of sight. . . . They go about naked, lacking clothes, and starving while they carry the sheaves. . . . From the towns come the groans of the dying and the gasp of the wounded crying for help. Yet God remains deaf to prayer!" (OJ, 33; Job 24:2–4, 7, 12). Job learns that however painful and distressing his own experience is, he is not alone. The wicked thrive and the good suffer—this state of affairs is more than Job's problem.

To be sure, Gutiérrez is painfully aware of the unjust suffering of the innocent in his own continent of Latin America. It is clear that the text of Job, as well as the other wisdom literature of the Old Testament, provides Gutiérrez and the people of Latin America (and throughout the globe) with classic narratives that represent their own voices of sufferings in an honest and compassionate manner. Without discounting personal anguish and torment, the unjust suffering of whole peoples and cultures is the central fact which Gutiérrez tackles. Reflection from the perspective of the oppression and exile of whole peoples is certainly at the core of much of the Old Testament. It is these experiences, Gutiérrez maintains, which cause the people of the third world to cry out to God. "In the Bible the revelation of God is given, and the most radical questions regarding it are asked, in a specific historical context. In this Psalm [Ps. 42:4–5, 11] they arise out of the experience of exile, suffering, and oppression that the Jewish people underwent in Babylon. It is in such circumstances that the just are forced to face up to the challenging question of their enemies: Where is your God?" (GL, 66).

As Gutiérrez shows, Bartolome de Las Casas was extraordinary in his attentiveness to the unjust plight of the Indian peoples. Las Casas tells of the suffering he witnessed: "From the discovery of the Indies up until our own day they [the Indians] have been made into mincemeat through wars most unjust—invasions perpetrated in contravention of all reason and justice and surpassing in cruelty all of the wars of the infidels and barbarians, indeed of the beasts themselves, in cruelty, in ugliness, in injustice, in wickedness, in horror and terror" (LC, 233). Neither the paganism nor the sacrificial practices of the Indians are justifications for this kind of violence and terror, contends Las Casas. It is the colonizers and not the Indians who are the true pagans and cannibals. It is against these vicious types that Micah uttered the following words: "Should you not know justice?—you who hate the good and love the evil, who tear the skin off my people, and the flesh off their bones; who eat the flesh of my people, flay their skin off them, break their bones in pieces, and chop them up like meat in a kettle, like flesh in a cauldron" (3:1-3).

According to Las Casas, the Indians suffer as innocent victims of these cannibalistic practices; they suffer as Christ did. Elsewhere Las Casas writes, "[T]he screams of so much spilled blood have now reached heaven. The earth can no longer bear such steeping in human blood. The angels of peace and even God, I think, must be weeping" (*LC*, 226). Without question, Las Casas denounces the nefarious and sinful actions of the conquistadors. In Gutiérrez the importance of this prophetic denunciation does not, however, preclude the element of crying and protesting unto God, and in this connection Gutiérrez mentions another extraordinary person: Guaman Poma de Ayala, a Peruvian Indian.

Poma de Ayala is harsh in condemning the individuals and groups responsible for acts of evil, but, equally, he does not restrain his tongue from interrogating God: "Where are you then, my God, will you not hear me and help your poor?" (*GL*, 66). He quotes Ps. 13:1-4, "Lord, how long shall I cry and thou not respond to me?," and then admonishes his readers, "Together with the prophets, speak with tearful voices, groaning with your heart and soul and mouth, tongue and eyes. . . . Cease not to weep with the prophets, who will help you . . ." (*LC*, 447-48). Gutiérrez explicitly notes that this tradition of lamentations and protests unto God has been neglected by Christians today. Gutiérrez comments on the above quote by Poma de Ayala: "Here is a prayer of protest. It recurs frequently in the Old Testament, but is neglected by Christians today" (*LC*, 448).

Gutiérrez then continues by speaking of Poma de Ayala's imitation of the hidden God. As with Jesus Christ, Ayala embodied in his life and thought a kenotic selflessness, a willingness to abandon his own social status and enter into the world of the exploited and poor. Ayala spent many years toiling and living with the Indian poor in order to write of their sufferings. As with the hidden God in Jesus Christ, Ayala emptied himself of his status and privilege in order to embrace the suffering of other human beings. In comparing the life of Christ to that of Ayala, Gutiérrez remarks: "He too has had his hidden life, to which he assigns the unlikely, but symbolic, duration of thirty years, the length of time he has wandered all up and down the Tawantinsuyu. He has lived among the poor, having abandoned his lofty social estate, has raised his protest to God for the sufferings of which he has been a witness and which he himself has suffered, and has been devoured by those who were abusing the Indian poor, taking him for one of them" (LC, 448). The lamentations of Poma de Ayala are nothing else, Gutiérrez maintains, than a sharing in the cry of Jesus on the cross, "My God, my God, why have you abandoned me?"

THE THREAT OF CHAOS

The experience of crisis in the above lamentations is one manifestation of Divine hiddenness. Another way in which Gutiérrez interprets the threat of death-dealing forces is in light of the presence of chaos and contingency in history. In many scriptural texts, there appears to be a conflict between the forces of chaos and those of order. Gutiérrez argues that Israel's history of suffering attests to this sense of chaos. The forces of oppression and affliction threaten to return Israel and God's creation to an unformed and precreated state of disorder. Oppression and violence are, thus, anticreation. The abyss or deep in Genesis symbolizes the anarchy prior to God's act of creation (just as the flood at the time of Noah undoes God's creation). In Exodus, God delivers the Israelites from the servitude of Egypt and overcomes the forces of disorder that threaten the existence of the nation. When God splits the Red Sea, God combats the forces of darkness and chaos. The nation of Israel is thereby recreated. This struggle against the forces of death suggests that in the Jewish tradition creation of the world and historical redemption are inextricably linked.

Gutiérrez explains these two elements in the Old Testament by making reference to Second Isaiah's interpretation of the Exodus. Second Isaiah, writing during the Babylonian Exile, calls upon God to intervene once again and deliver his nation from violence and death. "Awake, awake, put on your strength, O arm of the Lord," says Isaiah, "awake as you did long ago, in days gone by. Was it not you who hacked the Rahab in pieces and ran the dragon through? Was it not you who dried up the sea, the waters of the great abyss, and made the ocean depths a path for the ransomed" (Isa. 51:9-10). Gutiérrez comments: the "waters of the great abyss are those which enveloped the world and from which creation arose, but they are also the Red Sea which the Jews crossed to begin the Exodus" (TL, 155). The dragon Rahab represents both the chaotic threat of Egypt as well as the whore of Babylon in the context of Second Isaiah. No doubt, the sea and the dragon represent forces of anticreation and chaos.

In the context of Job's sufferings as well, the cosmos is seen as lacking order and reason. In Job's life, creation is noncreation, devoid of order; it is a continuation of the void and abyss prior to creation (*OJ*, 8, 80; Job 3:4–6). In Gutiérrez's daring reading of Job he suggests that the Scriptures (as well as human experience) disclose two sides of God: on the one side, order, beauty, and love; and on the other, disorder, violence, and anger. While Gutiérrez does not develop this idea, we might suggest that this vision of the divine is not entirely unlike the ambiguity of the Greek and pagan gods, as Simone Weil contends.

Biblical scholars, for example, have argued that Near Eastern mythical stories of conflict and violence within the divine are not entirely absent from the Bible. To be sure, the Bible clearly represents a demythologization of the stories of war and struggle among the gods. The ethical monotheism of Yahwistic religion, on the whole, does away with the polytheism and mythical stories of pagan religions (even if parts of the Old Testament seem to admit the existence of other gods, these gods clearly are not worshipped by the nation Israel and they are less powerful than Yahweh). Even with this admitted, however, there are intimations of a divine struggle with chaos in the Old Testament, of a rule of chaos or threat of evil that is anterior to creation and prior to the free human act of will against God.

In *The Symbolism of Evil* Paul Ricoeur explains that Near Eastern myths are significant for their mythical and symbolic interpretations of the experience of evil in human existence.[12] He interprets these Near Eastern myths under the rubric of the myth of chaos. To summarize his argument, Ricoeur contends that these stories about the genesis of the divine (theogony) express the possibility of a chaos anterior to order, that the principle of evil is primordial and coextensive with the generation of the divine. When creation is established, it is established only through conflict, violence, and battle. The assumption of these myths is that humanity is *not* the origin of evil; humanity finds evil and continues it. Are these myths compatible, however, with the Jewish and Christian claim that evil emerges with human sin, the Adamic myth?

Indeed, the confession of the holiness and goodness of God (not only in the Judeo-Christian tradition, but by Plato) and the confession of the sinfulness of humanity does in fact transform the pagan myths of the Greeks and Babylonians. It is certainly true that the traditions of ethical monotheism in the Old Testament represent an important break with mythical patterns of ancient Near Eastern theology. Yahweh is a transcendent God who is both personal love and, yet, resistant to the idolatrous tendencies to anthropomorphize the divine. Yahweh is not depicted at war with other gods, nor are we given any hint that Yahweh has a genealogy.

The Old Testament does not provide us with a theogony of the Most High. It is true that the abyss of the deep (in Hebrew *tehom*, not unlike the Babylonian Tiamat) is portrayed as a foe of Yahweh. In the Jewish tradition, nevertheless, the battles of Yahweh with the sea are combined with the historical traditions of the Exodus. It is crucial to note that this historical dimension distinguishes the Jewish tradition from Mesopotamian or Canaanite myths. Unlike these myths, there is no mythological combat between gods. Yahweh defeats historical, human enemies! Thus, while the Old Testament stands in continuity with mythical patterns of the ancient Near East, Judaism was transformed by formative historical events.

With this crucial caveat mentioned, it is the fundamental argument of Paul Ricoeur that the importance of the Adamic myth certainly transforms, but does not abolish, the insights and contributions of tragic myths and dramas. In the traditions of Israel, history and myth are combined. The idea that evil is prior to humanity is too deeply ingrained in human experience for this sentiment to be excised from the Jewish and Christian imagination. In the figure of the serpent, for example, we are reminded of a principle of evil that is always, already there, prior to the Fall. The serpent symbolizes a positive presence of evil that humanity is responsible for, no doubt, but not as the origin of this evil. Indeed, in some cases in the Old Testament, it is Yahweh who is depicted as the origin of evil, as when God hardens the hearts of Israel's enemies.[13] For Christians, this experience of an evil that one inherits is fundamental to the idea of original sin. In both of these cases, evil is disclosed as an ineluctable reality that is, in part, outside of our conscious, autonomous control. Evil limits, if it does not abolish, our freedom.

Tragedy articulates in a mythical and dramatic manner the experience of evil as fate, destiny, or divine will; that is, evil as nonhuman in origin. Not surprisingly Ricoeur turns to the book of Job as a case where "the moral vision of the world was wrecked by Jewish thought itself."[14] Since the suffering of Job upsets a clear and rational theory of just retribution, the reappearance of tragic elements should not surprise us.

For Ricoeur, then, while the confession of the holiness of God and, concomitantly, the sinfulness of humanity is central to the Adamic myth of the Fall, the Jewish and Christian traditions preserve elements that have affinities with tragic myth. The recognition of a less rational, more chaotic and senseless element to evil (as in the book of Job) is a serious challenge to the ethical, reward-punishment framework of the Adamic myth. The importance of recognizing some truth to the tragedy lays the foundation for a less judgmental and more compassionate embrace of the afflicted of history. "Hence, it may be asked whether the Hebrew and, more generally, the Near Eastern theme of the 'suffering Just One' does not lead back from the prophetic *accusation* to tragic *pity*."[15]

Thus, while there is a historicizing and demythologizing trend in Israelite traditions, archaic and pagan elements manifest themselves in Israel's history, especially through the nation's historical experiences of suffering and oppression. Even the sense of conflict in the divine realm and the ambiguity of God are not altogether absent from the Old Testament. The problem of theodicy emerges with Israel's monotheism since it can no longer account for conflicting human experiences (chaos and order; good and evil) vis-à-vis mythical narratives of warring gods. If God is the sole master of the universe, from where do violence, chaos, and affliction come? As Job asks, "If not he, Who else?" It seems to me—and I believe that Gutiérrez points to this—that the Old Testament still intimates that there is conflict in the cosmos, even if the conflict in history is most pronounced. Complaint, lamentation, and protest express the agony of God's apparent violence against the nation Israel. While the wrath of God, for instance, is often read in terms of human sin, it is also seen as the inscrutable and unpredictable action of God.

RECONCILIATION AND HOPE

However much the discussion of the hiddenness of God may resemble a Manichaean or Marcionite position (gods of good and evil), Gutiérrez clearly repudiates such a conclusion. To assert that there are two separate gods at work in creation and history not only debases the mystery of evil, for Gutiérrez, but also undermines the difficulty and tragic beauty of the struggle of Job. The problem of theodicy is, thus, eluded by an easy solution that precludes struggle, protest, and hope in God. Only with monotheism is the struggle with and against God possible. "Perhaps he [Job] will go away limping, like Jacob after his contest with God, but—again like Jacob—he believes that he will be declared the winner if he grapples with God in order to receive God's blessing and that he will therefore be able to say in the end: 'I have seen God face to face, and yet my life is preserved'" (*OJ*, 66).

In the final analysis, Gutiérrez claims, the major contrast between the God-talk of Job's friends and Job is that the friends only talk *about* God and never *to* God (*OJ*, 54). Job's God-talk is, conversely, a talk that proceeds by struggle, lament, and suffering. In the third world context of

Gutiérrez, the struggles and laments of the poor and oppressed share this kind of God-talk, this agonizing form of theology. While the complaints of the poor and oppressed may sound scandalous to some, they are simply communal expressions of Christ's cry of abandonment on the cross (OJ, 102-3). It is the cries of innocent sufferers that must nourish our theological efforts. In order to hear the almost inaudible cries of the afflicted we must silence our theological arguments (even those which ostensibly seek to defend God, as in modern theism), and resist seeking explanations and solutions for the problem of evil.

Gutiérrez suggests that the text of Job and a theology of the cross teach us that "the greatness of God is to be identified less with power than with freedom and gratuitous love—and with tenderness" (OJ, 68-69). The monotheistic God of Christianity, he says, is a weak God who passes unnoticed and hidden to those who only have eyes for a God of power and might (OJ, 100). The suffering God at the cross does not provide us with a solution to evil, but in the figure of the Crucified One Christians adore a God who empties himself of power and glory in order to be in solidarity with the afflicted of history.[16] For Gutiérrez the recognition of tenderness in this image of the weak God (not only of the cross but also of the babe at the manger) gives hope and joy to human history. In Gutiérrez's reading of Job we are left, then, with a profound sense of hope and beauty.

While this chapter has argued that there are affinities with tragedy in the thought of Gutiérrez, nevertheless, it is the prophetic element that dominates in Gutiérrez and includes an overriding sense of hope and joy even in human history. The reality of violence does not eclipse the reality of beauty and love in human experience. "There is evil in the world, but the world is not evil. There are chaotic forces within the cosmos, but the cosmos is not a chaos" (OJ, 80). While lamentations and suffering unto God is a means by which we come to know God, such protests and complaints give way, in certain epiphanic and graceful moments, to sheer gratitude, joy, and love for God and humanity.

Thus, there are times to face the dark and tragic reality of existence, and others when we are overwhelmed by beauty, consolation, and even ecstasy. The message of the prophets moves us by their heightened awareness of suffering, but they also do not fail to inspire us by their attestation of the redeeming and tender acts of God in history. In my view, Isaiah is exactly right when he speaks gentle words of tenderness to an afflicted people, a people who has suffered more than double for its sins.

Comfort, O comfort my people, says your God. Speak tenderly to Jerusalem, and cry to her that she has served her term, that her penalty is paid, that she has received from the Lord's hand double for all her sins. (Isa. 40:1–2)

VI ✍

The Mystical-Prophetic Thought of Weil and Gutiérrez: Reflections on the Mystery and Hiddenness of God

The thesis of this work can be summarized as follows: Simone Weil and Gustavo Gutiérrez both incorporate a prophetic sensitivity and attention to the hiddenness of God as well as a mystical vision of the wonder and beauty of a life formed by grace and attentive to the divine mystery. Both of these thinkers share a distrust in philosophies or theologies which place the mystical and prophetic forms of religion in binary opposition. For one thing, Weil and Gutiérrez reveal a critical suspicion of forms of mysticism that ignore or minimize the harsh and tragic reality of suffering and violence in history; conversely, they equally castigate prophetic traditions that deny the contributions of mystical interpretations, practices, and ways of speaking to and about divine mystery. An intense awareness of the mystery, beauty, and love of God is joined with a heightened awareness of power, conflict, suffering, and evil in human life. In this way, an awareness of both the mystery and hiddenness of God is central to their thought.

Another characteristic of the mystical and prophetic elements of their thought is the celebration of both love and justice. Within the prophetic tradition, justice is demanded by both of them as an ethic that serves to prevent sentimental and solely private versions of love, the kind of love exhibited in talk shows and popular magazines. The prophetic passion for justice infuses their thought with an attention to the inequalities, poverty, and abyss of suffering in the world around us. Love is celebrated as a mystical force that creates the possibility for forgiveness and mercy, even in the aftermath of conflict and war. The temptations of revenge, spite, and hatred toward one's enemies are overcome by hope in the redemptive power of love and goodness.

An emphasis on the shared characteristics of the thought of Simone Weil and Gustavo Gutiérrez cannot preclude attention to important differences, however. They embody distinct perspectives and interpretations, and this book contends that Simone Weil has a more intense and developed understanding of mysticism than Gutiérrez, while Gutiérrez contributes a more developed and persuasive account of the prophetic tradition. This does not mean that the mystical element is missing from Gutiérrez nor the prophetic element from Weil. Indeed, Gutiérrez and Weil make their own contributions to each tradition, especially with Gutiérrez's interest in the indigenous spiritualities of third world peoples and Weil's creative interpretation of Greek tragedy vis-à-vis the Christian passion narratives. This book contends that dialogue between these thinkers can contribute a more developed and comprehensive mystical-prophetic formulation than that of either Weil or Gutiérrez taken separately.

POINTS OF CONTACT IN WEIL AND GUTIÉRREZ

> Evil is to love what mystery is to the intelligence. Just as mystery
> constrains the virtue of faith to be supernatural, so likewise does
> evil act in regard to the virtue of charity. And to try to find
> compensations, justifications for evil is as harmful for the cause of
> charity as it is to try to expound the content of the mysteries on the
> plane of the human intelligence.
>
> —Simone Weil

For both Simone Weil and Gustavo Gutiérrez, the mystery of God and the mystery of evil are intractable to human understanding. Attempts to prove the existence of God are as misguided as attempts to explain and justify the presence of evil. Such attempts are potentially idolatrous insofar as they reduce God to human terms, images, metaphors (not only as rational arguments for God, but also where culture, race, class, or gender figure as privileged symbols of God). In a like manner, explanations for evil may become idols that profane the mystery of evil and the incomprehensibility of God (as with some theodicies). On the contrary, at the heart of the mystical and prophetic visions of Weil and Gutiérrez is a silencing and interruption of rational explanations and theories for both God and the presence of evil. Instead, a response that loves without a why, that seeks justice without a cause, and that expresses God's incomprehensibility is advocated by Weil and Gutiérrez.

The meaning of faith is defined in relation to both the mystical tradition, as a knowledge born of love and in relation to the prophetic and tragic traditions, as a knowledge born of suffering. In this sense, reflection on God in the thought of Weil and Gutiérrez is grounded in spiritual praxis and love *and* ethical-political praxis (justice) and the experience of suffering. Knowledge of the mystery and hiddenness of God is possible only through spiritual training and through struggle, suffering, and even confrontation with God. The sense of divine mystery in mysticism and divine hiddenness in prophecy demands a contemporary theological method that is not merely informational but primarily transformational. In this picture, religious reflection has the primary task of cultivating and inspiring particular forms of life (via spiritual exercises and attention to the nonpersons of history) in order to make a consciousness of God's presence possible. The path to God in this mystical-prophetic interpretation is through an entire way of life animated by acts of spirituality, love, compassion, and justice.

The creative incorporation of both mystical and prophetic elements in the thought of Weil and Gutiérrez seeks to do justice to the full diversity and ambiguity of human experience. Appreciation for the presence of beauty, love, joy, ecstasy in human life, on the one hand, and an honest recognition of suffering, violence, terror, on the other, is at the heart of their thought. The sense that there is much that is attractive, alluring, and beautiful in human life is combined with a feeling of exile, estrangement, and terror toward history and society (*mysterium et tremendum*).

Concerning their interpretation of God, Weil and Gutiérrez note a similar ambiguity. A consciousness of the tenderness and love of God is held in tension with a fearful and awesome awareness of the violence and wrath of God (divine hiddenness). Gutiérrez recognizes that in the Old Testament, for instance, the dual face of God is interpreted vis-à-vis both the positive fortunes and blessings of Israel as well as the experiences of exile and oppression. Here the face of God discloses a passionate love for the people and anger with, even abandonment of, Israel. Simone Weil notes that for Christians, also, the intimate relationship of Jesus of Nazareth with the Father reveals the tender face of God and yet it, too, gives way to Jesus' feeling of fear and abandonment in face of the harsh will of the Father.

For Simone Weil, an urgent and essential task of philosophy is to illuminate, not explain, the irreducible absurdities and contradictions of the human condition (*FLNB*, 182; *NB*, 411–12, 396). Weil interprets the contradictions between the gospel of John and the synoptic Gospels as a sign of their truth, not falsity (*NB*, 416). The Gospel of John expresses the

sheer beauty, joy, sweetness, and love inherent to Christian life, while the
synoptics emphasize the pain, struggle, and anguish of the Christian vocation (*WFG*, 83).[1] This tension between these contradictory elements in
human experience and Christian belief has led Gustavo Gutiérrez to insist on both mystical and prophetic language about God. For him, at the
very soul of liberation theology is the relationship between mystical language and experiences of God in a key of love, peace, and joy, on the one
hand, and prophetic speech and awareness of the harsh reality of exploitation, poverty, and oppression (*TSMYF*, 17; *MIC*, 81; *OJ*, 16, 88). While
mystical language acknowledges that everything comes from the free and
unmerited love of God, prophetic language denounces historical situations of injustice and despoliation. The interaction between mystical and
prophetic language is meant to avoid both a spiritualistic evasion of historical responsibility and a political reductionism (*OJ*, 16; *TSMYF*, 57).

The visions of mysticism and prophecy also remind us of the limits of
objective language about God. For Gutiérrez, understanding of God will
emerge when we are engaged in spiritual and prophetic actions. Spiritual
training and ethical-political commitment are conditions for theological
reflection. They comprise the moment of silence and prayer that is indispensable for reflection on God.

In the theology of Gutiérrez, an acknowledgment of God's love, though
not without pain and struggle, forms the cornerstone of theology and is
the crucial basis for the prophetic embrace of the poor and afflicted. The
pursuit of justice in the prophetic traditions must be situated within this
context of God's gratuitous love, or else the pursuit of justice is easily
debased into resentment and vengeance (*OJ*, 94–96). Gutiérrez suggests,
then, that the synthesis of mystical and prophetic language is at the heart
of his liberation theology (*GL*, 146, 162).

Prophecy and the Hiddenness of God

Throughout this book we have seen that an interpretation and struggle
with the hiddenness of God is at the heart of the thought of Simone Weil
and Gustavo Gutiérrez. Their reading of divine hiddenness incorporates
the following positions: (1) a theology of the cross in which God's *presence*
is located in the context of suffering, anguish, conflict, and oppression;
(2) a confrontation with God's *absence* and power, in which the problem
of evil comes to the forefront. Daringly, both Weil and Gutiérrez mention the apparent split between the God of goodness and the God of
power implicit in these two elements of the hidden God. With this sec-

ond element of God's absence or power, an awareness of the rule of force, violence, injustice, and war in history gives rise to Simone Weil's appreciation of tragedy and to Gutiérrez's reading of Job.

Here the struggle with God's absence or violence refuses explanation in terms of human sin or human freedom. Affliction strikes in a haphazard fashion and in a profoundly unwarranted and undeserved fashion. The dialectic between these two elements of the hiddenness of God prevents Weil and Gutiérrez from either a repudiation of God (atheism) or from a simplistic theism. The Christian confession in the revelation of God through the figure of Christ crucified is, no doubt, at odds with a secular atheism. On the other hand, the willingness to confront and struggle with the realities of tragic suffering and premature death in history (the apparent absence or violence of God) undermines any confident and optimistic theism. Weil and Gutiérrez both maintain this dialectic in manner that refuses to surrender either element of divine hiddenness.

Simone Weil insists that the truth of Christianity is confirmed not by the glorious or almighty face of God in Christ, but rather through the wretched, ignominious, and poor face of Christ the beggar. The grandeur of the Church and Christian society fail to recognize this hidden God, this Jesus who was a common convict, shamefully tortured and put to death (FLNB, 144-45). Christian society, instead, admires the grandeur of martyrs, those who went to their death with courage and flare. But this martyrdom is far from the experience of Christ. Christ lamented his fate and pleaded for his fate to be altered. The bitterness of Christ's cross lies precisely in the fact that it is something he endured against his will (FLNB, 415). At the moment of the cross, Christ feels the whole force and terror of his destiny. He feels abandoned by God and cries out to God (FLNB, 26).

For those who seek God in signs of wonder, power, and majesty this depiction of God is a stumbling block, shameful and foolish to human reason. For others, Weil suggests, this understanding of God is the gateway to knowledge; this theology articulates a wisdom born of suffering. Such wisdom shatters the normal faculties of human reason and discursive thought (FLNB, 483). It is a wisdom most poignantly perceived by those who themselves have endured affliction. Slaves, peasants, workers, colonized peoples, victims of violence, village idiots—such persons and groups are privy to a knowledge hidden from the wise and powerful (MA, 67, 70). They feel their own fragility and recognize their dependency. They are often more aware of the painful face of reality that others seek to deny with a veil of illusion or fantasy.

To be sure, Gutiérrez shares this theology of the cross. For him, the cry of Jesus on the cross must permeate all our theological efforts (*OJ*, 103). The task before theology is reflection on God from the garbage heaps, from the underside of history. God's face and actions are revealed on the margins of society and history. God hides his face from history and yet reveals it in the struggles and deaths of the disinherited and poor (*GL*, 90). For Las Casas, Gutiérrez shows, God is most profoundly manifested in the scourged and crucified bodies of the oppressed Indians (*LC*, 11, 13, 18). The cross of Christ echoes throughout history. For Gutiérrez, too, a wisdom born of suffering is insinuated in this perspective. While experiences of poverty and oppression may bring premature death to the victims, suffering also communicates a knowledge accessible to the uneducated and illiterate, to women, to third world peoples, and to those, as St. Paul says, of ignoble birth (1 Cor. 1-2).

In Weil and Gutiérrez, this understanding of God's presence in locations of suffering and poverty is joined with an awareness of the brutal reality of force, conflict, violence, and oppression in human history and society, and thereby they turn to consider divine absence or even the possibility of divine violence. In certain moments of intense crisis and anguish, then, a theology of the cross gives rise to the consideration of the problem of evil.

For Weil, Greek tragedy is unparalleled in unveiling the role of force and violence in human affairs. Greek tragedy exposes the bitter and destructive impact of force. It does so without diluting the weight of suffering by false illusions or consolations (*MA*, 164). Force crushes whatever is in its path; it destroys memories, identities, hope. It is a mistake to assume that force is powerless to annihilate spiritual values. Weil's consideration of force in human affairs owes much to her very concrete knowledge of violence and oppression in history, and thus her reflections on force are by no means simply determined by her reading of Greek tragedy. Her encounter with exploitative work in the factory forced upon her an existential contact with violence in human affairs. This experience instilled in her an indelible awareness not only of physical suffering, but of the humiliation and degradation that results from an encounter with force. This experience, she tells us, imprinted her with the mark of a slave.

Recognition of the reality of colonialism and imperialism is also at the heart of Weil's interpretation of force in human life. As her biographers point out, even when Weil became disillusioned with some of the labor unions, she never ceased to denounce and struggle against the colonization of non-European peoples.[2] Her reading of history is particularly sensitive to the historical events of oppression and subjugation, where force annihilates entire communities and spiritual traditions. The narrative of conquest in the book of Joshua, the imperial policies of Rome, the violence of Christendom in the Middle Ages or during the Conquest of the Americas, or the contemporary presence of France in third world countries—all received the harsh censure of Weil. Such histories of violence were all too successful in annihilating the victims in its path.

Any attempt to explain such affliction and evil in terms of human sin was abhorred by Weil. Affliction does not strike its victims in a rational and ethical manner in terms of reward-punishment. Force is blind and chaotic; it is anonymous and indifferent (*WFG*, 125, 135). The reality of such violence and power in creation leads her to suggest that creation is not only being, but also nonbeing or void. It is the arena in which God creates, but also withdraws and renounces his presence. Creation is also cross (*NB*, 191-92, 213; *FLNB*, 100, 120).

Given this tragic reading of affliction, Weil spurns those theodicies which attempt to explain or justify evil in simple terms of human sin or freedom. The words that comprise such theodicies are no more than idolatrous subterfuges that seek to divert our attention from suffering; they are obstacles to compassion for the afflicted (*NB*, 626-27). Indeed, the repudiation of some theodicies leads Weil to daringly challenge God. In this case, she suggests that the tender and personal God manifested in Jesus Christ is only one face of God in human experience. The more terrifying experiences in history and society provide a basis for perceiving an impersonal and indifferent face of God, one that destroys the righteous and wicked alike. Hence, metaphors of void, abyss, force, chaos are, at times, associated with God in the thought of Simone Weil. It is the wrath and violence of God that Prometheus and Jesus Christ confront (*ICAG*, 65, 67). It is against this hidden face of God that Job calls for a mediator, Weil remarks (*NB*, 525). In these instances, Simone Weil regards the disobedience of Prometheus and Job, and the cry of lament of Christ, as a "divine disobedience," one inspired by an excessive love of humanity (*FLNB*, 344).

While Weil turns in the direction of Greek tragedy, Gutiérrez draws his insights from the Scriptures, together with his own experiences of suffering and oppression in the third world. In both the Scriptures themselves (especially in the prophets, Job, and the passion narratives) and contemporary experience, Gutiérrez recognizes the dark face of human existence. In his theology, the vicious and devastating reality of power, conflict, and oppression in human history is faced without dilution. He belongs to a history of people who have suffered the effects of colonialism, capitalism, and oppression. For him, the crucifixion of Christ continues through the crucifixion of entire peoples. Even poverty itself means death, he never tires of saying.

While Gutiérrez continues to be insistent about human responsibility for much evil, whether personal or structural sin, he has also turned his attention to the problem of evil and the implications of evil for our understanding of God, and his work on the book of Job is crucial for understanding this dimension of his theology. In his work on Job, his uneasiness with the reductive explanation of evil in terms of human sin is substantiated. He moves to consider and defend the protests and laments of Job, even if they may sound harsh to our ears (OJ, 102). Along with Job he confirms the laments of the poor and afflicted who cry out, "How long O Lord?" Not unlike Simone Weil, he notices that the text of Job interprets God in terms of both friend and foe (OJ, 65–66). For Job and the innocent sufferers of history, the face of God is not only tender and intelligible but also indifferent and inscrutable. Job sees his plight (and the plight of the other innocent righteous) as the result of God's power and majesty. Job recoils in the face of the hidden God and calls out "violence" against God (OJ, 57,61). Through this encounter with his suffering, Job sees the world as void, chaos, abyss (OJ, 8, 98–100). This leads Job to curse the day he was born. What is particularly extraordinary about the text of Job, Gutiérrez continues, is the fact that it is Job, and not Job's friends (who call for Job to repent of his sins), who speaks correctly of God (OJ, 102–3). Gutiérrez might say with Simone Weil, then, that there are times when a disobedience of God is divine.

To be sure, neither Weil nor Gutiérrez believe that such a struggle with God leads to a final repudiation of God. Their reflections on the hiddenness of God are filled with pain, anguish, and struggle, but they also lay the foundation for an honest and hopeful love of God. For Weil and Gutiérrez alike, the figure of Jesus Christ provides an example and response to the tragic reality of violence and injustice in human life. The cross of Christ is the location not only of the redemption of human sin but also of the divine embrace of human alienation and estrangement. Without furnishing an explanation for evil, the example of Christ provides the basis for compassion, a compassion that loves without a why. This response silences accusations and complaints about the ostensible sins of the afflicted. Compassion gives of itself and seeks justice while silencing blame and while renouncing the fruits of action (FLNB, 94). It is the suffering, protesting, and yet loving example of Christ that is the key to mystical-prophetic thought of Weil and Gutiérrez.

In the thought of Weil, the pain, emptiness, and void of affliction (cross, dark night) is a moment of apprenticeship that, with proper attention, gives way to the manifestation of the divine emptiness, an emptiness that is fuller and more real than any worldly presence (NB, 531, 545). Weil suggests that the divine emptiness or the hidden God is more real than the false gods of the world. This divine emptiness disrupts our complacency and satisfaction with the ways of the world. Not only does the hidden God detach us from our false gods, but it also discloses itself in the form of gift, as an unwarranted and unexpected surprise. The divine void reveals itself as the Good and comes to us as pure joy, grace, and love. For Weil and Gutiérrez, this leads to a face-to-face encounter with God that validates and affirms the beauty, joy, and goodness of creation. It leads to an immediate and direct mystical knowledge of God that Jesus Christ possessed in an unsurpassable manner.

Mysticism and the Mystery of God

The theology of cross in Weil and Gutiérrez alike, as mentioned, affirms God's presence in locations of God's seeming absence. The interruptive presence of affliction and force, however, calls into question a confident affirmation of God and raises the more troubling question of God's absence or violence. What prevents this attention to divine hiddenness in Weil and Gutiérrez from becoming an outright repudiation of God as either nonexistent or evil? This book has tried to show that mysticism in Weil and Gutiérrez intensifies and validates a consciousness of God's presence. In this sense, the prophetic and tragic elements in their readings of the hidden God is incomplete without attention to the mystical elements in their thought. Weil and Gutiérrez will insist that the mystical traditions provide invaluable resources for articulating the passionate encounter of humanity with God. An attention and awareness of God's presence—even if it is a presence that is beyond being—is confirmed through the language, practices, experiences and lives of the mystics.

When the mystical tradition speaks of the absence of God, it is often in reference to a cognitive absence. In other words, mystical or apophatic theology portrays the absence of God in a way that indicates the potential idolatry of reducing the transcendent God to a "present" thing or element in the world. God is no-thingness. An affirmation of divine mystery acts to relativize and annul the tendency of language to literalize our concepts and images about God. For both Weil and Gutiérrez the critique of idols is an essential moment in our path to a consciousness of the true God. Weil declares that the false gods must be demolished before the true God will manifest himself (SNLG, 148, 155, 158). Atheism, then, can be considered a purification, as a cleansing of the concepts and images that we usually name God (GG, 103). Insofar as religion is solely a source of consolation, Weil continues, it too can only benefit from a deconstructive atheism (GG, 104). Moreover, for Weil, idolatry is a subtle and insidious temptation that goes beyond our concepts of God and religion; idolatry extends into many arenas of life, such as society and culture, race, class, nation, the ego.

Gutiérrez, as well, confirms this perspective and contends that idolatry is a more serious threat than atheism (TSMYF, 32; GL, 48). Idolatry places human security and hope in what is other than God: in wealth, power, glory, the ego. In his prophetic reading of idolatry, Gutiérrez insists that idolatry leads to the sacrifice of human lives for gain and power. In the book of Job, also, Gutiérrez discovers the words and explanations of Job's friends to be forms of idolatry: their words and ideas of just retribution prevent them from being attentive to the suffering of their friend. Here the idol of theodicy prevents Job's friends from compassionate attentiveness, while also reducing the transcendent God to their own theories and understandings of divine justice (OJ, 75).

The mystery of God, therefore, is at the heart of the mystical thought of Weil and Gutiérrez. It inspires and imbues their thought with beauty, joy, and love. When the false gods are annihilated, then contact with the Good beyond being is imaginable. In the thought of Weil, contact with the Good is partially realized (in an implicit manner) through love of neighbor, love of the beauty of the world, and through religious practices and friendship (WFG, 137–215). Such forms of love constitute the period of preparation, when God is present but only in a veiled manner (WFG, 138). When God comes in person, she continues, these loves and practices of preparation are intensified and heightened. Through such a loving adventure, God reveals himself/herself and a more immediate and explicit consciousness of God is born. Ecstasy, joy, and beauty overwhelms the human person and it becomes obvious that one has slept with God by the extraordinary life one leads (FLNB, 146).

Gutiérrez is no less insistent on the comprehensive character of the spiritual life. Christian spirituality involves a following of Christ that demands an alteration of all our ways of thinking, believing, and acting;

spirituality is an entire way of life (*WDOW*, 54,81). Mystical knowledge of God, in particular, makes our faces radiant through contemplation of the holiness of God, as it did to the face of Moses (*GL*, 31). For Christians, St. Paul argues, the veil that hides the face of Moses is removed by Christ once and for all, and the glory of the Lord is made accessible to the people (2 Cor. 3:18). This makes possible a more direct and immediate knowledge of God, Gutiérrez maintains (*WDOW*, 45).

The example of Job is unparalleled for Gutiérrez in illustrating the transforming impact of a human encounter with God. Job's mystical, face-to-face encounter with God brings an end to his dejected and despairing outlook. Bitterness and protest against God succumbs to a reverent love and hope in God (*OJ*, 85-87). Job's vision of God communicates the mysterious, alluring, and beautiful face of God that his suffering had veiled. In the thought of Gutiérrez, Christian faith is both an awareness of suffering, conflict, and cross in human life, on the one hand, and a direct and immediate consciousness of God's presence, on the other. The mystical element of Christian faith validates the goodness, love, and gratuitousness of God. The self-manifestation of God comes as pure gift and draws us out of ourselves and into God (*ekstasis*).

We have seen that for both Weil and Gutiérrez, mysticism cannot be reduced to extraordinary experiences and events. While it does not necessarily exclude such experiences, the heart of mysticism in their thought is an immediate or direct consciousness of God that is born of love. Weil contends that the mystical life is only authenticated by the entire life of the mystic. When one is pregnant and lives for the sake of others, then one will know that the soul has been united to God (*FLNB*, 146). Far from encouraging a withdrawal and escape from history and society, mysticism in the thought of Weil and Gutiérrez is inspiration for a life lived in the midst of the world. In Weil's reading of Plato, a vision of the Good only motivates a return to the cave and a life of worldly service (like that of the Buddhist bodhisattva) (*SNLG*, 111-12). For Gutiérrez, spirituality provides the sustenance and hope for struggle against the injustices of the world (*WDOW*, 13-17). The fruit of mysticism in Weil and Gutiérrez is, in short, a spiritual fecundity in history and society.

Finally, Weil and Gutiérrez share the promotion of a form of mysticism that attends to the well-being of the entire person, body and spirit. Material concerns of bread, water, shelter, security, freedom, and so forth fall within the purview of their understanding of spirituality (their mutual appreciation of Marx deserves mention here). Indeed, they both speak of cultivating the soil for the spiritual life (*NFR*, 6-7; *LC*, 79). Weil says the kind of spirituality that is entirely otherworldly is a spurious mysticism (*NFR*, 150-51). Only through concrete things and persons of this earth can we penetrate to that which lies beyond, Weil holds. The recognition of human dependency on material and spiritual conditions of life makes evident the role of necessity in human life.

Contact with necessity through the pain of work, for instance, instructs us about human limits and mortality. Workers are less likely to consider themselves autonomous masters of their lives. The worker's subjection to time and space is revealed through the burden and disgust of work (*NB*, 79, 170, 301). Work is participation in the cross through an acceptance of the death of the ego. With the proper attention and consent, Weil believes that work can become a spiritual exercise. When this happens, an equilibrium between freedom and necessity is established; here the human person is neither slave nor master (*FLNB*, 88-89). Consent to one's limits, to the vulnerable and mortal feature of human life, gives rise to decreation and to the birth of God within the soul (*NFR*, 286).

Gutiérrez develops a spirituality of labor in a similar manner. The dialectic between freedom and necessity is phrased in terms of creation and cross, respectively. As a participation in creation, work is an act of creative freedom, of human cooperation with God (*STH*, 24-26). In this sense, humanity is given the mandate of lordship over creation. In exploitative, oppressive work the human person is reduced to an inanimate object, the means rather than the end of production. A spirituality of labor seeks to reverse this perversion of means and ends and to reestablish the human person as coauthor of creation. Neither is the human being a simple master of creation for Gutiérrez, however. Labor, in this sense, makes evident our dependency. It is a sharing in the cross of Christ (*STH*, 60).

Weil and Gutiérrez alike are clear that a change in the actual conditions of work is a crucial step in cultivating the soil for spirituality. Oppressive work is more likely to lead to the destruction and degradation of a person than to a spiritual rebirth or moment of decreation. Spiritual training involves, then, the nurturing of roots and ethical-political analysis (*NFR*, 181, 207; *WDOW*, 3). Weil and Gutiérrez hope to make the mystical life accessible not only to laypeople but also to the masses of the poor and illiterate. The privileged insights of such groups concerning human misfortune and the tragic beauty of the human condition places them in a position that can lead, with the proper attention and consent, to an awareness of God's gift of love even in the midst of their pain and struggles.

POINTS OF DIVERGENCE IN WEIL AND GUTIÉRREZ

While the synthesis of the mystical and prophetic elements of religion is at the heart of Weil and Gutiérrez, there are important differences in their thought that cannot be overlooked. Indeed, the differences between Weil and Gutiérrez are an important aspect of the thesis of this book, namely, that the fruit of engaging these two thinkers will serve to enrich the reflections of both of these important thinkers considered separately.

Mysticism and the Contribution of Simone Weil

Gutiérrez admits the complexity and ambiguity of the term "spirituality." He argues that it is important to go back to the biblical and historical resources of Christian thought to refine our understanding of spirituality (*WDOW*, 54). For the meaning of spirituality and mysticism alike, Gutiérrez provides us with a reading of these terms which are biblically based. As such, his thoughts on these terms are important and accurate, but they are also limited. A study of Christian mysticism must involve an exploration of the history of Christian thought beyond biblical resources. A more exhaustive and complete study of the meaning of mysticism is still lacking in his thought. Since he regards spirituality and mysticism to be at the very heart of his thought, a further exploration and development of the meaning of mysticism can only refine and enrich the liberation theology of Gutiérrez. It seems to me that Simone Weil provides an excellent case of someone who can enrich and refine the meaning of mysticism in the thought of Gutiérrez. Exactly how might she do so?

Besides the fact that Weil claimed to have had certain transforming mystical experiences, what is quite extraordinary about Weil is the manner in which she internalizes and embodies major ideas of the mystical tradition. In ways that are often unconscious she articulates and develops themes that are central to the mystical tradition in the west. Much of this is due to the fact that she had a profound and penetrating knowledge and love of Plato and the Platonic tradition. Without a doubt the Platonic tradition deeply influenced the development of Christian mysticism. Weil's fascination with the Platonic tradition was not limited to Plato and the mainstream Christian mystics, however; in addition, she was attracted to marginal and "heretical" Christian Platonic groups, to spiritualities that have been almost obliterated from memory, such as that of the Cathars. The development of mysticism in the thought of Weil has much to do, therefore, with her attraction for Plato and the Christian Platonists. The development of her ideas of detachment, decreation, void, dark night, attention, waiting, obedience, inactive action, apophatic language of God, nuptial union, mysticism of work, and so forth owe much to the history of the interpretation of Plato and to the creative and novel reading of this tradition by Christian mystics.

Of course, her own autobiographical claims to mystical encounter with God equally enrich our understanding of mysticism. She states that God himself came down to her and possessed her during different times of physical suffering, durinf prayer, during the recitation of poems, and during her participation in Catholic liturgies and festivals (WFG, 67-72). In one of her notebooks she recorded a narrative of an incident in her life, a mysterious encounter with God (FLNB, 65-66).[3] She tells us that the fruit of such experiences was to increase her love of God and Christ. In fact, she exclaimed that she loved God, Christ, and the Catholic faith, especially the Catholic mystics, the Catholic liturgy, hymns, architecture, and rites "as much as it is possible for so miserably inadequate of creature to love them" (WFG, 49). Simone Weil is, indeed, an exemplary Christian mystic. The intensity and radical nature of her mystical thought is both enigmatic and alluring. Her actual thought as well as her person contributes much to a contemporary interpretation of the heritage of mysticism.

Let me briefly summarize some of the issues we have discussed. In her essay "God in Plato," Weil summarizes what she considers generations of mysticism (SNLG, 111). In her reading of Plato's cave metaphor in The Republic, she notes that the beginning of the mystical life is, first and foremost, a recognition of our life in the cave—that is, a recognition that we are born in illusion and falsehood, in a situation that she names original sin (SNLG, 108-9). In this situation, knowledge of our misery, of our exile and imprisonment, is concealed from us.

The beginning of the mystical life is, then, the perception that this world is not everything and that we must seek the Good elsewhere. Such a consciousness of the void leads to spiritual training in detachment. Detachment from the attractions of wealth, power, fame, worldly wisdom, and the passions brings pain and anguish. Here spiritual nakedness and death to the world are the result of this voiding and emptying of worldly attachments. At this level the will is employed to the point of exhaustion (*FLNB*, 326). Following this stage, the voiding of the idols of the world is joined to a voiding of conceptual and imaginative idols. Even the trust in ostensibly religious experiences must also be exhausted. Our conceptions of God and religion must be purified of false concepts and images. Weil interprets this moment of the void as an apophatic critique of speech about God as well as a critique of the tendency to ascribe truth to consolations, miracles, and religious fantasies.

A final moment of this training is the actual experience of affliction or "dark night." In this state, one suffers a loss of memory and hope, and even a loss of God. An awareness of our nothingness, our fragility, and our finitude is almost unavoidable here. With the proper attention, decreation occurs and we are assimilated to God, not by a recognition of our likeness to God, but by a consciousness of our misery (*NB*, 120, 236). Weil interprets human labor as a concrete practice of this moment of detachment and "dark night."

These elements of the void are the means of escaping from the cave and coming into the light. Once one is outside of the cave, a vision of the sun, the supreme Good, stuns the recipient. Weil contends that the vision of the Good corresponds to spiritual marriage with God (*SNLG*, 111). The ability to contemplate the Good, however, is dependent upon the faculty of attention. The dialectical moments of the process of detachment and decreation (a recognition of our nothingness) are conditions for an analogical moment in which an awareness and consciousness of the Good are born. For Plato, Weil says, this involves training in attention of an intellectual, aesthetical and ethical nature. This element of training is only the condition for the ascent, however; it is not the elevating force (*SNLG*, 157).

At the heart of the ascension is God's gift of grace. The wings by which we ascend grow only through passion, through a state akin to falling in love (*SNLG*, 118). The beauty and love of God suddenly come upon the recipient, they shock and transform her. Memory is roused and an awareness of our origin and destiny emerges. It is this passive moment in the spiritual journey, the moment when desire, and not will nor intellect, is effective, that proves that this is truly mysticism, Weil concludes (*SNLG*, 127).[4] Spiritual exercises may prepare for God's presence, but only desire draws God down (*WFG*, 111). For Weil, this moment of manifestation occurs through visible means: by an icon, image, or physical form. Salvation occurs through a contemplative and aesthetical process of looking (WFG, 193).

In a Christian manner, Weil insists that this process of ascension is not the final moment in the mystical life: an imitation of the descent of Jesus Christ into human form must follow the vision of God. Activity in the world is only intensified. The transformed person is one with God as the just person is one with Justice. Acts of charity flow freely from the pregnant and virgin soul; one loves and gives without a why (FLNB, 146–49). What Weil refers to as "inactive action" calls to mind the passivity and detachment of the individual ego and will. Renunciation of one's motives and fruits of action are performed while remaining active in the pursuit of justice and the well-being of others. Acts of charity are performed entirely for the sake of an-other. Compassion for another person even dispenses with the need to act "for God" (WFG, 151, 178). In short, the decreated person is no longer himself. The ecstatic grace of love displaces the ego and replaces it with Christ.

Prophecy and the Contribution of Gutiérrez

Needless to say, the interpretation of the prophetic tradition in Gutiérrez owes much to the Old Testament. In addition to a theology of the cross, the vision of the classic prophets is at the center of Gutiérrez's liberation theology. As we have seen, this element in the thought of Gutiérrez accounts for his attention to the revelation of God in concrete history. For the prophets, God is hidden in history and only recognizable in what is insignificant and unassuming, in the underside of history (GL, 80). Nevertheless, for those who have eyes to see and ears to hear, God is indeed revealed in the midst of the events of history. Thus, while the prophets manifest an extraordinary sensitivity to the dark and destructive face of history (historical experiences of oppression, slavery, exile), they also deem history to be the arena of God's saving acts.

The eschatological element in the prophets is the basis for a sense of hope in history. Gutiérrez clearly shares this hope in history and belief in (chastened) progress (GL, 93). Simone Weil, on the other hand, is far more skeptical and pessimistic about historical progress than Gutiérrez. We have seen that Simone Weil's contribution to our understanding of prophecy is her creative and persuasive reading of Greek tragedy vis-à-vis the Christian passion narratives. Her thoughts on the Old Testament, however, leave much to be desired and, more than such a deficiency, they are often prejudicial and shallow. It is precisely this fault in Weil that leads to the eclipse of the prophetic tradition at the hands of tragedy. In this sense, her reading of history is not only pessimistic, but at times fatalistic.

In his book *The Hidden God* Lucien Goldmann argues that the difference between dialectical thought and tragedy concerns, in part, their view of history. While dialectical thought contends that values and meaning can become incarnate in the real world of historical experience, tragic thought eliminates this possibility from history and places it in eternity.[5] In the tragic vision, the highest moment of redemption is an enlightened awareness and willing acceptance of human limits and the realities of suffering and death, while redemption in the prophetic tradition arouses a hope that the transformation and liberation of human bondage can occur even here and now, in the midst of real history.[6] With this broad distinction in mind, we might say that Simone Weil is more representative of the tragic vision and Gustavo Gutiérrez of dialectical thought.

Simone Weil often opposes history to the Good and contends that history is devoid of Good. Instead, history is the arena of force and violence. For Weil, the Old Testament makes temporal promises and by doing so it only affirms and perpetuates conquest and domination in history (*NB*, 570). Christianity as well is guilty of trying to discover final meaning and continuity within history. This is the problem with Hegel and Marx, she notes (*NB*, 616; *FLNB*, 308). She opposes this view of history to the timeless, eternal hope of the Good beyond history, intimated in the experience of beauty, love, or mystical union with God. In this reading, mystical religious traditions are aware of force, but repudiate force as well as trust in historical progress along with it. Redemption is eternal, not historical.

For these reasons, she is very critical of eschatology and apocalypticism. For her, eschatology confuses the Good with history; belief in the coming of God within history is an illusion that only fosters and promotes the will-to-power and rule of history. For Weil, it is this illusion which is responsible for Israel's violence against its enemies, for Rome's subjugation of nations, and for Christendom's persecution of "heretics," "infidels," and non-Christians. For Weil, either one renounces the will-to-power in history for a timeless and eternal Good or else one risks debasing the Good into an idol of conquest and military victory. "One's attitude was bound to be different according to whether one believed that the revelation referred to some approaching and general event, or to transcendent and eternal truths . . ." (*NB*, 353; also *NB*, 350; *FLNB*, 216; *NFR*, 219).

It should not be surprising that Gutiérrez is far more orthodox and hopeful about Jewish and Christians notions of history. He defends and advances the eschatological elements in Judaism and Christianity. For him, far from leading to the conquest and domination of history, eschatology is the interruptive event and word of God in history laying the foundation for justice, peace, and love. The eschatological promises of God subvert human complacency and apathy concerning history and announce good news for the poor and oppressed *even here and now* (*TL*, 160–68). The kingdom of God inaugurates a new covenant in which Good and justice will take root in history in a proleptic manner. The eschatological promises of God begin to flourish when the kingdom of peace and justice always/already enlivens the temporal, earthly, and social existence of humanity. In this sense, Gutiérrez argues that while they cannot be identified, temporal progress and the kingdom of God are related (*TL*, 171).

Again, while I consider the bias of Simone Weil concerning the Jewish prophetic tradition a serious fault that impoverishes her interpretation of the prophetic tradition, in a way it is also a strength, insofar as it leads to a creative and perspicacious reading of the prophetic tradition in relation to Greek tragedy. In the Christian passion narratives she detects an awareness of the disturbing reality of violence and suffering in human history akin to the representation of the dark face of human life in Greek tragedy. On his side, Gustavo Gutiérrez adds an invaluable contribution by considering the Old Testament narratives of Exodus, the Psalms, the prophets, and Job in a manner that creatively illuminates his own situation of oppression and poverty in the third world. Concerns with the destructive presence of evil steer Gutiérrez to engage the issue of theodicy in a way that has affinities with the tragic vision.

Nevertheless, Gutiérrez's profound and resolute hope in human history deserves to be called prophetic rather than tragic. With Simone Weil, on the other hand, it is the tragic tradition that is more dominant in her thought, even if the prophetic vision is far from absent. Her thoughts on work, her theology of the cross, her insistence on action and commitment in history and society, and even her reading of mysticism justify the claim that Weil is a prophetic-tragic thinker. Even if her historical pessimism draws her closer to tragedy, it does not entirely eliminate the prophetic tradition. Nor does her tragic vision end with total pessimism. Weil's mystical thought (allied with her theological aesthetics) affirms the redemptive hope and joy of God's love. Her trust in the gift of grace inspires and fills her with the faith-filled confidence that God is love, beauty, and good before God is power.

CONCLUSIONS

This book has tried to demonstrate the benefits and possibilities of reading Simone Weil and Gustavo Gutiérrez together. I have suggested that these thinkers share a concern with uniting the mystical and prophetic elements of religion. If this work succeeds in persuading the reader that the thought and lives of Simone Weil and Gustavo Gutiérrez are at all creative and alluring then these reflections will prove to be rewarding. An accomplishment of this sort is satisfying—even if, as we have learned throughout this book, the mystical tradition always reminds us that we are to live without a why, without anxious expectations of a return. In this light, T. S. Eliot may have had Simone Weil in mind when he wrote that we must wait.

> I said to my soul, be still, and wait without hope for hope would be hope for the wrong thing. . . . Wait without thought, for you are not ready for thought: So the darkness shall be the light, and the still-ness the dancing. Whisper of running streams, and winter lightning. The wild thyme unseen and the wild strawberry, the laughter in the garden, echoed ecstasy, not lost, but requiring, pointing to the agony of death and birth.[7]

Notes

INTRODUCTION

1. See Pierre Hadot, *Philosophy as a Way of Life*, ed. Arnold Davidson (Oxford: Blackwell, 1995), 155.

2. There have been several recent studies in philosophy interested in the style of lives that philosophers have led rather than simply the content of their ideas (i.e., philosophy as a form of training or an art of living). See Alexander Nehamas, *The Art of Living* (Berkeley and Los Angeles: University of California Press, 2000); Martha Nussbaum, *The Therapy of Desire* (Princeton: Princeton University Press, 1994); Alain de Botton, *The Consolations of Philosophy* (New York: Pantheon Books, 2000).

3. Simone Petremont, *Simone Weil: A Life*, trans. Raymond Rosenthal (New York: Pantheon Books, 1976), 37.

4. Ibid., 51.

5. Gabriella Fiori, *Simone Weil: An Intellectual Biography*, trans. Joseph Berrigan (Athens: University of Georgia Press, 1989), 43.

6. Petremont, *Simone Weil*, 204.

7. Robert Coles, *Simone Weil: A Modern Pilgrimage* (Reading, Mass.: Addison-Wesley, 1987), 10.

8. See Simone Petremont's discussion of Weil's thesis (*Simone Weil*, 64–68).

9. See Henry Leroy Finch, *Simone Weil and the Intellect of Grace* (New York: Continuum, 1999), 59.

10. Fiori, *Simone Weil*, 124–25.

11. J. B. Perrin and G. Thibon, *Simone Weil as We Knew Her* (London: Routledge and Kegan Paul, 1953), 135.

12. Interview entitled "Gutiérrez: Joy of the Poor Confounds the Powerful," *Latinamerica Press*, 10 May 1984, 3–6.

13. Ibid.

14. Ibid.

15. Ibid.

16. Interview entitled "Gutiérrez: Criticism Will Deepen, Clarify Liberation Theology," *Latinamerica Press*, 27 September 1984, 3.

17. Interview entitled, "Gutiérrez Looks toward a Theology from the Poor Themselves," *Latinamerica Press*, 21 February 1985, 4.

18. Robert McAfee Brown, *Gustavo Gutiérrez: An Introduction to Liberation Theology* (New York: Orbis Books, 1990), 34.

19. For a discussion of Weil's attitude toward utopianism, see David McLellan, *Utopian Pessimist* (New York: Poseidon Press, 1990).

20. Brown, *Gustavo Gutierrez*, 25.

CHAPTER I

1. The classic scholar of mysticism Baron von Hügel in *The Mystical Element of Religion*, vol. 2 (London: J. M. Dent and Sons, 1908), insists that mysticism must confront the dark and evil face of existence if it is to avoid being too optimistic and ahistorical. In his words: "First of all, I would strongly insist upon the following great fact to which human life and history bear witness. . . . It is, that not the smoother, easier times and circumstances in the lives of individuals and of peoples, but, on the contrary, the harder and hardest trials of every conceivable kind, and the unshrinking, full acceptance of these, as part of the price of conscience and of its growing light, have ever been the occasions of the deepest trust in and love of God to which man has attained" (291-92). Von Hugel even suggests that this confrontation with evil and suffering may even "seem to confirm Schopenhauer at his gloomiest" (ibid.).

2. For good discussions of this passage in the thought of Weil, see Fiori, *Simone Weil*, 223; and McLellan, *Utopian Pessimist*, 156-57.

3. Jacques Derrida, in *Specters of Marx*, trans. Peggy Kamuf (New York: Routledge, 1994), addresses the need to attend to the voices of spirits: of those spirits both dead and unborn. At the heart of this version of "spirituality" is a messianic, eschatological justice calling for attention to nonpresent spirits. "If I am getting ready to speak at length about ghosts, inheritance, and generations, generations of ghosts, which is to say about certain *others* who are not present, nor presently living, either to us, in us, or outside us, it is in the name of *justice*. . . . It is necessary to speak of the ghost, indeed to the ghost, and with it, from the moment that no ethics, no politics, whether revolutionary or not, seems possible and thinkable and just that does not recognize in its principle the respect for those others who are no longer or for those others who are not yet there, presently living, whether they are already dead or not yet born" (xix).

4. Alexander Nehamas also claims that there are two kinds of philosophers: one type envisions the philosophical enterprise as providing the most reasonable, analytical, and clear answers to fundamental questions. The other type sees

philosophy as furnishing the pupil with the type of questions and answers that might assist him or her in the training and formation of the self. It is the latter type that he names philosophers of the art of living. See Nehamas, *Art of Living.*

5. In his forthcoming book *On Naming and Thinking God,* David Tracy argues that modernity has separated the following three realms: theory and practice, reason and sensibility/feeling, and form and content.

6. See Hadot, *Philosophy as a Way of Life,* 59.

7. For helpful discussions of apophatic thought, see Deny Turner, *The Darkness of God: Negativity in Christian Mysticism* (Cambridge: Cambridge University Press, 1995), 20; Michael Sells, *Mystical Languages of Unsaying* (Chicago: University of Chicago Press, 1994), 3.

8. See chapter 2 for a fuller discussion of apophaticism in Weil's thought.

9. See Bernard McGinn, *The Foundations of Mysticism: Origins to the Fifth Century* (New York: Crossroad, 1991), xv–xvi.

10. Ibid., xvii.

11. McGinn's says, "The emphasis on mystical experience has led not only to a neglect of mystical hermeneutics but also to an emphasis on first-person, autobiographical accounts of special visionary or unitive experiences of God. First-person accounts are rare in the first millennium of Christian mysticism . . ." (ibid., xiv).

12. McGinn's says, "Isolation of the goal from the process and the effect has led to much misunderstanding of the nature of mysticism . . ." (ibid., xvi).

13. Andrew Louth explains the importance of descent in Christian mysticism. While Platonism depicts the soul's search for God in terms of ascent, Christianity insists that God's descent into human flesh (Incarnation) is indispensable for making possible human communion with God. See his *Origins of the Christian Mystical Tradition: From Plato to Denys* (Oxford: Clarendon Press, 1981), xiv.

14. See J. P. Little, *Simone Weil: Waiting on Truth* (New York: Berg Publishers, 1988), 115.

15. Meister Eckhart, *Meister Eckhart: The Essential Sermons, Commentaries, Treatises, and Defense,* trans. Edmund Colledge and Bernard McGinn (New York: Paulist Press, 1981), 183.

16. In Eckhart's words: "Do not be startled, for this joy is near you and is in you. There is no one of you so crude, or so small in understanding or so removed, that he cannot joyfully and intelligently find this joy within him in the truth in which it exists, even before you leave this church today . . ." Ibid., 61.

17. Petremont, *Simone Weil,* 204–6.

18. See ibid., 244.

19. While Weil does not explain what she means by "complaints of the Middle Ages," she may have in mind the discontent expressed by many of the peasants against the princes and large landowners. These feelings of complaint reached a peak on the eve of the Reformation and led to the Peasants Revolt of 1525. For an interesting anthology of such complaints and grievances, see Gerald

Strauss, ed., *Manifestations of Discontent on the Eve of the Reformation* (Bloomington: Indiana University Press, 1971).

20. See Fiori, *Simone Weil*, 226.

21. See Miklos Veto, *The Religious Metaphysics of Simone Weil*, trans. Joan Dargan (Albany: State University of New York Press, 1994), 27.

22. Miklos Veto interprets the renunciation of the fruits of action in relation to Weil's reading of the *Bhagavad Gita*. In the *Gita* Krishna tells Arjuna: "It is the action that is your concern, never its fruits; let the fruit of action never be your motive." Veto, *Religious Metaphysics of Simone Weil*, 144.

23. Veto, *Religious Metaphysics of Simone Weil*, 128.

24. Marguerite of Porete, *The Mirror of Simple Souls*, trans. Ellen Babinsky (New York: Paulist Press, 1993), chap. 48, 126–27.

25. See Sells, *Mystical Languages of Unsaying*, 122.

26. One of Weil's major criticisms of Russian communists was that they delivered the factories and machines of the industrial age from private owners to collective ownership while overlooking the necessity for change in the actual conditions of labor themselves. Social oppression of the workers continued, but now under the yoke of the bureaucratic state (OL, 15,40).

27. See Bernard McGinn, "Introduction: Theological Summary," in Eckhart, *Meister Eckhart*, 60.

CHAPTER II

1. In a similar manner Emmanuel Levinas claims that the infinite Good beyond being cannot be reduced to human material needs, but rather rouses the insatiable desire for Infinity. This desire is excessive and infinite. No finite worldly good ultimately quenches this desire. "The infinite in the finite, the more in the less, which is accomplished by the idea of Infinity, is produced as Desire—not a Desire that the possession of the Desirable slakes, but the Desire for the Infinite which the desirable arouses rather than satisfies. A Desire perfectly disinterested—goodness." See *Totality and Infinity* (Pittsburgh: Duquesne University Press, 1969), 50. In Levinas, as with Weil, this is associated with the "void," or the presence of absence. Levinas calls this the *there is*.

2. See chapter 4 for a development of Weil's understanding of the hiddenness of God.

3. McGinn, *Foundations of Mysticism*, xviii–xix.

4. Denys Turner, *The Darkness of God* (Cambridge: Cambridge University Press, 1995), 17. In reference to the intellectual character of Pseudo-Dionysius, Turner writes: "It is therefore the *eros* of knowing, the passion and yearning for the vision of the One, which projects the mind up the scale; it is the dialectics of 'knowing and unknowing' which govern that progress, and it is not in the traditional metaphors of affectivity, touch, taste and smell, but in the visual meta-

phors of light and dark, seeing and unseeing, that progress is described" (ibid., 47).

5. Louth, *Origins of the Christian Mystical Tradition*, 182, 186.

6. John of the Cross, *Selected Writings*, trans. Kieran Kavanaugh (New York: Paulist Press, 1987), 201.

7. Ibid.

8. Ibid., 202.

9. I should note that Weil reads the ideas and practices of void, dark night, detachment, and decreation in very similar manners. They all function as deconstructing the idols of worldly attachments including desires, material possessions, concepts and images of God, and the egoistic self. Finally a confrontation with actual affliction plays an important role in all of these ideas.

10. John of the Cross, *Selected Writings*, 64.

11. Ibid., 71.

12. Ibid., 65.

13. Along with the Stoics, moreover, Weil sought to cultivate detachment from the conventions of society through spiritual exercises. "A smile from Louis XIV, considered as an object of desire, is the shadow of a manufactured object. The manufactured object is the institution of royalty—an arbitrary institution, a convention. . . . Must continually make this analysis with regard to every object of desire . . ." (*NB*, 563). A consideration of the arbitrary and conventional character of social and cultural practices was to lead to the emptying of our attachments (e.g., Marx on fetishism).

14. John of the Cross, *Selected Writings*, 168.

15. Eckhart, *Meister Eckhart*, 183.

16. Ibid., 201.

17. Eckhart insists that God is beyond names. "I say that whoever perceives something in God and attaches thereby some name to him, that is not God. God is above names and above nature." (ibid., 204). In spite of this, Eckhart speaks of God in terms of the Simple One or Naked Unity.

18. John of the Cross, *Selected Writings*, 85.

19. Ibid., 95.

20. Ibid., 125.

21. Ibid., 128-29.

22. Ibid., 106.

23. Ibid., 108, 110.

24. Differences between John and Eckhart are important. For Eckhart recollection or awareness of our preexistent self in God is the central end of the mystical life. In John, the establishment of hope for a new future is crucial. The loss of memory in John occurs through crisis, conflict, suffering. See Turner, *Darkness of God*, 177-78.

25. Eckhart, *Meister Eckhart*, 183-84.

26. This voiding of our conceptions of God may also include a detachment

from conceptions of morality. Weil claims that there is a certain kind of morality that is more pernicious to good than amorality (*SNLG*, 169). In her writings on Marx, for example, she maintains that morality is often defined by the ruling groups of society. "Furthermore, all the conceptions that are current in any society whatsoever are influenced by the specific morality of the group which dominates that society" (*OL*, 156). When God acts to legitimize such a notion of morality, our idea of God is in need of purification.

27. Eckhart, *Meister Eckhart*, 200.

28. Heiko A. Oberman, *The Dawn of the Reformation* (Edinburgh: T. and T. Clark, 1986), 132.

29. For a more developed analysis of the notion of the hiddenness of God in Simone Weil, see chapter 4.

30. Oberman, *Dawn of the Reformation*, 143.

31. Ibid.

32. Ibid., 147. Oberman explains that "excessus" in Luther also implies the humbling knowledge of human misery.

33. Ibid., 149.

34. Ibid., 150.

35. Ibid., 97.

36. Ibid., 97–98.

37. The contrast that I have noted between decreation and destruction in Simone Weil is similar to the contrast between the dark night and depression in John of the Cross. The major difference is that Simone Weil extends the analysis of destruction to include the oppressive effects of force and violence in history and society. In regard to Luther, I would say that his understanding of the hiddenness of God is *not* simply individualistic, even if faith is a personal struggle. In the *Bondage of the Will*, for example, the hidden God is faced as an honest attempt to deal with the injustices of history and nature. The injustices of history and nature (i.e., that the wicked prosper and the good suffer) has led the great minds, Luther says, to deny the existence of God and to imagine that "chance governs all things at random" See *Martin Luther: Selections from His Writings*, trans. John Dillenberger (New York: Anchor Books, 1962), 201.

38. Bernard insists that arrogance born of ignorance (of self) is the most dangerous sin. "This arrogance born of the last ignorance is worse and more dangerous because while the second kind of ignorance causes us to ignore God, this leads us to despise him. . . . It is pride, the greatest sin, to use gifts you have been given as though you were born with them, and to arrogate to yourself the glory which belongs to the generous giver." See *On Loving God*, in *Bernard of Clairvaux: Selected Works*, trans. Gillian Evans (New York: Paulist Press, 1987), 177. In a similar manner Pascal notes that conversion to God occurs through self-annihilation and recognition of human nothingness or misery. "True conversion consists in self-annihilation before the universal being whom we have so often vexed. . . . It consists in knowing that there is an irreconcilable opposition

between God and us, and that without a mediator there can be no exchange." See his *Pensées*, trans. A. J. Krailsheimer (London: Penguin Books, 1966) 137.

39. John of the Cross, *Selected Writings*, 190.

40. For good discussions of Weil on decreation, see Veto, *Religious Metaphysics of Simone Weil*, chap. 1.

41. Eckhart interprets the just person as one who has annihilated her or his will to such an extent that whatever God wills is the same to them. He goes further and says that this person is "equal to nothing," suggesting a notion of not only human equality, but an equality that includes an equality with the "nothingness" of the Godhead. One is united with the God beyond God, where God's ground and my ground are one and the same. See *Meister Eckhart*, 185-87.

42. In another text Weil asserts that through decreation the soul becomes "the same thing as the soul of the divine Persons" (*FLNB*, 132). Here she seems to imply that the soul is taken up into the relations of the Trinity. She continues that, in this life, such a possibility is very rare and brief. The exiled nature of human life permits nothing more.

43. Eckhart, *Meister Eckhart*, 127.

44. This is true also of what John of the Cross calls "loving attention." The memory, will, and intellect must be purged in order to make room for hope, love, and faith.

45. I certainly think that it is appropriate to consider Weil in relation to the hermeneutical thinkers. Attention to an-Other may include a person, text, event, myth, symbol, narrative, and so forth. Her notion of "reading" certainly would agree with the hermeneutical insistence on the interpretation-mediated character of all reality and experience. See *NB*, 23, 39, 43, 45.

46. See Peter Winch, *Simone Weil: The Just Balance* (Cambridge: Cambridge University Press, 1989), 209-10. This quote is taken from Ludwig Wittgenstein, *Culture and Value*, trans. Peter Winch (Chicago: University of Chicago Press, 1980), 85e.

47. This quote is taken from the *Tractatus Logico-Philosophicus*, trans. D. F. Pears and B. McGuiness (London: Routledge and Kegan Paul, 1961). See Art Monk's biography of Wittgenstein entitled *The Duty of Genius* (New York: Penguin Books, 1990), 156 for a good description of this element of Wittgenstein.

48. Weil also says in this context that divination is predicated upon the patterns and order of nature. Other gifts given by Prometheus were reason, numbers, letters, medicine, the practical ability to build homes and domesticate horses, and so on. All such gifts presuppose some order and harmony in the universe. See *Aeschylus*, trans. David Grene and Richmond Lattimore, vol. 2 (Chicago: University of Chicago Press, 1991), 155-56.

49. While Levinas would not be considered an analogical thinker, he does interpret the manifestation of Infinity in the face of the Other as a kind of iconic manifestation. "The way in which the other presents himself, exceeding *the idea of the other in me*, we here name face. This mode does not consist in figuring as a

theme under my gaze, in spreading itself forth as a set of qualities forming an image" (Levinas, *Totality and Infinity*, 50). The gaze isn't under the control of the self, but rather, in Levinas's words, "the gaze is precisely the epiphany of the face" (ibid., 75).

50. Bernard McGinn has mentioned to me that this passage echoes the thought of Angela of Foligno, whom Simone Weil may have read.

51. See Louth, *Origins of the Christian Mystical Tradition*, 2–3.

52. "As a stage on the way, it is a good thing that in any activity there should be a part of the soul that remains withdrawn and concentrated in God, but it is not the end of the way. A very different relation is needed between worldly activity and the spiritual part of the soul. Every worldly activity should be so performed that there appears in it the meaning with which God created it" (FLNB 268).

53. Eckhart suggests that the breakthrough to the ground of the soul is not only dependent upon detachment ("virginity"), but more significantly, upon becoming a fruitful wife and mother. "This virgin who is a wife brings this fruit and this birth about, and every day she produces fruit, a hundred or a thousand times, yes, more than can be counted, giving birth and becoming fruitful from the noblest ground of all—or, to put it better, from that same ground where the Father is bearing his eternal Word, from that ground is she fruitfully bearing with him" (*Meister Eckhart*, 178–79). In a different and more daring fashion than Weil, Eckhart contends that through this breakthrough, God and the soul will be one. "Out of the purity he everlasting bore me, his only-born Son, into that same image of his eternal Fatherhood, that I may be Father and give birth to him of whom I am born" (ibid., 194).

54. Ibid., 188.

55. Ibid., 186.

CHAPTER III

1. Carl Braaten, for example, claims that "liberation theology flattens out certain dimensions of Christian theology. Think of the liturgical and mystical dimensions of the Christian faith. The abysmal aspect in the experience of God as the *mysterium tremendum et fascinosum* is conspicuously absent in liberation theology" (*The Apostolic Imperative* [Minneapolis: Augsburg Publishing House, 1985], 101). For this quote and my discussion of mysticism in liberation theology I have been aided by the dissertation of Gary Marshall, "The Mysticism of Liberation: The Mystical Theory of Encounter with God in Latin American Theology of Liberation" (diss., University of Chicago, 1995).

2. For a classic work that demonstrates the importance of biblical exegesis in the Middle Ages, see Beryl Smalley *The Study of the Bible in the Middle Ages* (Notre Dame, Ind.: University of Notre Dame Press, 1964).

3. Bernard of Clairvaux's teaching on the Redemption suggests that what is deformed (human nature after the Fall) must be reformed by conforming to the Form of God. See Bernard McGinn, *The Growth of Mysticism* (New York: Crossroad, 1994), 174–76.

4. See David Tracy, *Plurality and Ambiguity: Hermeneutics, Religion, Hope* (Chicago: University of Chicago Press, 1987) for a development of the hermeneutical understanding of truth as manifestation (esp. 28–29).

5. In addition to this understanding of faith being close to Simone Weil, I have also mentioned that Ludwig Wittgenstein understands the heart of Christianity to involve such a view of faith. He asks: "How do I know that two people mean the same when each says he believes in God? . . . A theology which insists on the use of certain particular words and phrases, and outlaws others, does not make anything clearer. . . . Practice gives words their sense." *Culture and Value*, trans. Peter Winch (Chicago: University of Chicago Press, 1980), 85e.

6. Augustine, *Confessions*, trans. R. S. Pine-Coffin (London: Penguin Books, 1961) also expresses beautifully the interchange of forms of predication. Augustine's theological reflections about God are often interrupted to give way to prayer and confession to God (though also "to and with" the Christian community).

7. "No mystics (at least before the present century) believed in or practiced 'mysticism.' They believed in or practiced Christianity (or Judaism, or Islam, or Hinduism), that is, religions that contained mystical elements as parts of a wider historical whole." See McGinn, *Foundations of Mysticism*, xvi.

8. It is important to make clear what these helpful models of "first and second act" do not mean. We would be mistaken to simply assume that the first act is devoid of an intellectual element, while the second act is purely an intellectual act. The first act of spiritual, contemplative praxis and ethical-political praxis do indeed embody and express intellectual reflection. There is no strict separation between the first and second act. With the second act, the point is, theological reflection takes a more systematic and reflective form. In the second act, questions of coherency, consistency, and rationality are important norms that are to check naive or careless positions. Nevertheless, there is already present reflection on truth, justice, and God in the first act of theology.

9. Augustine remarks that while God is strictly ineffable, God wishes us to speak in order to praise him. "For God, although nothing worthy may be spoken of Him, has accepted the tribute of the human voice and wished us to take joy in praising Him with our words" *On Christian Doctrine*, trans. D. W. Robertson Jr. (New York: Macmillan, 1958), 11.

10. The dialectical mystical theology of John Scotus Erigena insists that creation is a theophany, but a theophany that still hides the essence of God. All of reality is an "apparition of what is non-apparent, the manifestation of the hidden, the affirmation of the negated, the comprehension of the incomprehensible. . . ." Thus the tension between the *proodos* of God as going forth into all

things, on the one hand, and the *epistrophe* of God returning and negating all things, on the other, reminds us of God's immanence and God's transcendent Nothingness. See McGinn, *Growth of Mysticism*, 99.

11. See *The Summa Theologica*, bk. 1, q. 3, trans. Anton C. Pegis, in *Introduction to St. Thomas Aquinas* (New York: Random House, 1945), 28. Aquinas also says that the human mind can only know *that* God is, not *what* God is (94–95). Aquinas does suggest that God may be able to be known by the intellect and, thus, it is the use of the intellect that is the highest beatitude for humanity (71). However, it is only possible to see God by the graced intellect not by the natural intellect (77).

12. Bernard McGinn argues that the contrast between intellectual and affective mysticism may be misleading and too general. McGinn insists that even when there are differences concerning the nature of love and knowledge in the path to mystical union with God, the fact remains that for Christian mysticism both love and knowledge play a pivotal role. See his essay "Love, Knowledge, and Unio Mystica in the Western Christian Tradition," in *Mystical Union in Judaism, Christianity, and Islam*, ed. Moshe Idel and Bernard McGinn (New York: Continuum, 1996), 59–86.

13. McGinn cites the influential expression of Gregory the Great, "amor ipse notitia est" (ibid., 63, 81). The theologian Bernard Lonergan understands faith as a "knowledge born of love." He interprets the experience of conversion in relation to the dynamic state of "being in love." See *Method in Theology* (Toronto: University of Toronto Press, 1971), 115.

14. McGinn, "Love, Knowledge, and Unio Mystica," 59.

15. Ibid.

16. See references to Jean Gerson, *De mystica theologia speculativa*, in Steven Ozment, *The Age of Reform: 1250–1550* (New Haven: Yale University Press, 1980), 74. Also see Ozment's discussion of the late medieval lay movements such as the "Modern Devotion" and the Beguines (91–98).

17. McGinn, *Foundations of Mysticism*, 106.

18. Concerning the importance of social and historical context for the study of mysticism, Bernard McGinn says the following: "The paradoxical intersection of the timeless and time implied in the mystery of the Incarnation is nowhere more evident than in the ways in which 'timeless' mystical consciousness of God's presence has been conditioned by changes and developments in the church and in society at large" (ibid., xv).

19. In traditional Marxist terms, this kind of idolatry is named "ideology"; ideology in this tradition is certain ideas, beliefs, patterns of interpreting and acting that conceal and legitimate the power and economic interests of particular groups and classes in society over against those of others.

20. Las Casas insists that even the barbarians "have been created in the image of God and are never so utterly abandoned by divine providence as to be incapable of entering the Kingdom of Christ—as they are our siblings—and re-

deemed by the most precious blood of Christ" (LC, 296). Las Casas contends that Aristotle lacked the light of the Christian truth and charity and, thus, was unable to recognize the truth implicit in this thesis, namely, that all human beings, including slaves and women, are equally formed in the image of God (LC, 297).

CHAPTER IV

1. "Why, O Lord, do you stand far off? Why do you hide yourself in times of trouble? In arrogance the wicked persecute the poor—let them be caught in the schemes they have devised. . . . Rise up, O Lord; O God, lift up your hand; do not forget the oppressed" (Ps. 10:1-2, 12). With the prophets the hiddenness of God often expresses God's anger at the sins of the people. Isaiah pleads with God to forget his anger and to return to God's people. "There is no one who calls on your name, or attempts to take hold of you; for you have hidden your face from us, and have delivered us into the hand of our iniquity" (Isa. 64:7).

2. This phrase the "presence of absence" is taken from Levinas. His understanding of the "there is" is very similar to the understanding of the void or the hiddenness of God in Simone Weil. Levinas explains that 'there is' is an impersonal and anonymous darkness. This absence interrupts all totalizing systems of rational thought. It is a silence. "But this universal absence is in its turn a presence, an absolutely unavoidable presence. It is not the dialectical counterpart of absence, and we do not grasp it through a thought. It is immediately there. There is no discourse. Nothing responds to us, but this silence; the voice of this silence is understood and frightens like the silence of those infinite spaces Pascal speaks of." See his essay "There Is: Existence without Existents," in The Levinas Reader ed. Sean Hand (Oxford: Blackwell, 1989), 30.

3. I am indebted to David Tracy's unpublished essay "Evil, Suffering, Hope: The Search for New Forms of Contemporary Theodicy."

4. Weil often mentions Aeschylus in this regard. See Aeschylus, The Oresteia: Agamemnon, trans. Richmond Lattimore, ed. David Grene and Richmond Lattimore (Chicago: University of Chicago Press, 1953), 40, vv. 176-83. Weil also mentions Hesiod for the expression of "a wisdom born of suffering." See Work and Days, trans. Dorothea Wender (London: Penguin Books, 1973), 65, vv. 195-223.

5. Lucien Goldmann in The Hidden God: A Study of Tragic Vision in the Pensées of Pascal and the Tragedies of Racine (London: Routledge and Kegan Paul, 1964) claims that the tension between God's absence and presence is central to a tragic vision. He especially thinks such is the case in Pascal. "But we must add that for Pascal, and for tragic man in general, this hidden God is present in a more real and more important way than any empirical and perceptible being, and that His is the only essential presence that exists. That God should be always absent and always present is the real center of the tragic vision" (37).

6. See Michael Fishbane, "Biblical Prophecy as a Religious Phenomena," in *Jewish Spirituality: From the Bible to the Middle Ages*, ed. Arthur Green (New York: Crossroad, 1994), 63.

7. In *Bondage of the Will* Luther says: "God governs the external affairs of the world is such a way that, if you regard and follow the judgement of human reason, you are forced to say, either that there is not God, or that God is unjust. . . ." See *Martin Luther: Selections from his Writings*, 201. Calvin, too, insists that contemplation on history and nature (without Scripture) leads, if not to atheism, then to the worship of an unknown god (idolatry). See William Bouwsma, *John Calvin: A Sixteenth-Century Portrait* (New York: Oxford University Press, 1988), 154.

8. As is well known, Luther's breakthrough supposedly occurred at the toilet or *cloaca*. Whether or not Luther was actually referring to a toilet (more than likely it was a reference to the study room above the toilet), Luther's point is clear: where humanity is most weak, vulnerable, and filthy, there God is most strong. See Heiko A. Oberman, *Luther: Man Between God and the Devil* (New Haven: Yale University Press, 1989), 155–56.

9. Yet again I am indebted to the insight of David Tracy in his reading of Greek tragedy. See his forthcoming book on naming and thinking God.

10. Louis Ruprecht, in *Tragic Posture and Tragic Vision* (New York: Continuum, 1994), has argued that the belief that tragedy is simply fatalistic is a tragic posture, not an honest tragic vision. He is right to insist that one can take suffering very seriously without having an understanding of life that ends in despair and gloom (101).

11. While there are many differences in their thought, Weil would have benefited from Nietzsche's interpretation of Greek tragedy. Nietzsche contends that, far from being a nihilistic genre, tragedy is an elevating genre that leads to an embrace of the world in all its beauty and suffering. See his *Birth of Tragedy*, trans. Walter Kaufmann (New York: Random House, 1967).

12. Paul Ricoeur, *The Symbolism of Evil* (Boston: Beacon Press, 1967).

13. Ibid., 214. Ricoeur notes that Babylonian myth expresses a similar ambiguity of the divine. Enlil, for instance, by turns spreads terror and trust (181). Marduk also is interpreted as the cause of both creation and destruction (182).

14. Ibid., 219. As an example, Ricoeur mentions the extraordinary ability of Aeschylus in *The Persians* to rise above a celebration of Greek victory and to lament the catastrophe of the Persians. In the figure of Xerxes, Aeschylus does not see a mere enemy, but rather one who has been crushed by the gods.

15. Ibid., 218. Ricoeur mentions the case of the hero Prometheus confronting and resisting the will of Zeus in Aeschylus's *Prometheus Bound*.

16. Ibid., 327.

17. See Goldmann, *Hidden God*, 42. Goldmann also makes a contrast between a dialectical and tragic vision. Whereas dialectical thought interprets God's presence in actual historical events and occurrences, tragedy is more mythical

and ahistorical. See chapter 6 of the present work for the development of this contrast in relation to Gustavo Gutiérrez and Simone Weil.

18. See B. A. Gerrish, *The Old Protestantism and the New: Essays on the Reformation Heritage* (Chicago: University of Chicago Press, 1982), 134.

19. Ibid., 136. See Luther's *Bondage of the Will*, in *Martin Luther: Selections from His Writings*.

20. Ibid., 137.

21. See David Tracy, "The Tenderness and Violence of God: The Return of the Hidden God in Contemporary Theology," *Lumière et vie* 20, no. 1 (spring 1996). Luther did, indeed, understand the tragic vision of fate. In *Bondage of the Will* Luther explicitly discusses fate in the poets (he mentions Vergil, in particular). In his words: "Those wise men knew, what experience of life proves, that no man's purposes ever go forward as planned, but events overtake all men contrary to their expectation." See *Martin Luther: Selections from His Writings*, 183–84.

22. Lucien Goldmann claims that notice of an ostensible conflict in God is the mark of a tragic vision. Goldmann maintains that while Christian orthodoxy "tends to bring together the two concepts of God . . . the tragic vision tends to separate them from each other" (*Hidden God*, 78).

23. While this may seem quite foreign to the notion of the Christian God, it is not as far removed as one might think. The story of Noah is nothing else than a narrative of the destruction of the human race. Moses also pleads with God not to destroy the Israelites in the desert; Abraham persuades God not to destroy the city of Sodom. Weil is aware of these aspects of the Bible and compares the ambiguity of the Greek gods to these elements. She especially notes 1 Kings 22:21, in which God sends Ahab a "lying spirit" (*NB*, 580).

24. "Jesus will be in agony until the end of the world. There must be no sleeping during that time." Pascal, *Pensées*, trans. Krailsheimer, 313.

25. An interpretation of the hidden God is not unique to Christianity, according to Weil. She believes that there have been intimations of the cross of Christ in various traditions and cultures, but especially among Plato and Greek tragedy. See especially her *Intimations of Christianity among the Greeks*.

26. Kierkegaard charges Christendom with the same idolatry, namely, the worship of the glorified and powerful Christ and neglect of the *deus incognito*. See *Practice in Christianity*, ed. and trans. Howard Hong and Edna Hong (Princeton: Princeton University Press, 1991), 24–25, 35–36, 107, and elsewhere.

27. Wittgenstein shares Weil's sense of the wisdom inherent in suffering and life experience. Wittgenstein insists that intellectual arguments or proofs will do little to convince a person of the significance of God. Instead, life can "educate one to a belief in God. And *experiences* too are what bring this about; but I don't mean visions and other forms of sense experience which show us the 'existence of this being', but, e.g., sufferings of various sorts. . . . Experiences, thoughts,—life can force this concept on us." See Wittgenstein, *Culture and Value*,

86e. We would do well to note that the same skepticism Weil demonstrates toward special visions or supernatural communications is shared by Wittgenstein.

28. I would argue, as Weil does, that this availability of truth beyond the elite and privileged groups of society is central to origins of the Christian tradition. The Gospels speak from the vantage point of the poor, excluded, and marginalized peoples. As is well known, one of the major attractions of Christianity to Weil was the fact that Christianity was, before anything else, a religion of slaves (*WFG*, 67). It is this character of Christianity which Nietzsche repudiated.

29. Luther's statement "We are all beggars" was written two days before his death. It was preceded by the following words: "No one can understand Virgil in his *Bucolics* and *Georgics* unless he has spent five years as a shepherd or farmer. No one understands Cicero in his letters unless he has served under an outstanding government for twenty years. No one should believe that he has tasted the Holy Scriptures sufficiently unless he has spent one hundred years leading churches with the prophets." Besides wanting to convey the inexhaustible richness of Scripture, Luther insists that true wisdom is born of doing, not speculating. See Oberman, *Luther*, 166.

30. See David Tracy, "The Hidden God: The Divine Other of Liberation," *Cross Currents* 46, no. 1 (spring 1996).

31. See John of the Cross, *Selected Writings*, 199.

32. See Petremont, *Simone Weil*, 297.

33. John of the Cross reproaches those spiritual advisors who associate all suffering with sin. He says that they are no different than Job's sorry comforters. See *Selected Writings*, 189–91.

34. Margaret Farley, *Tragic Vision and Divine Compassion: A Contemporary Theodicy* (Louisville, Ky.: Westminster/John Knox Press, 1990), 63–64.

35. The impersonal face of God is not merely read by Weil in terms of the power of God and inscrutable presence of evil in history and nature, however. The impartiality of God (the sun) is also the basis for a divine love that refuses to choose between friend and enemy. It is the basis of agape. Along these lines, Weil mentions the text of Matthew (*NB*, 106; *FLNB*, 129).

36. While there is no evidence that Weil read the Lurianic Kabbalah, this text expresses a similar vision of the divine act of creation.

37. From Nietzsche, *Birth of Tragedy*, 43.

38. The contrast between the deaths of Christ and Socrates is well known. Socrates is far less troubled and is relatively tranquil and serene about his imminent death. Margaret Farley in *Tragic Vision and Divine Compassion*, quotes the reading of Socrates' heroic death by Levinas. Contrary to the suffering of Socrates, Levinas says, "we know that the possibilities of tyranny are much more extensive. . . . It can exterminate in the tyrannized soul even the very capacity to be struck. . . . To have a servile soul is to be incapable of being jarred, incapable of being ordered" (55). Even Nietzsche contrasts the tragic vision with the theoretical and

scientific vision of Socrates. With regard to the death of Socrates, the optimistic character of theoretical man is unveiled. "Hence the image of the dying Socrates, as the human being whom knowledge and reasons have liberated from the fear of death . . ." (*Birth of Tragedy*, 96–97). Knowledge has liberated Socrates, Nietzsche contends, from a tragic struggle with death.

39. Luther makes a very similar point that God manifested in the powerless figure of Christ is the only model for faith, not God-in-his-power. See his *Bondage of the Will*, in *Martin Luther: Selections from His Writings*, 190–91.

CHAPTER V

1. While Gutiérrez does not appropriate the term "postmodernity," he does share the suspicion and critique of modern forms of thought. He wants to make evident, for example, the ways in which the ostensible progress and evolution of Western European civilization has, at the same time, brought about the subjugation and colonization of entire groups and races of peoples. "It will no longer do simply to continue to think in the modern mold, refusing to accept the theological datum that that mold, that mentality, has accompanied and justified the historical process that creates this new world of spoliation and injustice" (*PPH*, 231). Many of the ideas lauded by the Enlightenment (rationality, freedom, individuality, progress) are shown to be deeply ambiguous. In the case of freedom, for example, Gutiérrez argues that liberal notions of freedom, while important for inspiring liberation and resistance, at the same time may be partners in oppression and exploitation. Laissez-faire capitalism, private property rights: in these cases, freedom is often an instrument of the powerful and wealthy to maintain their privileged status and position.

2. John Baptist Metz, "Suffering Unto God," *Critical Inquiry* 20, no. 4 (spring 1994): 620–21.

3. Hans Blumenberg speaks of an absolutizing of sin in Christianity due to the dominant influence of Augustine. In his words: "The answer that Augustine gave to this question [theodicy] was to have the most important consequences of all the decisions that he made for the Middle Ages. With a gesture just as stirring as it was fateful, he took for man and upon man the responsibility for the burden oppressing the world. Now, in the aftermath of Gnosticism, the problem of the justification of God has become overwhelming, and that justification is accomplished at the expense of man, to whom a new concept of freedom is ascribed expressly in order to let the whole of an enormous responsibility and guilt be imputed to it." See *The Legitimacy of the Modern Age* (Cambridge: MIT Press, 1983), 133.

4. In *The God of Life* and *On Job* the manifestation of God through the form and beauty of the cosmos is central to his understanding of Christianity. The strong contrast between the element of history in the Jewish traditions and

that of nature in the pagan traditions is overstated in A *Theology of Liberation.* Biblical scholars have pointed out the complexity of the Jewish traditions and have especially made us more aware of the relationship of Israel with God through the order and regularity of nature and the seasons. Mount Zion, for example, is interpreted as a manifestation of beauty of the whole cosmos. Metaphors of vision, rather than mere hearing, take center stage with the sacred space of Zion. See Jon Levenson, *Sinai and Zion* (New York: HarperCollins, 1985).

5. The prophet Isaiah expresses a similar sentiment. Addressing himself to God, he declares that "there is no one who calls on your name, or attempts to take hold of you, for you have hidden your face from us, and have delivered us into the hand of our iniquity" (Isa. 64:7). In this context, however, Isaiah does not merely relate God's hiddenness to human sin. Indeed, he complains that God has hardened the hearts of Israel and causes people to turn away from him. "Why, O Lord, do you make us stray from your ways and harden our heart, so that we do not fear you?" (Isa. 63:17).

6. One could argue that this prophetic sense of conflict is at the heart of Marx's interpretation of history. In Hegel one could argue that this sense of prophetic conflict in history (that history is a slaughter-bench) is related to Hegel's theology of the cross. For an interesting work that traces the origins of dialectic in Marx to the Christian Platonists (e.g., Erigena, Eckhart, Nicholas of Cusa), see Leszek Kolakowski, *Main Currents of Marxism*, vol. 1: *The Founders* (Oxford: Oxford University Press, 1978).

7. "For he grew up before him like a young plant, and like a root out of dry ground; he had no form or majesty that we should look at him, nothing in his appearance that we should desire him. He was despised and rejected by others; a man of suffering . . ." (Isa. 53:2–3).

8. "Why have you forgotten us completely? Why have you forsaken us these many days?" (Lam. 5:20).

9. It should be noted that Gen. 20:7 calls Abraham a prophet for his ability to intercede with Yahweh.

10. In commenting on the protests of Moses against God, Luther daringly suggests that such complaint may be justified. "Therefore how can human nature bear to think of God's wrath without tears, without muttering, without the most vigorous protest?" See *Luther's Works*, ed. Jaroslav Pelikan (St. Louis: Concordia Publishing House, 1956), 13:106–7.

11. Ibid., 14:156.

12. Ricoeur, *Symbolism of Evil.*

13. Ricoeur says: "There is no great difference in this respect between the 'hardness' of certain texts of the Old Testament and the 'blindness' of the Homeric writings and the Greek tragedians" (ibid., 89).

14. Ibid., 314.

15. Ibid.

16. Paul Ricoeur also contends that in the figure of Christ crucified, there is

a reconciliation of both the Adamic and tragic myth. Christianity is, thus, a prophetic-tragic religion (ibid., 328).

CHAPTER VI

1. Differences in Christianity are also evident in terms of Christology, Weil claims. John's gospel highlights the freedom and authority of Christ, who is portrayed as controlling his destiny, while the synoptics depict a more vulnerable Christ at the mercy of his destiny (NB, 538).

2. See Petremont, Simone Weil, 207, 325.

3. While I will not quote the entire text, it begins with the following description: "He came into my room and said: 'You poor wretch, who understand nothing and know nothing—come with me and I will teach you things you have no idea of.' I followed him. He took me into a church. It was new and ugly. He led me before the altar and said: 'Kneel.' I told him: 'I have not been baptized.' He said: 'Fall on your knees before this place, with love, as before the place where truth exists.' I obeyed." Weil continues that they then began to have a conversation, broke bread, and drank wine. She concludes with the following words: "Sometimes I cannot prevent myself from repeating, in fear and compunction, a little of what he said to me. How am I to know if I remember it correctly? He is not there to tell me. I well know that he doesn't love me. How could he love me? And yet there is something deep in me, some point of myself, which cannot prevent itself from thinking, with fear and trembling, that perhaps, in spite of everything, he does love me" (FLNB, 65-66).

4. In the mystical vision of Bonaventure, the seventh day of rest is also a stage in which union with God occurs through "grace not instruction, desire not understanding, the groaning of prayer not diligent reading, the Spouse not the teacher, God not man, darkness not clarity, not light but the fire that totally inflames and carries us into God by ecstatic unctions and burning affections." See The Soul's Journey into God, trans. Ewert Cousins (New York: Paulist Press, 1978), 115.

5. See Goldmann, Hidden God,:59.

6. Ibid., 81.

7, T. S. Eliot. The Four Quartets (New York: Harcourt, 1971), 28.

Bibliography

WORKS BY GUSTAVO GUTIERREZ

Beber en su propio pozo. Lima: Centro de Estudios y Publicaciones (CEP), 1983. Translated by Matthew J. O'Connell as *We Drink from Our Own Wells* (New York: Orbis Books, 1984).

"El Evangelio del Trabajo." In *Sobre el trabajo humano*, edited by Gustavo Gutierrez et al. Lima: CEP, 1982.

En busca de los pobres de Jesucristo. Lima: CEP, 1992. Translated by Robert Barr as *Las Casas: In Search of the Poor of Jesus Christ* (New York: Orbis Books, 1993).

Entre las calandrias: En ensayo sobre Jose Maria Arguedas. Lima: CEP, 1990.

"From Exclusion to Discipleship." In *Mysticism and Institutional Crisis*, edited by Christian Duquoc and Gustavo Gutiérrez. Special issue of *Concilium* 4 (1994).

Hablar de Dios desde el sufrimiento del inocente. Lima: CEP, 1986. Translated by Matthew J. O'Connell as *On Job* (New York: Orbis Books, 1987).

El Dios de la vida. Lima: CEP, 1989. Translated by Matthew J. O'Connell as *The God of Life* (New York: Orbis Books, 1991).

La fuerza historica de los pobres. Lima: CEP, 1979. Translated by Robert R. Barr as *The Power of the Poor in History* (New York: Orbis Books, 1983).

La verdad los hara libres: Confrontaciones. Lima: CEP, 1986. Translated by Matthew J. O'Connell as *The Truth Shall Make You Free* (New York: Orbis Books, 1990).

Liberation and Change. With Richard Shaull. Atlanta, Ga.: John Knox Press, 1977.

"Liberation Praxis and Christian Faith." In *Frontiers of Theology in Latin America*, edited by Rosino Gibellini. New York: Orbis Books, 1978.

"Liberation, Theology, and Proclamation." In *The Mystical and Political Dimensions of the Christian Faith*, edited by Claude Geffre and Gustavo Gutiérrez. Special issue of *Concilium* 96 (1974).

Teologia de la Liberacion: Perspectivas. Lima: CEP, 1971. Translated by Caridad Inda and John Eagleson as *A Theology of Liberation* (New York: Orbis Books, 1973).

"Two Theological Perspectives: Liberation Theology and Progressivist Theology."

In *The Emergent Gospel*, edited by **Sergio** Torres and Veronica Fabella. New York: Orbis Books, 1978.

WORKS BY SIMONE WEIL

Attente de Dieu. Paris: La Colombe, 1950. Translated by Emma Craufurd as *Waiting for God* (New York: Harper and Row, 1951).

Cahiers. 3 vols. Paris: Plon, 1956. Translated by Arthur Wills as *The Notebooks of Simone Weil*, 2 vols. (London: Routledge and Kegan Paul, 1956).

Escrits de Londres et dernières lettres. Paris: Gallimard, 1957.

Escrits historiques et politiques. Paris: Gallimard, 1960.

Formative Writings: 1929–1941. Edited by Dorothy Tuck McFarland and Wilhelmina Van Ness. Amherst: University of Massachusetts Press, 1987.

Intuitions prechretiennes. Paris: La Colombe, 1951. Translated by Emma Craufurd as *Intimations of Christianity among the Ancient Greeks* (London: Ark Paperbacks, 1987).

La condition ouvrière. Paris: Gallimard, 1951.

La Connaissance surnaturelle. Paris: Gallimard, 1950. Translated by Richard Rees in *The First and Last Notebooks* (London: Oxford University Press, 1970).

La pesanteur et la grâce. Paris: Plon, 1947. Translated by Emma Craufurd as *Gravity and Grace* (London: Ark Paperbacks, 1987).

La Source grecque. Paris: Gallimard, 1953. Translated by Emma Craufurd as *Intimations of Christianity among the Ancient Greeks* (London: Ark Paperbacks, 1987).

Leçons de philosophie de Simone Weil. Edited by A. Reynaud. Paris: Plon, 1959. Translated by Hugh Price as *Lectures on Philosophy* (Cambridge: Cambridge University Press, 1978).

L'Enracinement: Prelude à une declaration des devoirs envers l'être humain. Paris: Gallimard, 1949. Translated by Arthur Wills as *The Need for Roots* (London: Ark Paperbacks, 1987).

Lettre à un religieux. Paris: Gallimard, 1951. Translated by Arthur Wills as *Letter to a Priest* (London: Routledge and Kegan Paul, 1953).

Oppression et liberté. Paris: Gallimard, 1955. Translated by Arthur Wills and John Petrie as *Oppression and Liberty* (Amherst: University of Massachusetts Press, 1973).

Pensées sans ordre concernant l'amour de Dieu. Paris: Gallimard, 1962. Translated by Richard Rees in *On Science, Necessity, and the Love of God* (London: Oxford University Press, 1968).

Selected Essays. Translated by Richard Rees. London: Oxford University Press, 1962.

Simone Weil: An Anthology. Translated by Sian Miles. New York: Weidenfeld and Nicholson, 1986.

The Simone Weil Reader. Edited by George Panichas. New York: Moyer Bell, 1977.

Simone Weil: Seventy Letters. Translated by Richard Rees. London: Oxford University Press, 1965.

OTHER WORKS CONSULTED

Aeschylus. *The Oresteia.* Translated by Richmond Lattimore. Chicago: University of Chicago Press, 1953.
———. *Prometheus Bound.* Translated by David Grene. Chicago: University of Chicago Press, 1956.
Allen, Diogenes, and Eric O. Springstead. *Spirit, Nature, and Community: Issues in the Thought of Simone Weil.* Albany: State University of New York Press, 1994.
Augustine. *On Christian Doctrine.* Translated by D. W. Robertson Jr. New York: Macmillan, 1958.
Balthasar, Hans Urs Von. *Explorations in Theology.* Vol. 1: *The Word Made Flesh.* San Francisco: Ignatius Press, 1989.
———. *The Glory of the Lord: A Theological Aesthetics.* Vol. 1: *Seeing the Form.* Translated by Erasmo Leiva-Merikakis. San Francisco: Ignatius Press, 1982.
Barth, Karl. *The Epistle to the Romans.* Translated by Edwyn C. Hoskyns. London: Oxford University Press, 1933.
Bell, Richard, edited by *Simone Weil's Philosophy of Culture.* Cambridge: Cambridge University Press, 1993.
Benjamin, Walter. *Illuminations.* Edited by Hannah Arendt. Translated by Harry Zohn. New York: Schocken Books, 1968.
Bernard of Clairvaux. *On Loving God.* In *Bernard of Clairvaux: Selected Works,* translated by G. R. Evans. New York: Paulist Press, 1987.
Blenkinsopp, Joseph. *A History of Prophecy in Israel.* Philadelphia: Westminster, 1983.
Blumenberg, Hans. *The Legitimacy of the Modern Age.* Translated by Robert M. Wallace. Cambridge: MIT Press, 1983.
Bonaventure. *The Soul's Journey into God.* In *Bonaventure,* translated by Ewert Cousins. New York: Paulist Press, 1978.
Botton, Alain de. *The Consolations of Philosophy.* New York: Pantheon Books, 2000.
Blum, Lawrence, and Victor Seidler. *A Truer Liberty: Simone Weil and Marxism.* London: Routledge Press, 1989.
Brueck, Katherine. *The Redemption of Tragedy: The Literary Vision of Simone Weil.* Albany: State University of New York Press, 1995.
Brueggemann, Walter. *The Prophetic Imagination.* Philadelphia: Fortress Press, 1978.
Cabaud, Jacques. *Simone Weil.* New York: Channel Press, 1964.
Carr, Anne. *A Search for Wisdom and Spirit: Thomas Merton's Theology of the Self* . Notre Dame, Ind.: University of Notre Dame Press, 1988.
Certeau, Michel de. *The Mystic Fable,* vol. 1: *The Sixteenth and Seventeenth Centuries.* Translated by Michael Smith. Chicago: University of Chicago Press, 1992.

——. *The Practice of Everyday Life.* Translated by Steven Rendall. Berkeley: University of California Press, 1984.

Cohen, Arthur. *The Tremendum.* New York: Continuum, 1993.

Collins, John. *The Apocalyptic Imagination.* New York: Crossroad, 1992.

Cross, Frank Moore. *Canaanite Myth and Hebrew Epic.* Cambridge: Harvard University Press, 1973.

Davy, M. M. *The Mysticism of Simone Weil.* Translated by Cynthia Rowland. London: Rockliff Publishing, 1951.

Derrida, Jacques. *Specters of Marx.* Translated by Peggy Kamuf. New York: Routledge, 1994.

Dupre, Louis. "Mysticism." In vol. 10 of *The Encyclopedia of Religion*, edited by Mircea Eliade. New York: Macmillan, 1987.

——. "*Unio Mystica*: The State and the Experience." In *Mystical Union in Judaism, Christianity, and Islam: An Ecumenical Dialogue*, edited by Moshe Idel and Bernard McGinn. New York: Continuum, 1996.

Farley, Wendy. *Tragic Vision and Divine Compassion: A Contemporary Theodicy.* Louisville, Ky.: Westminster/John Knox Press, 1990.

Fiori, Gabriella. *Simone Weil: An Intellectual Biography.* Translated by Joseph Berrigan. Athens: University of Georgia Press, 1989.

Fishbane, Michael. "Biblical Prophecy as a Religious Phenomenon." In *Jewish Spirituality: From the Bible through the Middle Ages*, edited by Arthur Green. New York: Crossroad, 1994.

Friedman, Richard Elliot. *The Hidden Face of God: A Divine Mystery.* Boston: Little, Brown, 1995.

Gerrish, B. A. *The Old Protestantism and the New: Essays on the Reformation Heritage*. Chicago: University of Chicago Press, 1982.

Goldmann, Lucien. *The Hidden God: A Study of Tragic Vision in the Pensées of Pascal and the Tragedies of Racine.* London: Routledge and Kegan Paul, 1964.

Grant, Robert, with David Tracy. *A Short History of the Interpretation of the Bible*. Philadelphia: Fortress Press, 1984.

Gregory of Nyssa. *The Life of Moses* in *Gregory of Nyssa*. Translated by Abraham Malherbe and Everett Ferguson. New York: Paulist Press, 1978.

Hadot, Pierre. *Philosophy as a Way of Life.* Translated by Michael Chase. Oxford: Blackwell Publishers, 1995.

——. *Plotinus or The Simplicity of Vision.* Translated by Michael Chase. Chicago: University of Chicago Press, 1993.

Hegel. *Hegel On Tragedy.* Edited by Anne Paolucci and Henry Paolucci. New York: Harper and Row, 1962.

Heidegger, Martin. *Being and Time.* Translated by John Macquarrie and Edward Robinson. New York: Harper and Row, 1962.

Heschel, Abraham Joshua. *The Prophets.* Vol. 1. New York: Harper and Row, 1962.

Horsley, Richard, with John Hanson. *Bandits, Prophets, and Messiahs*. New York: Harper Collins, 1985.

Hugel, Baron von. *The Mystical Element of Religion*. Vol. 2. London: J. M. Dent and Sons, 1908.

Jay, Martin. *The Dialectic Imagination*. Berkeley: University of California Press, 1973.

John of the Cross. *The Dark Night* and *The Ascent of Mount Carmel*. In *Selected Writings*, translated by Kieran Kavanaugh. New York: Paulist Press, 1987.

Katz, Steven, ed. *Mysticism and Philosophical Analysis*. New York: Oxford University Press, 1978.

Kierkegaard, Søren. *Practice in Christianity*. Translated by Howard Hong and Edna Hong. Princeton: Princeton University Press, 1991.

Kolakowski, Leszek. *Main Currents of Marxism*, vol. 1: *The Founders*. Translated by P. S. Falla. Oxford: Oxford University Press, 1978.

Levenson, Jon. *Sinai and Zion*. New York: Harper Collins, 1985.

Levinas, Emmanuel. *Totality and Infinity*. Pittsburgh: Duquesne University Press, 1969.

——. *The Levinas Reader*. Edited by Sean Hand. Oxford: Blackwell Publishers, 1989.

Little, J. P. *Waiting On Truth*. Oxford: Berg Publishers, 1988.

Louth, Andrew. *The Origins of the Christian Mystical Tradition: From Plato to Denys*. Oxford: Clarendon Press, 1981.

Luther, Martin. *Bondage of the Will*. In *Martin Luther: Selections from His Writings*, edited by John Dillenberger. New York: Anchor Books, 1962.

——. *Lectures on Isaiah, Chapters 1–39*. In vol. 16 of *Luther's Works*, edited by Jaroslav Pelikan, translated by Herbert Bouman. St. Louis: Concordia Publishing House, 1969.

Marguerite of Porete. *The Mirror of Simple of Souls*. In *Marguerite of Porete*, translated by Ellen Babinsky. New York: Paulist Press, 1993.

Marion, Jean-Luc. *God Without Being*. Translated by Thomas Carlson. Chicago: University of Chicago Press, 1991.

Mays, James Luther, and Paul Achtemeier, eds. *Interpreting the Prophets*. Philadelphia: Fortress Press, 1987.

McGinn, Bernard. *The Anti-Christ: Two Thousand Years of the Human Fascination with Evil*. New York: HarperSanFrancisco, 1994.

——. *The Foundations of Mysticism: Origins to the Fifth Century*. New York: Crossroad, 1991.

——. *The Growth of Mysticism: Gregory the Great through the Twelfth Century*. New York: Crossroad, 1994.

——. "The Letter and the Spirit: Spirituality as an Academic Discipline." *Christian Spirituality Bulletin: Journal of the Society for the Study of Christian Spirituality* 1, no. 2 (fall 1993).

McLellan, David. *Utopian Pessimist: The Life and Thought of Simone Weil*. New York: Poseidon Press, 1990.

Meister Eckhart. *Meister Eckhart*. Translated by Edmund Colledge and Bernard McGinn. New York: Paulist Press, 1981.

Metz, Johann Baptist. *Faith in History and Society*. Translated by David Smith. New York: Seabury Press, 1980.

Monk, Ray. *Ludwig Wittgenstein: The Duty of Genius*. New York: Penguin Books, 1990.

Nehamas, Alexander. *The Art of Living: Socratic Reflections from Plato to Foucault*. Berkeley: University of California Press, 1998.

Nietzsche, Friedrich. *The Birth of Tragedy*. Translated by Walter Kaufmann. New York: Vintage Books, 1967.

———. *Twilight of the Idols/The Anti-Christ*. Translated by R. J. Hollingdale. London: Penguin Books, 1968.

Nevin, Thomas. *Simone Weil: Portrait of a Self-Exiled Jew*. Chapel Hill: University of North Carolina Press, 1991.

Oberman, Heiko. *The Dawn of the Reformation*. Edinburgh: T. and T. Clark, 1986.

———. *Luther: Man between God and the Devil*. Translated by Eileen Walliser-Schwarzbart. New Haven: Yale University Press, 1989.

Origen. *Commentary on the Song of Songs*. In *Origen*, translated by Rowan Greer. New York: Paulist Press, 1979.

Ozment, Steven. *The Age of Reform: 1250–1550*. New Haven: Yale University Press, 1980.

Pascal, Blaise. *Pensées*. Translated by A. J. Krailsheimer. London: Penguin Books, 1966.

Perrin, J. B., and G. Thibon. *Simone Weil As We Knew Her*. Translated by Emma Craufurd. London: Routledge and Kegan Paul, 1953.

Petremont, Simone. *Simone Weil: A Life*. Translated by Raymond Rosenthal. New York: Pantheon Books, 1976.

Plato. *The Republic* and *The Symposium*. Translated by B. Jowett. New York: Anchor Books, 1973.

Pseudo-Dionysius. *The Divine Names, The Celestial Hierarchy*, and *The Ecclesiastical Hierarchy*. In *Pseudo-Dionysius*, translated by Colm Luibheid. New York: Paulist Press, 1987.

Ricoeur, Paul. *The Symbolism of Evil*. Translated by E. Buchanan. Boston: Beacon Press, 1967.

Ruprecht, Louis. *Tragic Posture and Tragic Vision*. New York: Continuum, 1994.

Segundo, Juan Luis. *The Christ of the Ignatian Exercises*. Translated by John Drury. New York: Orbis Books, 1987.

Sells, Michael. *Mystical Languages of Unsaying*. Chicago: University of Chicago Press, 1994.

Smalley, Beryl. *The Study of the Bible in the Middle Ages*. Notre Dame, Ind.: Notre Dame University Press, 1964.

Sobrino, Jon. *Spirituality of Liberation: Toward a Political Holiness.* Translated by Robert Barr. New York: Orbis Books, 1988.

Springstead, Eric. *Christus Mediator: Platonic Mediation in the Thought of Simone Weil.* Chico, Calif.: Scholars Press, 1983.

Steiner, George. *Martin Heidegger.* Chicago: University of Chicago Press, 1989.

Tracy, David. *The Analogical Imagination: Christian Theology and the Culture of Pluralism.* New York: Crossroad, 1991.

———. *Blessed Rage For Order: The New Pluralism in Theology.* Chicago: University of Chicago Press, 1996.

———. *Dialogue with the Other: The Inter-Religious Dialogue.* Louvain: Peeters Press, 1990.

———. "The Hidden God: The Divine Other of Liberation." *Cross Currents: The Journal of the Association for Religion and Intellectual Life* 46, no. 1 (spring 1996).

———. "Literary Theory and Return of the Forms for Naming and Thinking God in Theology." *The Journal of Religion* 74, no. 3 (July 1994).

———. *On Naming the Present: God, Hermeneutics, Church.* New York: Orbis Books, 1994.

———. "On the Origins of Philosophy of Religion: The Need for a New Narrative of Its Founding." In *Myth and Philosophy,* edited by Frank Reynolds and David Tracy. Albany: State University of New York Press, 1990.

———. *Plurality and Ambiguity: Hermeneutics, Religion, Hope.* Chicago: University of Chicago Press, 1994.

Turner, Denys. *The Darkness of God: Negativity in Christian Mysticism.* Cambridge: Cambridge University Press, 1995.

Veto, Miklos. *The Religious Metaphysics of Simone Weil.* Translated by Joan Dargan. Albany: State University of New York Press, 1994.

West, Cornel. *Prophesy Deliverance!* Philadelphia: Westminster Press, 1982.

Wiesel, Elie. *Souls on Fire.* New York: Random House, 1972.

Williams, Bernard. *Shame and Necessity.* Berkeley: University of California Press, 1993.

Wilson, Robert. *Prophecy and Society in Ancient Israel.* Philadelphia: Fortress Press, 1980.

Winch, Peter. *Simone Weil: The Just Balance.* Cambridge: Cambridge University Press, 1989.

Wittgenstein, Ludwig. *Culture and Value.* Chicago: University of Chicago Press, 1980.

Index